THE
RUNNER'S BOOK OF
DAILY INSPIRATION

*A Year of Motivation,
Revelation, and Instruction*

KEVIN NELSON

CONTEMPORARY BOOKS

Library of Congress Cataloging-in-Publication Data

Nelson, Kevin, 1953–
    The runner's book of daily inspiration : a year of motivation,
  revelation, and instruction / Kevin Nelson.
      p.   cm.
   Includes index.
   ISBN 0-8092-2962-5
    1. Running—Quotations, maxims, etc.   2. Running—Miscellanea.
 I. Title.
 GV1061.N396   1999
 796.42—dc21
                                    98-33517
                                        CIP

Jacket design by Monica Baziuk, based on a design by Amy Nathan
Jacket illustration copyright © 1998 Allen Garns
Interior design by Kim Bartko

Published by Contemporary Books
A division of NTC/Contemporary Publishing Group, Inc.
4255 West Touhy Avenue, Lincolnwood (Chicago), Illinois 60712-1975 U.S.A.
Printed in the United States of America
International Standard Book Number: 0-8092-2962-5
99 00 01 02 03 04 QP 19 18 17 16 15 14 13 12 11 10 9 8 7 6 5 4 3 2

Preface

"I have found that encouraging people to exercise when they have not expressed the desire to is useless. It has been my experience that the average person needs a source of inspiration more than a source of information."

—Dr. Max L. Irick, physician

One of the best things about running is that you can do it every day. Rain or shine, snow or slush, you can lace up your running shoes and take a spin around the block and through the park.

It is a delightfully simple pastime. You don't need a coach or a guru. You can run by yourself—although running with others is great fun, too—for as long or as little as you please. While many runners work out on a track from time to time, the overwhelming majority do not. They run along courses of their own devising: along the waterfront, past the projects, on dirt trails and pavement, up hills and down, across bridges, and around the neighborhoods, wherever they choose.

There is a marvelous serendipity to running that does not exist in other sports that take place on established playing fields according to codified rules and regulations. There are precious few rules in running, and you are free to do it almost anywhere. Nor is there need for a lot of expensive equipment, despite what the shoe manufacturers say. Abebe Bikila of Ethiopia won the Olympic Games Marathon in his bare feet.

Running takes place outdoors—yet another of its virtues. When you run, you tune in not just to your own body and mind but also to the greater world around you. You breathe in great gulps of fresh air, while listening to the red-winged blackbirds chirp and watching the clouds sweep across the sky.

The health benefits of running are well known and hardly need any explanation here. Your heart and lungs and bodily systems all work better when you run. It improves the quality of your life. And when you feel better physically, your mental life becomes richer and more rewarding. You think more *clearly*.

So, with all these extraordinary benefits, how come everyone doesn't run? Well, there's this little matter of motivation, and that's where *The Runner's Book of Daily Inspiration* comes in. It's the goal of this book to inspire people to run every day they possibly can.

You can rant at people until you're blue in the face that a certain activity such as running is good for them. But if they don't want to do it, for whatever reason, they're not going to. They have to find the desire within themselves and then be willing to keep at it even after the initial enthusiasm has faded away.

For longtime runners, novices, marathoners, ultramarathoners, sprinters, weekend runners, joggers, walkers, older runners, younger runners, it's all the same. If you're enjoying yourself, you're going to do it. Enjoyment fuels desire. Follow your joy, and you will be just fine.

That's the unadorned message of this book: running is fun. It's not all drudgery and discipline and pounding the pavement. You *can* do it every day—or every other day, or whatever works in your schedule. And you can have a good time while you're at it. And meet some good people and learn things about yourself, as well.

The Runner's Book of Daily Inspiration is the third in a series, preceded by similar books on fishing and golf. I sometimes fantasize that after glancing at the daily entries for each of these books, a person will run, play golf, and fish all in the same day. Now, that would be a day well spent!

In any case, it is hoped that runners receive pleasure and inspiration from these pages, just as they receive pleasure and inspiration from their sport. If you don't feel in the mood to run someday, and yet you open this book, and it changes your mind, and you decide to give it a go after all—well then, as the author, I can think of no higher compliment. Happy running.

January 1

"Know yourself, so you may live that life peculiar to you, the one and only life you were born to live. Know yourself, that you may perfect your body and find your play."

—George Sheehan, philosopher-runner

It is the first day of the new year. What better thing to do than go for a run?

It's a holiday; there's plenty of time. After your run you can come back and watch the bowl games . . . or *not*. Whatever you do, you'll feel better about it after working up a good honest sweat.

This is the time of year for resolutions, so let today be the start of something grand. Set your sights this year on a far target, such as running a marathon, or better still, running a personal best in a marathon.

Or perhaps you like to run only for the sake of running, to feel fit and healthy and to hold a good opinion of yourself. Well, then, let this be the year for *that*.

Running is a thing worth doing not because of the future rewards it bestows, but because of how it feeds our bodies and minds and souls in the present. Go out for a run today, and let it be the start of something grand.

Resolved: I make this year the greatest year of my running life.

January 2

*"How much happiness is gained, and how much misery escaped,
by frequent and violent agitation of the body."*

—Samuel Johnson

The main goal of running is not to finish first, or run faster
than you ever have before, or beat your competitors, although
any one of these can be, at times, a very worthy goal.

The main goal of running is to enjoy yourself. Whenever
you run, keep that in mind.

There is one indisputable rule of the roads: If you do not
enjoy running, you will not run. If you do not run, you will
not reap any benefits from it.

Everything starts with fun, a sense of play. Lacking that, all
is lost. Though runners often work desperately hard at it, most
love what they do and get an elemental charge from it. To borrow a line, at the heart of every runner is a little boy or girl.

Inevitably some days seem more like work than pleasure.
When this occurs, ask yourself, Are you focusing too much on
duty and routine, times and mileage? Every day is a good day
when you run. Remember that, and you'll be fine.

Resolved: I remember to enjoy myself when I run.

January 3

"It is the illusion that we can go no faster that holds us back."
—Kenny Moore, marathoner and writer

You can go faster. However fast you run, you can run faster.

Just ran a 2:25 marathon? You can go 2:20. Just ran a 33-minute 10K? You can run it in 32, or even 30.

These are fast times for fast runners. This truism nonetheless applies to all: no matter how fast you've run, you can run faster.

You may still be trying to break the magical three-hour barrier in the marathon. Heck, you may still be trying to break the not-so-magical six-hour barrier or finish a marathon in the same day. Even so, the illusion that you can go no faster is just that: an illusion. It's a barrier in your mind that you can overcome. The breakthrough you're looking for lies on the other side.

This wondrous breakthrough is more than possible. It's a reality that's within your grasp. Enlarge your perception of yourself and what you can do. Identify whatever illusions are holding you back, and let go of them. Free your mind, and your feet will follow.

Resolved: I let go of the illusion that I can run no faster.

January 4

"Running is a gift I give myself almost every day. Even on those days when things haven't gone great, I can come home and give myself the accomplishment of a 30- or 40-minute run."

—Arthur Blank, businessman and runner

Running is a kind of investment in yourself. Make it a daily investment, and you will be even better off than you are today.

Nonrunners cannot see how they can afford the time to run every day. But runners cannot imagine getting through a single day without it.

Is that because runners have lighter schedules than nonrunners and thus more free time? Hardly. Every runner will tell you that, once you start running and enjoying it, once you start giving yourself the gift, you will find ways to make the time. Your priorities will shift slightly, perhaps even radically. You will realize that some of what seems important in your life is just clutter, and it will blow away like dry leaves in your desire to run.

Even if you don't run every day, take an "every day" approach to it. See it as something you'll do next week and next month and next year. There *are* immediate, short-term benefits to running, but all in all, the benefits are of the type that accrue over time. Look for long-term results, not quick fixes. With this attitude you'll be less prone to burn out, or to do too much too suddenly.

Resolved: I take an every day approach to running.

January 5

Never be afraid to stop, whether you're Lois Scheffelin or Bill Rodgers. Rodgers once set a Boston Marathon record while stopping five times during the race at the water stations. When asked why he stopped to drink, Rodgers said, "The cup spills if I run."

Stopping is an honorable tradition in running. Even great runners like Rodgers stop in the middle of a race. Some days you just don't have it, and there's no sense in forcing it. The great runners know this and accept it. Only a fool keeps charging forward when all the signs are telling him or her to stop.

Stopping means that you've recognized your limits, which is always good. It indicates self-knowledge and self-control and shows that you know what's best for yourself. You're in charge of your running, not the other way around.

Everyone needs to take a break from time to time. If you're running with a partner, he or she will understand.

After all, the purpose of stopping is to enable you to continue to run. You stop in order to start again. Whether you stop for a few minutes or a few days, you *will* resume running again.

Resolved: I stop if I need to.

January 6

"Running should be a relief from stress, a way to help cope with it, not another added stress."

—Bob Glover, runner

Life is stressful enough without adding another stress to it. So, don't beat yourself up about your running. That's missing the point.

Unless you're training for the Olympics, running is not an end in itself. It's a means to an end, a thing you do to help you do other things better.

Running is the one surefire method that you have found to help you manage the many stresses that populate your everyday life. Running works better than champagne or coffee. It is better than drugs. And it helps keep you sane.

So, don't let it make you crazy.

If you miss a day, don't sweat it. If one day becomes two days, or three days, or even a week, that's OK, too. You'll get back to it. Sooner or later (and probably sooner) your body will start crying out for you to do something, and you will respond.

Running is not like some sort of exotic food diet in which you need to follow certain strict rules. It's not punishment or self-denial. On the contrary, it's self-enhancement, and everyone who runs, from the jogger to that Olympic athlete in training, gets benefits from it.

So, if running ever becomes stressful to you, take a step back from it. Let its benefits come to you, rather than zealously pursuing them.

Resolved: I take it easy on myself and on my running.

January 7

"For me, a seven-minute-a-mile pace is fast enough, and I often run slower. I'll sometimes start a workout running an eight-minute or nine-minute pace. You can achieve a lot with slow workouts."

—Doug Kurtis, marathoner

Slow is good. Slower is even better. And slowest? Why, that's the best of all.

So much of modern life requires speed. Everyone zips here and zaps there, and there's hardly time to catch your breath.

Running is a glorious exception to that. If you insist on running fast all the time, all you will get for your trouble is shinsplints. And you always must breathe when you run, or else you won't get very far.

Slow runners have it all over the fast ones. Fast runners pour over a course, hardly noticing the scenery. Slow runners have the leisure to see a northern harrier hovering above its prey in a field, or observe the lovely quality of stratus clouds in an azure sky.

The great genius of running is that the plow horses can get just as much out of it as the fleet-footed Thoroughbreds, aerobically speaking. And they can carry on a conversation and catch up on all the gossip, to boot.

But don't misunderstand. Slow runners are savvier than you think. Long, slow distances are, as the fastest runners will tell you, a respected race-training technique, increasing your endurance and establishing a base that will help you run faster, if you wish.

Resolved: I run slowly and build my endurance.

January 8

"I don't make a decision every morning. I made a decision once, long ago, to run every day. When I wake up, the decision is already made."

—Walt Guzzardi, runner

Inspiration comes and goes. You can never be sure where, or when, it will alight.

Inspiration is like a hummingbird, constantly in motion. When it finally lands, it's only for the briefest of instants. One small noise and it flashes away so quickly that you wonder if it was there at all.

Every runner needs inspiration, but the best runners and the ones who have been doing it a long time mainly get their inspiration from running. The act itself is what gives them the motivation.

Some days you're not going to feel like it. You're going to feel like practicing your avoidance techniques rather than your running techniques. That's inevitable—and normal.

But if you can find the wherewithal to drag yourself out of bed or the office (or wherever you happen to be) and run, you will receive an instant supply of motivation. You will be flooded with motivation; it will surge through your veins like a drug. You will be reminded once more why you run and why you make the effort. And you will wonder why you hesitated at all.

Remember that feeling—and how good you feel after a run—the next time your wellspring of inspiration seems dried up.

Resolved: When inspiration's lacking, I get my inspiration from running.

January 9

When you have a pebble in your shoe, what do you do? Stop, and take it out. When your shoelace is untied, what do you do? Stop, and tie it. It makes sense, right? If something is wrong, you stop and fix it.

Apply this simple rule to running, and you will be a better runner. You may have a feeling that something you're doing isn't quite right. Well, then, stop and fix it.

You do not have to continue down a path that is not giving you the results you want. Know that you have the capacity for change. Know that when you're on the wrong track, you can stop and get on the right one.

It's natural to want to find the right thing immediately and stay there and not think about it until you've reached your goal at the end. But how realistic is that? You've got to expect a few wrong turns along the way. But after you make one mistake, you do not have to follow it with another.

It may be frustrating, and it may seem as if it's slowing you down, but stopping to get on the right track will save you time and plenty of trouble in the end. After all, if you ignore a pebble in your shoe, it can develop into a painful blister or bruise. But if you stop and take it out, after a temporary pause, you can keep right on running.

Resolved: If something's not quite right with my running, I stop and fix it.

January 10

> "I never say, 'Don't do' anything. I say, 'Take care of the ball; hold onto the ball.' I never say, 'Don't jump offside or 'Don't get beat deep' or 'Don't throw interceptions.' I say, 'Throw it to our guys. Hang onto it.'"
>
> —Steve Mariucci, football coach

The language is football, but this positivist philosophy applies equally well to running and other forms of endeavor: banish the negatives from your vocabulary and thus put a limit on negative thinking.

Instead of saying, "I don't want to run hard," say, "I am going to run under control today."

Instead of saying, "I don't want to run today," say, "I'm going to take the day off and give my body a rest."

Instead of saying, "I didn't run very far," say, "I did a shorter workout today."

Words matter. Words are the way we express our thoughts. On some level, words *are* thoughts. What does this say, then, about a runner who constantly puts himself or herself down?

Of course, you may not be aware of how you talk about yourself. That's the first step: listen to yourself and how you talk about your running. Talking in positive terms will help change the way you think about yourself and the way others view you.

Take a cue from the great runners—indeed, all great athletes. They focus on the positive, on what they can do. To be great in your own way, do the same.

Resolved: I talk positively about my running.

January 11

"My method of encouraging people to run is by running myself."
—Peggy Blount, runner

The truth is, if you want to run, you may have to strike out on your own.

This is a big step for many people, particularly those without an athletic background. You have no personal history of running or any other form of athletics, and you've never done anything like it before.

Your spouse may think you're being silly. Your friends and coworkers may make jokes about it.

To be a runner is to be a leader of sorts—or a loner. It's very brave, issuing out on your own. Even if you find someone to run with, there will be days when he or she isn't available and you're on your own. You may feel funny about the way you look when you run. You may feel slow or clumsy.

Make a pact with yourself: you're going to run, no matter what. Whether or not anyone goes with you or not, you're going to run. You've made up your mind to do this thing and darned if you aren't going to do it.

By small victories are larger ones made. Now that you have made the decision, who knows where it will lead?

Resolved: I run, by myself or with others. But I run.

January 12

"My first understanding was that you could not become a distance runner quickly. I began gradually, not doing too much."

—Henry Rono, champion runner

Running is a wonderful sport because you can do very little and still get a lot from it. By giving only the minimum, you can almost get the maximum. In what other activity can you say that?

One of the oldest and tiredest clichés in sports is about the athlete who gives "110 percent." If you give 110 percent in running, you're giving way too much.

It makes no sense to push that hard, especially in a workout. When training, put forth only 60 or 70 percent of your capacity on average. Start low and build your endurance, and over time your capacity will grow.

A little bit counts for a lot in running, like putting the small change that's in your pocket into a coin bank at the end of each day. Those dimes and quarters may not seem like much at first, but you'll be surprised how fast they can accumulate.

Running a little every day—not doing too much—is a sure-fire way to build wealth, wealth of body and mind.

Resolved: I run today, but I don't do too much.

January 13

*"Young people tell me, 'I want to be just like you.' I tell them,
'No, you want to be different from me. Define yourself. What
can you give that I can't?'"*

—Yo-Yo Ma, cellist

You will never know who you are until you first admit who
you are not.

What are your strengths and weaknesses as a runner (and
a human being)? What do you do well? Is it your unwilling-
ness to quit, your toughness, your speed, your ability to work
hard? You must know the answers to these types of questions
to achieve your running goals.

This process of self-examination can be pretty brutal at
times. It's hard to face facts about yourself. You have to recognize your limits—what you wish you could do, perhaps, but
can't. You may compare yourself with other runners and find
yourself lacking in some respect.

But remember: no one else has your unique gifts. You possess talents and capabilities that other people, including the
ones you admire, can only dream of. And those unique gifts
are what you must bring to the world.

When you're young, you think you can do everything. As
you get older, you realize you have to pick your spots. It's the
same idea. The better you know yourself, the better a runner
you will be. You will know when to ease off or push. You will
know that you can go farther or that it's time to turn around.
Definition leads to growth. Once you know your limits, you
can expand your limits.

Resolved: I define myself as a runner and, in doing so, find
myself.

January 14

"Every time I bomb out, I have to come back. I have a feeling after a bad race that my next one will be good."

—Bill Rodgers, marathoner

It's a given that there are going to be good days and bad days when you run.

There are good days and bad days when you do *anything*. Why should running be any different?

It's like the old saw about being thrown off a horse. What do you do when it happens? You get back on and try it again. It's the same with running.

You may have a string of good days in a row. But inevitably you're going to hit a rough patch that knocks you off your stride. Since you know that already—that there will be good days and bad—why not convert that knowledge into power?

The low-energy days won't get you down for long because you know they will inevitably end. And if you're on a hot streak, you won't be disheartened or shocked at its end because that's part of the process, too.

Good, bad, up, down. It's all part of the bipolar nature of things. Understanding this will help you keep your long-term goals on track. You will be able to make adjustments more quickly, remain flexible, and keep a good attitude throughout.

Resolved: I have good days and bad. But I keep running.

January 15

"Running gives me confidence."

—Steve Prefontaine

When the great middle-distance runner Steve Prefontaine was growing up in Coos Bay, a small fishing town on the Oregon coast, he was considered a slow learner. He was too hyper to sit still for long in class, and he did poorly in school.

When he reached junior high, he discovered running, and it changed his life. Now he had an outlet for his energies. He found something that he was good at, and his self-esteem, his belief in himself, and his abilities grew.

There is a lot of Steve Prefontaine in every runner. Pre was extraordinarily gifted as a runner, a young Amadeus on the track. Now a figure of near mythic proportions, he died tragically in a car crash in his early 20s. While most runners do not share his gifts, every runner knows how he felt when he ran. Every runner gets a similar boost of self-confidence from running.

Don't you? Don't you feel better about yourself when you run? Don't you feel that there are more possibilities to your life, and that you have a better chance to exploit those possibilities?

If you get a charge from running, if it gives you self-confidence and helps build your self-esteem, if it makes you feel good about yourself and about what you can accomplish in this life, you owe it to yourself to run. It's as simple as that.

Resolved: I run because it gives me confidence, and I have confidence because I run.

January 16

"I love to run. This is just part of my life. It's the way I live. You put in so much effort and the rewards are so little, you might as well enjoy it and make lots of friends."

—Johnny Kelley, venerable Boston Marathon fixture

Make friends and enjoy it. That was old Johnny Kelley's philosophy of running and life, and it's as good as any that's ever been uttered.

What do you want out of running? To break records, set personal records (PRS), win trophies? You probably won't get too many of the latter, to be honest.

But you might meet some real nice people and have some extremely fun times. Running is filled with those.

There's a lot of effort involved in running. Let's be honest. You have to drag yourself out of bed or wherever you happen to be and fling yourself down some long and lonely road where you expose yourself to the elements and yapping dogs and who knows what else.

Nor are there many rewards except those of the personal kind. Nobody will probably ever interview you for the newspapers or TV. You will never be called to come up to the victory stand at the end of a race. Chances are, when they're handing out the awards, you will still be out on the course.

Even so, there are plenty of good times and good people to keep you busy in running for a lifetime or two.

Resolved: I make friends and enjoy running and let the rest take care of itself.

January 17

"My body immediately reacts to a lack of exercise. 'Take me outside,' it cries; 'let me out.'"

—Paula Zahn, broadcaster and runner

Your problems will seem more manageable. Your work will be more productive. Your thinking will be clearer. You will be more tuned in to your relationships. Your emotional state of being will be richer and fuller.

Everything about your life will seem better somehow if, instead of ignoring your body's pleas for exercise, you respond to them.

Your body is like any tool: leave it sitting in the garage collecting rust, and after a while, it's not going to be able to do what it was designed to do.

Every day your body actively communicates with you. And its message is potent. It says, "Use me. Work me." You'll see: the more you do, the better off you will be.

Some people have ignored these signals for so long that their bodies have to shout at them in the form of back pain or ulcers or a heart murmur. But it's never too late to learn. Once you get into the habit of listening to your body, you will find it to be a wise and effective teacher.

Resolved: When my body cries out for exercise, like today, I respond.

January 18

"Deep down I always believe I can win."

—Francie Larrieu Smith, runner

There is a great story about the golfer Jack Nicklaus, who was lining up a crucial putt on the 18th hole of a big PGA tournament. If he could sink the putt, he would win the title. If he missed it, he'd finish second.

He took a long time (as is Jack's tendency) sizing up the putt. He walked it off and thought about it. Then he got over the ball and stroked it firmly.

The cup was 10 feet away. The ball rolled 9 feet, 11 inches and hung on the lip. A baby's breath would have blown it in, but alas, there were no babies around, and the ball stubbornly stayed up.

Despite losing the tournament, Nicklaus was not disappointed with his effort. "I hit the ball in," he said afterward. "It just didn't go in."

That's the attitude of a winner. The ball did not go in. But in his heart, Nicklaus knew he hit it in. You must have the same sort of confidence when you compete. Even if you do not win, know always that you have the ability to win. And even if you are a back-of-the-pack runner, deep down, believe in your capacity to do well. After all, if you don't believe in yourself, who else is going to?

Resolved: I always believe in my ability to do well.

January 19

*"Not a shred of evidence exists in favor of the argument that
life is serious, though it is often hard and even terrible. It
seems obvious that the first rule of life is to have a good time."*
—Brendan Gill, writer

It is rainy and wet. What better thing to do than go for a run?

The weather is almost never as bad as it seems when you're staring at it from the sensible comfort of indoors. Indeed, some rainy days are quite pleasant.

Often when you run in the rain, you make the cheery discovery that those drops you're feeling on your tongue and cheeks can't be classified as rain; they're really more of a light mist. The wind also barely registers, and because other, more pusillanimous, souls are hiding indoors, you have your usual running trail all to yourself.

That is, except for the birds. Apparently unruffled by the weather, they are out in abundance. You run past a flock of snowy egrets in the wetlands area where you go, their white feathers a sharp contrast against the dull brown marsh. Next to this patch of white is one of black—a group of blackbirds feeding and moving along the marsh in their characteristic hopscotch patterns.

By the end of your run, you feel as good as you have in a long, long time. You've thumbed your nose at convention and had a surprisingly strong workout besides. Nearing home, you think, "What the hell" and splash through a series of puddles like a water-loving Labrador. Once indoors again, thoroughly satisfied, you shed your soaked shoes and get dry.

Resolved: Next time it rains, I run through a puddle.

January 20

Michael Jordan is not a "runner," although he does run up and down the court plenty and is in terrific physical shape. Still, runners and nonrunners alike can learn a valuable lesson from him.

Michael Jordan was cut from his high-school basketball team.

Michael Jordan is the greatest basketball player in the history of the planet. His statue outside the United Center in Chicago reads, "The greatest there ever was. The greatest there ever will be." It's not a boast.

But when he was a young man, Michael Jordan was cut from his high-school basketball team.

What was that coach thinking? The future Einstein of basketball players was trying out for his squad, and the coach just couldn't see it. Apparently, he could see only a gawky, unseasoned kid who wasn't good enough even to ride the bench.

And how did the schoolboy Michael Jordan respond to this insult? Not by quitting or conceding defeat. He did not cave in to his coach's assessment of his abilities; he stuck to his own vision of himself and turned a loss into a win. He used it as motivation to keep trying, to keep getting better, and always, always, to keep playing and pursuing his joy.

Resolved: I keep running and pursuing my joy, no matter what.

January 21

"Running is the greatest thing that ever happened to me. It's the focus of my daily routine, the source of everything. It gives my life a sense of rhythm."

—Allan Ripp, runner

Easy-hard is one of the oldest and most trusted maxims of training. Follow a hard day of running by an easy day (or even an off day). After an easy day comes a hard day.

What's hard, and what's easy? That's up to you. An easy workout for Alberto Salazar in his prime would surely unhinge the average runner.

Easy-hard will fit snugly into your goals as a runner, whatever they are. Easy-hard is the basis for every high-level training program.

It just makes sense. You can't test the same set of muscles in the same way every day. You're courting injuries if you do. One way to vary the routine is to swim or bicycle—activities that use different muscle groups from running—on your easy days.

Easy-hard prevents you from putting undue pressure on yourself. The easy days give you a needed mental break as well as a physical one.

If this concept is new to you, give it a try. Like so many other runners and athletes, you'll soon find yourself falling naturally into an easy-hard rhythm.

Resolved: I get into the rhythm of easy, followed by hard.

January 22

"Running is a childish and primitive thing to do. That's its appeal, I think. You strip away all the chains of civilization. While you're running, you go way back in history."

—Joe Henderson, runner and writer

When you run, you go back in your own *personal* history as well.

You may not have been a runner or competed in organized sports when you were young. But almost assuredly you loved to run as a child. You ran around in the backyard, playing tag. You skipped down the sidewalk or chased your friends around the school playground.

Running is truly one of the joys of being a child. There's no pain in motion, nor even thought of potential injury. Muscles and ligaments are as elastic as rubber bands. You take a fall, and after Mom or Dad applies the necessary bandage and TLC to your skinned knee, you're up and running again with nary a thought for the consequences.

It's a goofy cliché to talk about discovering (or rediscovering) your "inner child." But that is precisely what happens when you strip off your adult workaday wardrobe, lace up your running shoes, and take off on a run.

That feeling you feel when you run and it's good—that surge of energy, that giddy elation—that's not a new feeling. You felt it as a child on those days when you were running around the park or a playground, unburdened by care or worry.

Resolved: I strip off my adult wardrobe and go for a run.

January 23

"Every calling is great, when greatly pursued."

—Oliver Wendell Holmes

Some runners have a tendency to trivialize themselves and what they do. When they do this, they cut themselves off from the potential to learn and grow.

You can learn from everything you do, including and especially running. Running is a frivolous activity only if you engage in it frivolously. That's not to equate it with curing AIDS or exploring space. But it's hardly a meaningless exercise.

It's a safe bet that many of the scientists now researching AIDS or involved in the space program are runners. When they need to clear their heads at the end of the day or on the weekends, they go out for a run.

If others make jokes about your running, let them. There's nothing you can do about that. You can, however, control your own internal self-criticism, or at least be aware of it. Unless you're possessed of a strong will, constantly second-guessing what you do leads only in the direction of disappointment and, ultimately, quitting.

Running is a way to help yourself and to achieve the things you want. That's hardly trivial. Running clears the mind the way a summer storm blows the smog and haze from the sky. And with a clear mind and strong heart, what isn't possible in this life?

Resolved: I ease up on the self-criticism and stop putting down the things I do.

January 24

"He who has health has hope; and he who has hope has everything."

—Arab proverb

Today's message may be more cautionary than inspirational in nature. So be it.

Some people decide to plunge feetfirst into running, regardless of whether they've been working out or not. While their enthusiasm is to be admired, is this entirely wise? If you're fit and you know your body, that's one thing. But if you've been playing couch potato over the winter (or longer), it behooves you to check in first with a physician.

Certainly the last thing you want to do is fling yourself off the couch, throw down the channel changer (knocking over the chips and beer in the process), and suddenly enter a local race. You're just looking for trouble if you do that.

Let reality catch up with self-perception. You may be thinking of yourself as the athlete you used to be, not the one you currently are. You can get back into shape (possibly even better than you used to be), but it will take some time.

Even if you've stayed active, you may be due for a baseline physical. There's no harm in getting a reading on where you stand now, in case something comes up in the future. A doctor can advise you on a potential fitness program. Almost assuredly he or she will tell you to take it slow at first and to build gradually.

Resolved: I pay a visit to my doctor before I jump feetfirst into a training program.

January 25

"Methinks that the moment my legs begin to move, my thoughts begin to flow."

—Henry David Thoreau

If you're a writer, and you can't decide what your next sentence is, take a break and run. When you come back, you'll know your next chapter, let alone your next sentence.

If you're a thinker, and your thoughts aren't flowing, get up and run. A run will make your thoughts pour out of you like lava from Mount Etna.

Whoever you are, whatever you do, you will think sharper and clearer thoughts when you run. So, always take a break and go run.

Some people may have to debate about it. But you've already figured it out. When you're feeling stalled, or even when you're not, take a break and run.

It's lunchtime. You've just gotten out of a long, boring meeting where they've stuck you with yet another assignment that you didn't want or ask for. What do you do? You take a break and run, that's what. When you come back, you'll be in a far better mood to handle that new assignment, and you'll probably have developed ideas on how to do it, besides.

When you run, you think. A runner is always sorting out his or her thoughts, feelings, and ideas. A running break is a thinking break. Isn't it about time for one?

Resolved: I always take a break and go run.

January 26

"What do I get from running? Joy and pain, good health and injuries, exhilaration and despair, a feeling of accomplishment and waste. The sunrise and the sunset."

—Amby Burfoot, marathoner

Ok, so you had a bad workout. Shake it off. That's the great thing about running: it's something you do every day. Tomorrow is another day, and it will be better.

Could you possibly be overdramatizing, at least a little? What is the difference, really, between what you call a "good" workout and a "bad" one? The difference is probably not that huge after all.

There's definitely a yin-and-yang aspect to running. Some bad has to be mixed in with the good. Bad days help you appreciate the good.

What are your goals as a runner anyhow? Was it your ambition to run a terrific workout today, or give your all at Boston three months from now? They don't give any awards for training.

Let today be a lesson. A bad workout teaches you what you need to do, or avoid, tomorrow. And if you've faced these problems before, then why let it get you down? You know that this malaise is only temporary and that tomorrow, or very soon, you will be back on the road again, ripping it up.

Resolved: I let go of a bad day and look for better things tomorrow.

January 27

"Now when I'm asked why I run, the answer comes quickly. I run because through running, I find answers to many of the other questions in my life."

—John Bingham, runner

If you're like most runners, you've found a route that works for you. It's comfortable as a worn slipper. You run there all the time. You know where it starts and ends, where to turn around, what the surface is like, what to look for on the route, about how long it will take, and how much effort you need to put forth.

It's reassuring to run in a familiar, safe place. Every runner has a regular route that he or she likes and follows.

But every now and then, especially if your motivation is starting to flag a little, you may want to bust out of your familiar patterns and run someplace where you've never run before.

Obviously, in order to do this, it will take an added effort on your part. You may have to drive farther to get there. The course will be new and different and contain elements of the unknown. There may be hills, and at first you won't know where everything is. Unlike your home course, it will take some getting used to.

But almost immediately, the benefits will be plain. Your mundane daily run will suddenly take on the trappings of adventure. You will be glad you made the effort, and you'll want to go back there again as soon as you can.

Resolved: This weekend I find a new place to run, somewhere I've never run before.

January 28

"One can always trust to time. Insert a wedge of time, and nearly everything straightens itself out."

—Norman Douglas, thinker

One of the reasons people give for not running or exercising is lack of time. But if you say to these same people, "Not even five minutes?" they will probably respond that that's not enough time to do any good; a person needs a half hour or more to get in a good cardiovascular workout.

The truth is, five minutes is a lot. Five minutes is a start. You can get a lot accomplished in five minutes. And no one's schedule is so tight that he or she can't spare five minutes.

Longtime serious runners may skip over this advice as being not relevant to them. They're already committing an hour or two a day to their workouts.

But the five-minute rule applies to any project that you may want to tackle but seem to lack the time for. Want to write a novel or screenplay? Learn a foreign language? Improve your carpentering skills? Become a better cook?

Start with five minutes a day. Though it may seem like nothing, it is actually something—and it has a way of expanding. Once you make room for 5 minutes, 10 minutes and then 20 minutes will be a snap, and with hardly any effort at all your schedule will have somehow found room to accommodate all your desires.

Resolved: I start with five minutes of running or walking a day.

January 29

"There are no split-second decisions as in other sports. While you're running you don't have to think about anything."

—Dr. Victor A. Altshul, on running

When you play softball, you have to think about hitting, catching, and throwing. You need to know where to throw the ball if it's hit to you when you're in the field. If you're at bat, you need to be aware of where the ball goes after you hit it and how many bases you can safely take.

In softball as in many other games, there's a lot to think about. In running, however, all you have to do is run. Isn't that wonderful?

Altshul, who's done research on running, coined a phrase about it: "contentless character." For him it is what distinguishes running from other sports. There are a minimum of rules. You basically go out there and put one foot in front of the other. That's it. That's basically all you need to know (except watch out for dogs).

This quality frees you to think about other things besides the act itself. You don't have to worry about the rules or performing according to certain guidelines and expectations. There is a kind of vacuum to the sport that is filled by the runner him- or herself.

Running is like jazz: you can make it up as you go along. There are no rules about where to go or how far. You can do as you please, for as long as you want. It's your run. Fill the vacuum any way you like. It's all up to you.

Resolved: I appreciate the contentless character of running and run today for as long as I please.

January 30

"Think of the world you carry within you. What happens in your innermost being is worthy of your whole love."

—Rainer Maria Rilke, poet

A running journal can be a wonderful motivator, if used wisely. Some runners keep a journal to record their training times, mileage, and workouts—the prose of running, if you will.

But a more inspired use for a journal would also record the poetry of running—your thoughts and impressions, places you've run, people you've run with, birds or animals seen while running, nature observed, and unusual or humorous occurrences.

Let your journal take the form it will. It doesn't have to follow a script; it can be a record of whatever you want. Running is more than just times and mileage; let your journal reflect that. Don't let it become a burden, a thing you must do; add to it whenever you feel like it, not necessarily every day. Let it be a record of your internal life, even as it charts the progress of your external one.

You don't have to be a Toni Morrison or Richard Ford when you write; just get it down on paper.

Your journal can include pictures and newspaper clippings. Make it a kind of running scrapbook, though its chief use is personal, a method to help you understand the world you carry within you. A running journal will enable you to compare where you've been with where you are, while keeping in mind where you're going.

Resolved: I keep a running journal that records not only my running but my thoughts and observations, too.

January 31

"I knew I had disciplined myself, that running was my own doing, that no one had pushed me to do it. I knew that I was able to accomplish what I had because I had worked on it. It was very clearcut."

—Nina Kuscik, marathoner

Life is complicated. Running is simple. Is it any wonder that people like to run?

Running is very clear. It has a definite beginning and end. We start running at the beginning, and when we reach the finish, we stop.

In work and in other areas of life, we don't always get to see the results of what we do. The rewards are murky, if there are rewards at all. Running is different. We charge ourselves with a specific task—to run a certain distance—and we achieve it.

Running has clear, unchallenged benefits. When we run, we feel better. We look better. Our heart and lungs function the way they were designed to. There's nothing murky about it.

You can count on running; it won't disappoint. If you work at it, if you discipline yourself to run while continuing to enjoy it and have fun, you will become a stronger and faster runner. You will accomplish things. The rewards will be clear.

Don't complicate the simple joys of running. Keep it free of tangles. Set clear, simple goals for yourself and pursue them in a clear, straightforward way.

Resolved: I set clear, simple goals for myself in running, and I take satisfaction when I achieve them.

February I

That may be the hardest thing: accepting all with joy.

Some days you're flat-out miserable when you run. But
that's what you must learn: to accept it with joy.

You enter a race with high hopes. Those hopes are cruelly
dashed, like a bottle broken on the pavement. You run a terrible race, and you don't understand why. But still you must
learn to accept it with joy.

The worst may be when you strain a tendon or pull a muscle that stops you from running for a while. Or your knee
begins to hurt. Yes, even a bum knee. You have to accept that
with joy, too.

Acceptance without joy is a kind of resigned sadness. You
have no choice in the matter, so you go along with it. Some
tortured souls practice a form of acceptance by turning to
drugs and alcohol for consolation. But there's no joy in their
acceptance.

As long as you're alive, you have the capacity to learn and
grow. Your aching knee may be a disappointment to you, but
your situation could be worse. Maybe the knee has forced you
to sit down and saved you from even greater injury. Learn
what you can from whatever life hands you, whatever sadness
befalls you, and buried deep within that sadness will be ker-
nels of joy.

Resolved: I learn to accept all that happens to me in running
with joy.

February 2

*"A man too busy to take care of his health is like a mechanic
too busy to take care of his tools."*

—Spanish proverb

So, how are *your* tools holding up? Are you putting them to
use, or are you letting them gather dust in the garage?

It's an axiom that people take their health for granted until
they get sick or injured. Then they realize what a gift it is.
Nothing, especially not money or success or fame, compares
to it.

Good health is a matter of priorities. If you value it as a priority, you'll find the time for it. That's why running is such an
ideal way to improve your health. It takes so little time to do,
and it's marvelously convenient at that.

Are you busier than the president of the United States? He
runs. He seems to be able to fit it into his schedule. He realizes that without your health, you've got nothing.

But you know that. Everyone knows that. There's no great
secret there. That ranks up there with "an apple a day keeps
the doctor away" for depth of insight.

Well, then. Your running shoes are in the closet. Your
sweats and sock cap and mittens are in the drawer. The open
road beckons. What's stopping you?

Resolved: I think about my priorities. I take my tools out of
storage and go for a run.

February 3

The point is to run.

The lucky ones have arranged their lives in such a way that running is a natural and integral part of it. It's an everyday fact of life.

The rest of us, however, may have to work harder at it.

There are those inevitable distractions. Things getting in the way of what we want to do. What things? You know, *things*. Phone calls, kids, knocks at the door, people poking their heads into the office, car not starting, daily distractions too numerous to mention.

Some way, somehow, you have to shut those things out and give yourself time to run.

You may need to be rude about it. "Enough is enough," you must say to yourself as you wave good-bye to the distractions. You've decided that whatever they are, they are ultimately not as important as running.

And when you run, when you give yourself the chance, it's amazing how fast the distractions melt away. You see how unimportant they really are. And as you concentrate on the road ahead, you realize what you've been missing all this time: a sense of calm.

Resolved: I never let the distractions stop me from running.

February 4

Whoever you are, whatever kind of runner you are or want to be, you have possibilities that demand to be explored.

Only you can be you. Only you can explore your possibilities as a runner and as a human being. There's no sense even comparing yourself with anyone else, because only you possess your unique set of possibilities.

There are better and worse runners than you, of course. That's not the point. Each person has his or her own possibilities, which are distinct from anyone else's. Only you can be the person—and the runner—you were meant to be.

Does that mean the sky's the limit and anything's possible? No. You may not have it in you to become a 2:10 marathoner or win the 10,000 Meters in the Sydney Olympics.

But you most certainly do have it in you to get the most out of yourself, to examine and explore all your possibilities as a runner, whatever they may be. The happiest runners are the ones who are exploring all their possibilities.

Resolved: I make a commitment to explore my possibilities as a runner.

February 5

*"Effort is the one strictly undervalued and original contribution
we make to this world."*

—William James, philosopher

You may start the day feeling rotten. But that doesn't mean you
have to end the day that way. You can put out the effort and
feel better because of it.

Forget inspiration. All you need is effort.

Your effort will create good works. Your good works will
make you feel better. Feeling better will help you create more
good works, and so it goes.

Feelings change. Meanwhile, let your effort be constant and
unflagging. It's impossible to summon up inspiration every
day. But you can almost always summon up the effort, and the
effort will in itself motivate you.

Effort is a product of will. Some days you are just going to
have to slog away. If you make the effort, inspiration will follow. And if it doesn't, well, at least you will have done the
work, made the effort—and you can be proud of that.

Work breeds inspiration. The more you work, the more
effort you put forth, the more inspired you will be.

Resolved: I put out the effort. I run.

February 6

*"If you become restless, speed up. If you become winded, slow
down. You climb the mountain in an equilibrium between
restlessness and exhaustion."*

—Robert Pirsig, writer

A well-known novelist once advised young writers never to
write when they're tired. Tired writers make for tired writing,
she said.

Runners may do well to heed this lesson. Running is wonderful in that you can be tired before you do it but feel ener-
gized afterward. It revives flagging spirits and defeats fatigue.

Still, fatigue is cumulative. If you feel tired day after day
after day yet continue to log your usual miles, you may be
ignoring what your body is telling you and risking injury or
burnout or both.

Overtraining has both a mental and a physical component.
Your body wears down over time, but so does your mind.
There's nothing at all wrong with taking a day off if you're just
not into it mentally for whatever reason, though you may feel
fine physically.

You must learn to trust yourself in this regard. If you take
off a day and it leads to a week, what's wrong with that?
Maybe you need the week off, after all. See how that feels.
Enjoy the inactivity for a change. You'll know when it's time
to come back.

Never run "through" your fatigue. Listen to it as you would
any other signal from your body, and put it to good use.

Resolved: I watch how tired I'm becoming, and if I need to
take a day or two off, I take it.

February 7

"I have loved the feel of the green grass under my feet, and the sound of the running stream by my side, and the face of the fields has often comforted me more than the faces of men."

—John Burroughs, philosopher

Many runners are forced to run on city streets. The sounds accompanying them are the growls and grunts of trucks and cars hurtling by. Then there are the smells, not to mention the potential danger from those same vehicles, barely noticing the lone defenseless runner passing by in the brightly colored parka.

Now and then it's worthwhile to take a run where vehicles never go, where emerald green rolling hills flank you on either side and water runs nearby.

When there's running water, there are almost certainly trees and soothing greenery. Scrub jays skitter in and out of the underbrush. You may even sight a doe and her fawns come down to the water in twilight.

As Melville said, meditation and water are wedded forever. If the running itself does not put you in a thoughtful state, the water will. There is something reassuring about the sound of it. It seems of a different category altogether from the harsh cacophony emanating from those cars and trucks.

Without water, there is no life. Water *is* life. If you are lucky enough to be able to run by running water, or even if you have to make a special trip to do it, it will invigorate your senses and fill you with robust energy.

Resolved: I find a way to run by running water.

February 8

"If someone says 'can't,' that shows you what to do."

—John Cage, composer

If someone says to you, "You can't run a marathon under three hours," make that your goal.

Or if someone says, "You'll never be able to finish a marathon, *ever*," resolve to yourself, right then and there, that that is what you must do.

Or if someone laughs and says, "You'll never finish in the top 100 in the Cherry Blossom 5K. You're not fast enough," set your sights on doing just that.

Draw your inspiration from "can't." No matter who says it, do just the opposite.

Now, it's a much trickier situation if the person who is telling you "can't" is located inside your head. Examine the voice. Who does it belong to? Your mother or father? Sister or brother? A former spouse or an old high-school teacher or coach?

Whoever it is, tell that person what you would any other. Tell him or her, "Yes, I can. You're not going to stop me, not this time. This is too important. I want to do this thing. I want to set a clear goal for myself and achieve it. I know I can, and I will. With your help or without it. Now, if you'll just shut your trap, I'm going to go for a run."

Resolved: I turn every "can't" into a "can."

February 9

"It is better, I think, to begin easily and get your running to be smooth and relaxed and then to go faster and faster."

—Henry Rono, champion runner

Think of a runner whom you admire. Put a picture of that runner in your head when you run, and it will help you be smooth and relaxed.

The very best runners make it look easy. Their stride is long and relaxed. They resemble a metronome in their easy-limbed consistency. They look the same at mile 16 as they did at mile 6.

Keep that image in mind at the start of a race. Or if you get off track while you're running and lose concentration, bring the image back, and it will help you get comfortable again.

Athletes in every sport use this simple visualization technique. Young golfers envision Tiger Woods on the tee before they swing. Basketball players picture themselves as Michael Jordan when they go up for a jump shot.

You may not have a lovely, long-legged stride when you run. Very few people do, in fact. But having a picture of grace in your mind will make you a more graceful person in reality. Once you get into that smooth and steady pace, there is always the possibility that you can build on it and go faster.

Resolved: When I run, I form a mental picture of a runner whom I admire and see if that helps my own stride.

February 10

"Running gives me a sense of controlling my life. I like the finiteness of runs, the fact that I have a clear beginning and end. I set a goal and I achieve it. A good run makes you feel sort of holy."

—Nancy Gerstein, runner

What's your regular route? An out and back to the end of the point? A loop through the park? Around the neighborhood and up the parkway along the river?

Wherever you run, you've probably come to take it for granted on some level. You've run there so long, you no longer see it as special. But it *is* special. It's where you run, and that alone makes it an honored place.

Why not? The feeling you get when you run is similar to the feeling some people get when they go to church or synagogue. People who don't know any better may see your regular route only as a clutter of streets, signs, traffic lights, houses, parkland, apartment buildings, and whatnot. But you know different. It's where you run, the place where you hook into the source.

After all, take away the stained-glass windows and the iconography, and a church is just another building, except for what people bring to it. Bring your whole self to where you run, even if it's the same old spot. It's only natural to take the familiar for granted. But true wisdom comes when you see the extraordinary nature of ordinary things, the divine genius underlying a field of wild hay or a rock dove cooing on a telephone wire.

Resolved: I run my regular route today and feel good about it.

February 11

"Strange what a difference a glorious day can make! How one revels in life, in being, in poetry, in the holy ridiculousness of things."

—Lionel Johnson, poet

It's Sherlock Holmes weather. Fog is everywhere and thick as cake frosting.

It's so thick and gray, it's almost ridiculous. But there is something wonderful about it, too, something strange and otherworldly.

A hill that you know is there isn't there, vanished in the fog. You run along a path with a ridge that slopes away to your right. But that's on a normal day, and today's not normal. Today, the entire ridge is missing, disappeared from view.

Twenty yards ahead of you is nothing but fog. When you reach this spot, the fog magically falls away, and you can see the surroundings—trees, grasses, rocks—for what they are. But the fog has only shifted. Another 20 yards ahead it has materialized anew, and you peer into this murky, insubstantial curtain of gray wondering if it's safe to even go there.

But you keep running, and when you reach that next spot and the fog falls away again, only to re-form once more in the distance, a surge of excitement rushes through you, and you realize how wonderful it is to be out in weather like this, doing something that some people view as crazy, living life fully.

Resolved: I run in and through the fog.

February 12

"Running is a statement to society. It is saying 'no' to always being on call, to sacrificing our daily runs for others' needs. When we run we are doing something for ourselves."

—Phoebe Jones, runner

It's easy to find impediments to running. Such impediments are everywhere and readily available to anyone who wants to make use of them.

It's easy to make excuses. Other people will certainly understand, because they're making excuses for themselves as well.

It's easy not to find the time. Time is almost as precious as Mideast oil these days, and no one will blame you for not having enough of it in your schedule.

Finding reasons not to run is, in fact, easy. What's harder—although it's never as hard as you think it is once you get going—is actually doing it. At some point you just have to dump all the excuses in the trash and run. You've got to say, "Yes, there are obstacles, but I'm going to find a way around them or over them, if necessary, and make time for what I really want to do."

Perhaps you have real ambitions as a runner and need to make not just a little time for yourself every day, but a lot of time. All right, then, do it.

Do what you have to do to run. Do what you have to do to run a lot.

Make a statement to yourself and to society, and do it.

Resolved: I dump all the excuses in the trash, and I start running . . . a lot.

February 13

"So much in life seems inflexible and unchangeable, and part of the joy of running and especially racing is the realization that improvement and progress can be achieved."

—Nancy Anderson, runner

Runners are like any other dream seekers. They have their sights set on a high and lofty goal, and they want to achieve it.

Sometimes you get discouraged, though, because the dream seems so far away and so impossibly hard to achieve. It's a little like the way mountaineers must feel when they climb Mount Everest. Base camp on the tallest mountain in the world is at 17,600 feet elevation, but you still have nearly 12,000 more feet to climb before you reach the summit at 29,028 feet. That's enough to discourage anyone.

Running can feel like that sometimes. As daunting as Everest. But if you're discouraged, it may be because you're looking too far ahead. You need to quit judging yourself by where you're going and the fact that you haven't yet achieved it. Instead, look at how far you've come and appreciate what it's taken to get there.

Progress is being made. It may seem slow and incremental at times, but you are gaining ground. Refuse to be discouraged by your seeming lack of progress. That's only your perception in the moment; that's not necessarily the reality.

You *can* get better. You *will* get better. You *are* getting better. And you will get to the top of that mountain.

Resolved: I keep making progress as a runner, even as I appreciate how far I've already come.

February 14

"It's nice to feel the atmosphere of love round you once in a while, and nobody out of tune."

—George Woodberry, writer

The benefits of running with a friend or partner are obvious. But running with your lover? Ah, that's more problematic.

There is seldom complete equality when lovers are runners. One is usually faster than the other, and this can lead to difficulties.

What if Runner No. 1 (the faster runner) refuses to wait for No. 2 or makes No. 2 feel ashamed or inferior in some way? What if No. 1 slows down to accommodate No. 2, but instead of being comforted, No. 2 feels patronized?

But what if slowpoke No. 2 holds No. 1 back with little ailments or complaints and deprives No. 1 of the joy of running? What if No. 1 wants to go out alone, but No. 2 thinks they should spend this time together?

There are many possible scenarios when lovers run together, and some of them are quite complicated. Nevertheless, when it works, when the two of you are striding together as one, running is a most pleasant pastime for lovers.

You stretch together. You run together, at a pleasant conversational pace, each respecting the other's strengths and weaknesses. And, when you are done, you warm down together. Then you walk off together, happy in each other's arms, comforted and excited by your lover's sweat and smell and glowing physicality.

Resolved: I take a Valentine's Day run with my lover.

February 15

"I take what opportunities I have and try to make the best out of them. You take what you have, and you turn that into a soufflé."

—Lionel Bea, comedy promoter

Opportunities come in many forms, and one of those forms may be a simple break in the weather.

No winter storm is ever uniform. Anyone who spends much time outside, runners included, can tell you that. There are lulls and breaks and changes even in the midst of real gully washers.

This may be hard to believe, though, as you sit forlornly looking out the window, staring at the rain coming down in frozen sheets. You're not going to get to run, at least not today. No way, nohow.

Then something magical happens. An unexplained pause. The sky still looks ominous, the clouds dark and foreboding, but at least for the moment the storm has stopped, as if catching its breath. Can you trust it? How long will the respite last? What if the sky opens up again and dumps on you? What do you do?

To borrow a phrase, you make a soufflé; that's what you do. You make your move: you seize the moment. Make that your philosophy of running. Hell, let it be a philosophy of life. When you see an opening, when you see a chance to get yours, grab it. Because before long, who knows? It may start raining again, or another larger storm may be on its way.

Resolved: I take advantage of a break in the weather (or in anything else), and I run.

February 16

"Always stretch your hamstrings before you run. Spend a half hour on it. Stretch those hamstrings especially."

—DeAndra Carter, sprinter

A half hour for stretching? She's got to be kidding. Sometimes it's hard to find a half hour to run, let alone to spend it unkinking your hammies.

Nevertheless, it's a given that stretching makes good sense for runners. Not only for what it does for you physically, but also because of its relationship to time.

When you have time, you stretch. When you don't have the time, you tend to move through the stretching so you can get on the road faster.

Stretching, then, is nearly always a function of time. Runners with time can do a thorough job of stretching. Runners in a hurry tend not to do such a good job of it and probably expose themselves to a greater risk of injury.

Stretching may seem a routine chore, and at times it is. But there's nothing routine about the idea of not just giving yourself time to run, but giving yourself *plenty* of time.

There's a bonus to this gift of extra time you've given yourself. Not only do you feel more relaxed about stretching, but also you feel more relaxed about your running, and that can translate into an easy, smooth-striding workout.

Resolved: I give myself extra time to warm up and warm down.

February 17

"You should run your first marathon for the right reasons, because you'll never be the same person again. You must want to do it, not do it because your boss did it or your spouse did it."

—Bill Wenmark, running coach

What's true for running marathons is true for running in general: do it because you want to.

Don't do it because your friends do it. Don't do it to impress the boss. Don't do it because your spouse does it. Don't even do it because you think it's the right thing to do and it will be good for you.

Ultimately none of that matters. What matters is you and your desire. It's like that old joke: How many therapists does it take to change a lightbulb? Just one. But the lightbulb has to want to change.

You have to want to run. Nobody can force you to do it. Your doctor could hold an all-day sit-down with you, explaining the medical benefits of running, but if you're not interested, it's all so much hot air.

Let freedom—the idea that you don't have to run if you don't want to—be a motivating influence. You can quit anytime. Run only as long as you're having fun, as long as you're getting something out of it. When you're not, stop. It's your call.

You make your own rules in running. It isn't like when your parents told you to finish what's on your plate or you wouldn't get dessert. Nobody's forcing you to do it. That's what's so great about it.

Resolved: I run because I want to. As simple as that.

February 18

"There is only one big thing—desire. And before it, when it is big, all is little."

—Willa Cather

When you have desire, you have everything.

There are small races and big races within every running race. The big races are in the front of the pack; they decide the men's and women's winners. Smaller races take place throughout the field. These consist of middle- or back-of-the-pack runners struggling to keep pace with one another.

You sometimes see the painful end of these smaller races at the finish line: one runner putting on a kick and straining to edge out another for the right to finish 898 in a field of 5,000.

Then there are the individual races that may not be visible to the spectators. These races are simply to finish, or to finish under a certain time, or to establish a new PR, and triumphing in these contests may bestow the greatest rewards of all.

But one emotion unifies all these runners: desire. Desire is not a substitute for miles. You must do the work. But conversely, hard training alone will never take the place of desire. In the end, the runner with the most desire—who wants it the most—will be the one who accomplishes his or her goals.

You can overcome any obstacle in your path with desire. Big obstacles become small or disappear altogether.

Resolved: I let nothing stop me from achieving my running goals.

February 19

"When adversity strikes, it may be what is needed to be successful."

—Inspirational message in football locker room

At one time or another, every runner takes a tumble. No, really, an actual tumble. He or she is going along fine, striding smoothly and gracefully like Grete Waitz, and then—kersplatt!

It may be the most painful thing that can happen to a runner. Ask Mary Decker Slaney about it. It's humiliating and embarrassing even when it's not in the Olympics. It's impossible to feel dignified when you're splayed across the pavement with your chin and knees bloodied.

It's painful, too. Dirt and mud are smeared across your sweats and shirt. You feel like crying. You feel like the clumsiest, stupidest oaf on the planet.

But there's really nothing else for you to do except get back up and start running again.

Maybe you walk a little to get your legs back under you. Instead of continuing on your regular run, maybe you even turn back around to your car. You go home and lick your wounds for the day. But at some point, assuming you're not badly hurt, you go out running again. There's really no other option.

In a perfect world, none of us would ever fall. But this isn't a perfect world, and when we fall, there's only one choice: get up and start running again.

Resolved: When I fall, I get back up—in running, as in life.

February 20

"I think there is too much emphasis placed on the distinction between the people in the front and the people in the back. I happen to feel that the sensations are exactly the same for all of us."

—Kenny Moore, marathoner and writer

A runner is a runner is a runner. Even if you're a two-legged traffic jam, you're still a runner. You can take pride in that.

The important thing is that you're out there giving it your all, even if your all isn't as much as someone else's. As a runner, you're probably in better physical shape than most of the nonrunners you meet. That alone raises you into the ranks of the elite.

As you continue to run, it's natural to focus more on your times and the other runners in the pack and how you stack up against them. Just don't let that overwhelm the simple knowledge of why you run and what brought you to it in the first place. Ultimately what matters is not when you cross the finish line but how you get there and what it means to you when you do.

There's an old saying: It's not the size of the dog in the fight that matters; it's the size of the fight in the dog. Ditto for runners. A runner who finishes 5,000th can show more heart, more pluck, and more gritty determination than the runner who finishes 5th.

And that's what's so great about this arguably odd, sometimes lonely, utterly compelling pursuit. It's very democratic. The joy of it is freely available to all.

Resolved: I relish my place in the field, even if that place happens to be far behind the leaders.

February 21

"We know, we affirm, I know and I affirm that at the very core of our being, of my being, there is the fact of responsibility."
—Eric Gill, commentator

There is a time-honored tradition among carpenters: when they're building a house, if they make a mistake somewhere, they write their name on it.

If you botch the job, you claim it. That's a good rule for runners, too.

Don't blame what happens on the weather or bad conditions or a crowded field or your shoes or the other runners or any other scapegoat you can think of. Just accept what you did—and if what you did was a mistake, accept that, too.

It's impossible to truly move on until you accept your mistakes. Otherwise you're doomed to repeat them, because you're always blaming what happens to you on some external condition or circumstance. You look everywhere but to yourself for the reason.

You can't always be looking back at what went wrong. That leads only to greater self-doubt, which causes you to repeat your mistakes.

Look your mistake squarely in the eye, however small or large. Own it. Write your name on it metaphorically. Then you don't have to think about it anymore, at least not in the same way, and you can go back to that beautiful house of running that you're building.

Resolved: I own my mistakes as a runner (and as a human being).

February 22

"Heroism is the will to be oneself."

—José Ortega y Gasset, philosopher

Most sports stories are admittedly pretty corny. They include anecdotes about girls stricken with polio who come back to win gold medals in the Olympics, boys cut from their high-school basketball teams who grow up to be NBA stars, men and women who recover from near-fatal accidents to win championships in their field.

There are lots of reasons why these stories, however corny, grab our hearts and uplift us, and one of those reasons is this: they're true. They are not fairy tales; they occur in real life. So-called ordinary people do overcome grinding poverty, disease, injury, and other overwhelming obstacles to achieve amazing things. They do make miracle comebacks. They do set impossible goals for themselves, and despite the cluck-clucking of conventional wisdom, they achieve them.

So, why not you, too? Why not be the hero of your story? It's not such a crazy idea. Imagine your story as a novel or film. See yourself as the main character. Put yourself in a race or some other scenario, and conceive of a script in which you emerge victorious.

Before they were told in books, television shows, and movies, all great sports stories started in the same place: the heart of an individual. You can be that individual. Whatever your dream, whatever your goal, it is possible. It is not fantasy. You can make it happen in the real world in which we live.

Resolved: I become the hero of my own improbable running story.

February 23

"I loved testing myself more than I feared being beaten."

—Ron Clarke

Ron Clarke was a great New Zealand middle-distance runner of another generation. He loved running at the front of the pack as a means, not only of testing the rest of the field, but also of testing himself.

Whether you run in the front of the pack or the rear, you must, from time to time, test yourself. How else are you going to know how you fare as a runner?

Testing yourself does not mean punishing yourself. It does not mean pushing yourself so hard that you cause an injury. Testing yourself is an information-gathering process, a matter of finding out about an important subject: you.

Now, some runners may associate testing with school or work and want nothing to do with it. They'd rather run sheerly for pleasure and not be so serious about it.

What they may not realize, though, is that there is pleasure in testing yourself. You learn when you test yourself, and learning can be a pleasure. You may enter a race and be found wanting. But that's not a loss, if you view it in the right way. How else would you have learned that you need to get more fit or follow a more even pace? In any case, you now have more information than you did before, information that can be put to use in the future.

And, then, there's always the possibility that you will put yourself to the test and surpass expectations. What a supreme pleasure that is!

Resolved: When I feel ready and well prepared, I test myself.

February 24

"At any given time we are the sum of all our new beginnings."
—Charles Gaines, writer

Many people think that you must always be at the beginning in order to begin. That's not true at all. You can make a fresh start even if you're almost at the end.

Let's say you're reading a book and get bogged down halfway through. Now, you may choose not to return to the book and finish it. But if you do choose to finish, you will have to pick up the book and make a fresh start at the point where you left off—that is, in the middle.

Another example, with a running hook: A man is leading a 10K race and has done so from the very start. Then, with 1,000 meters to go, another runner overtakes him and goes into the lead. What the former leader must do, if he can, is clear: realize that circumstances have changed and make a new start.

He must make a new start very nearly at the end of the race. If he doesn't, he has no chance of overtaking the new leader and winning the race.

Today may seem the most ordinary of days. But it really isn't. Today is when you make a new beginning in running, whether you're the rankest beginner, the oldest and craggiest veteran in the business, or somewhere in between. It's always possible to start afresh.

Resolved: I make a new beginning, even if I'm in the middle or near the end.

February 25

"Until you are willing to be confused about what you already know, what you know will never grow bigger, better or more useful."

—Milton Erickson, philosopher

Many runners find themselves stuck on a plateau. Whatever they do, they don't seem to be able to go any faster.

They need to reexamine their assumptions. They need to challenge what they do and why they do it. If they don't, they're going to remain on that plateau while others climb past them.

When you're having no success, it's easy to question your methods. Clearly something isn't working and needs to be changed. You're willing to try new techniques because the old ones have failed.

It's much harder to change your patterns when they've brought some success. You're invested in them. They're comfortable, and not only that, but they also work to some degree. You've achieved a level of success, and there's satisfaction in that.

There *is* satisfaction in that, and you should feel good about it. Still, you have to accept the fact that if you maintain those old patterns, what you do in the future will closely resemble what you've done in the past. The past foretells the future.

If you want to do better, you're going to have to reexamine those comfortable old assumptions. Change may be required. A new way of doing may be in order. Look at what you've done in the past, and challenge it. The road to a brighter future— getting off that plateau—lies in that direction.

Resolved: I reexamine what I take for granted about my running.

February 26

*"I frequently tramped eight or ten miles through the deepest
snow to keep an appointment with a beech tree, or a yellow
birch, or an old acquaintance among the pines."*

—Henry David Thoreau

Thoreau was a walker, not a runner, but like him, you have
numerous acquaintances in the places where you run.

There is that rock outcropping near the edge of the marsh.
Most every time you run by, a ground squirrel mounts one of
the rocks and stands on its hind legs, sounding a warning to
its compatriates about the approach of this large, plodding,
two-footed creature.

You need to say hello to that squirrel. For that matter, you
need to keep your appointment with those rocks, too.

Farther along the way you see a small furry animal moving
in the high grass. This is strange. You've seen black-tailed
jackrabbits in this area, but never anything like this, moving
so slowly.

Then you see a white stripe with black fur, and you realize
it's . . . a skunk. You give it a wide margin and keep going.

But still, it's your duty to keep your appointment with that
skunk. Just not too close.

Even a runner who is running alone has friends among the
squirrels, rocks, snowy egrets, pines, eucalyptus, and wild
hay. Running is a way to stay in touch with them.

Resolved: I keep my daily running appointment with the
beech, the yellow birch, and my friends among the pines.

February 27

"Too rapid a buildup is critical in injuries. You need to know your limitations."

—Russell Pate, exercise physiologist

Listen to that little pain. Listen to it before it becomes a big one. That's common sense.

Everyone must pay attention to a big pain. Big pains give you no choice in the matter. They demand that you stop and sit down. Little pains are quieter yet often more insidious. They don't demand anything at first. They speak in a whisper, a whisper that's easy to ignore.

Listening to a little pain is about learning to accept limits. Everyone has limits. That little pain you're feeling may be a flare on the outer territorial edge of your limits as a runner.

It's possible to rebel against those limits, just as you can rebel against those little pains. Possible and understandable. Limits are anathema to someone on a mission. You want to think and believe that there are no limits, that anything's possible.

That doesn't make much sense if you're in it for the long run, which is the only way to be in it when you're a runner. A little pain is a statement about limits. Not a big Gettysburg Address type of statement, more of an E-mail between friends. Don't ignore those little pains. They may be telling you something big.

Resolved: If I get a little pain from running, I pay attention to it.

February 28

"Running gives you freedom. When you run, you can go at your own speed. You can go where you want to go and think your own thoughts. Nobody has any claim on you."

—Nina Kuscik, marathoner

What a rare concept these days: going at your own speed.

When you drive a car, you must travel at the designated speed limits. When you come to a red light, you must stop. When it turns green, you may resume.

You must appear at work at a certain time. You cannot leave until a certain number of hours pass. You eat lunch at the established time and return to the job after an agreed-upon interval.

Everywhere you go, whatever you do, there are rules governing your conduct. Sometimes the rules are unspoken, such as when you eat dinner at a restaurant. Exceed the tacitly understood limit of how long you can sit at your table, and your waiter will soon be giving you the evil eye from the corner.

In running, however, these rules do not apply. Or rather: you make the rules. You can run fast or slow. You can speed up or ease off the pedal. You can run long or short. You can do whatever suits you at that moment, for as long or as short as you like. You make your own hours, and you set the pace. Is it any wonder people feel free when they run?

Resolved: I go for a run today, contentedly traveling at my own speed.

February 29

"I talk to myself when I train. The year I ran best at Boston, I focused on what to tell myself during those last few miles when it hurts. I told myself, 'Keep going' and 'I'm a tough dude.'"
—Paul Thompson, runner

When you run a big race, there are often people along the way cheering for you. Their enthusiasm gives you a boost and helps transport you along, especially near the end when you need it the most.

But your greatest cheerleader in any race will always be you. Truth is, you never have to go far to find moral support when you begin to drag or hit a rough patch.

The person who will get you through that rough patch is the same one who has gotten you through all those other rough spots in the past. It's the same one who cheers for you when you're on a run and no one else is around. You can always count on that person, even if everyone else has deserted you.

You're a tough dude.

Keep going.

Come on, you can do it.

You probably have your own personal mantra, something you say to yourself to keep running after the well has seemingly been tapped dry. But no, the well isn't dry, at least not yet. You have more left, and a few simple encouraging words can help you find it.

Every time you enter a race or go on a run, take along your personal cheerleading section. Sometimes you really need it.

Resolved: I give myself personal pep talks to keep going when I'm tired.

March 1

"I run because I enjoy it—not always, but most of the time. I run because I've always run—not trained, but run."

—Amby Burfoot, marathoner

Always, always, run. But be wary when your running turns into training.

Training implies work and duty, which are fine and noble concepts that will kill your enjoyment of running if you let them.

Running is a choice. Training is mandatory, an obligation. That makes all the difference in the world.

When you freely choose to do an activity, you come to it with enthusiasm and energy. An activity that is forced upon you saps your strength.

Training is like a foul-tasting pill that you must take because it's supposedly "good" for you. First chance you get, you're going to flush those pills down the toilet.

Training is a whip, and sooner or later you will rebel against it. It is a form of self-denial, harsh and unyielding. Athletes who begin training at too early an age are prime candidates for burnout. Their spent and discouraged carcasses litter every sport, including running.

Keep enjoyment and fun in the forefront of your running, and you will be better for it. You may even find yourself passing all those hard-trainers in the race.

Resolved: I never train. I run.

March 2

"It's all right to have a good time. That's one of the most important messages of enlightenment."

—Thaddeus Golas, philosopher

Let your running life be filled with pleasure. Let it be a gateway to good times.

After a good run, take a long, hot shower. Few things in life are more pleasurable than that.

Run to the pastry shop and back. Then sit down with a caffe latte and croissant, and read the morning paper.

Sunday is always a lovely day for running. There's more time, the runs tend to be longer, and you feel more relaxed. Afterward go down to that great breakfast place with your friends and feast on eggs Benedict and fresh-squeezed juice.

Invite some members of your running club over for a spaghetti feed one evening. Make a mockery of the solitary nature of running with lots of good talk and good cheer.

After all, it is not only running neophytes who sometimes feel bored. Anytime you do something day after day after day, it's going to be hard to keep it fresh.

The answer is in association. Do fun things when you run. Or do them after or before. The more you associate running with pleasure, the more pleasurable it becomes.

Resolved: I keep those good times coming and always associate running with pleasure.

March 3

"If it's the ultimate game, why are they playing it again next year?"

—Duane Thomas, former running back, on the Super Bowl

In football as in running, there are no ultimate tests. You're not going to war or fighting for your life. You're running a footrace. There's nothing ultimate about it.

Flip to the calendar pages of any running magazine. The pages are filled with race listings. If these are ultimate tests, why are there so many of them?

If you focus too much on a given race, you're putting unnecessary pressure on yourself. That will likely make you tie up when you run, and you won't turn in your best performance.

Better to see individual races merely as segments of one lifelong race that is your running career. If it doesn't go as well as planned, or you have to drop out, as occurs with even the best runners, see it only as an unwelcome interruption, like being washed into an eddy while rafting a river. As soon as you can, rejoin the current and continue down the stream.

Finish what you start. That's as good a rule in running as it is in life. On the other hand, if you don't, it's not the end of the world. There will be other tests to come.

Resolved: I try to finish every race I start. But if I don't, I keep it in perspective.

March 4

"To an imagination of any scope the most far-reaching form of power is not money, it is the command of ideas."

—Oliver Wendell Holmes

First you conceive, then you write it down.

Einstein's relativity theory was just an idea until he wrote it down. Then it became more solid somehow, more real. By writing it down, he gave his idea a life outside himself. Others could read it and judge for themselves. It was no longer just a thought bouncing around in his head; it was a thing of substance.

So it must be with your goals as a runner. Having them in your head is a good start; that's where all great schemes, dreams, and plans are hatched. Now you must take command of them. Write them down, and give them heft and substance.

You can write your goals in your runner's journal, if you have started one of those. If not, write your goal on a slip of paper—Boston, 2:35—and display it in a place where you'll see it every day. Your cubicle at work, perhaps. Make it a screen saver on your PC. Tape it to your bathroom mirror, post it under a refrigerator magnet, or tack it to a bulletin board.

Great ideas must be circulated. Write your goal down, and make sure that you circulate it to the one person who needs to see it: you.

Resolved: I write my running goals on paper, and I put it where I can see it every day.

March 5

"If you want to be a better runner, you've got to run more. It's as simple as that."

—Tom Fleming, running coach

It *is* simple, really. The more you run, the better you will be.

The more you run, the more fit you become. As your fitness improves, so will the quality of your running. You can go to the bank on it.

How much you run varies with your age, conditioning, and goals. But almost everyone will improve by running more. You may not become Joan Samuelson or Frank Shorter. But you will get better.

If you're stuck on a plateau and you feel frustrated, running more is a possible solution. Running more will improve your endurance, which can bring down your times. If you need speed work, add it to your regular workout. That is a form of running more.

Running more doesn't mean you stop listening to your body. Making a sudden jump from 10 miles a week to 100 miles is obviously foolhardy. Running more can be just a little bit more.

Not faster, not harder, not too much, not straining. But more.

Resolved: I run more.

March 6

"Spend at least some of your training time, and other parts of your day, concentrating on what you are doing in training and visualizing your success."

—Grete Waitz, champion runner

Here's an excellent visualization (and motivation) technique: before you run, imagine a race or workout from the end to the beginning.

See yourself crossing the finish line, checking your watch for the time and receiving the cheers of the spectators. Work back from there. Imagine yourself rounding the last turn to come down that last straightaway. Keep going back. If it's a marathon you're staging in your mind (and planning to run), picture yourself at the 20-mile mark—sweating, fighting, making it through the wall.

The length of the race doesn't matter; the technique applies to all distances, from 5K to ultra. See yourself at a water station, drinking from a paper cup and pouring it over your head. There you are, in full stride, running alongside another whose pace resembles yours. Going back further, see yourself wading through the bodies at the start, before the pack has thinned out. See yourself standing, milling among the other runners, waiting for the race to get going.

Even envision the drive to the race. Imagine quickly finding a parking space (a miracle!), then jogging lightly over to the start. Spend a few minutes with this exercise; athletes in all sports use it. See what you are about to do as a thing that has already been accomplished; it will in fact help you do it. The race will already be run before you run it.

Resolved: I visualize a race from end to beginning, in order to help me run it.

March 7

"The ability to concentrate is the single element that separates the merely good athlete from the great ones. Concentration is the hallmark of the elite runner."

—William P. Morgan, Ed.D.

How do you improve your concentration as a runner? Focus on what you can control. What can you control? The task at hand. That task, as Hal Higdon says, is represented by the "narrow corridor of the road ahead." Put everything else aside.

What occurred behind you is gone. It may be educational after a run to look back and learn from it. But worrying about it while you are running will only divert your focus from that narrow corridor ahead.

Thinking ahead is something every runner must do to some degree. But thinking too far ahead—say, to the finish line—will only dull your psychological edge and distract you from what you need to do in the moment. Think about the finish when you come to it.

You can't control what's happened in the past. That's over and done. Nor can you control what will occur in the future. That's only a matter of speculation.

Accept that the world is always going to be a little crazy and out of control. Sometimes it's going to go positively bonkers, in fact. There is very little you can do about that.

So, what can you do? Focus on what you can control, right here and right now, and keep yourself fixed on the narrow road ahead.

Resolved: I focus on what I can control and fix on the narrow corridor ahead.

March 8

"Run into peace. The man who is in the state of running, of continuous running into peace, is a heavenly man. He continually runs and moves and seeks peace in running."
—Meister Eckhart, 14th-century philosopher

We cruise the Net and read the morning paper. We fax, we phone, we E-mail. We check in with CNN and listen to drive-time radio.

We're a tuned-in culture, all right. We're so tuned in that sometimes we forget to pay attention to ourselves and what really matters.

Running is a way to do that. It takes you both out of yourself and into yourself. It's how you get away from all the busyness of modern life, as well as how to cope with it.

When you run, you log on to yourself. You flip through the pages of your being. You take a letter from your psyche and find out what the real news is. That may be why some people find it hard to run. They don't want to check in with themselves, afraid of what they may find out.

There's no reason to be afraid. If you contracted a rare disease—heaven forbid—wouldn't you rather know about it than not? The worst thing is not knowing. When you have information, you have power. The possibility for healing exists. You can't get on the road to a cure or recovery when you're still in ignorance.

For most of us, thankfully, the circumstances are not so dire. All we need to do is check in with ourselves, and the answers we're looking for will be there.

Resolved: I always run, because running is one of the ways I pay attention to myself.

March 9

"We must mix victory with defeat. If you have a salad that is all lettuce, that is not good. It has no flavor, it's flat. Victory is the same. You must mix in defeat to gain the flavor of victory."

—Gerard Cote, French Canadian marathoner

Everybody loses. If you haven't lost, you're not trying.

Every success story is a story of losses converted into gain. One must fail before one can succeed. Losses can occur repeatedly, over a period of years. Every "overnight success" will tell you that. It's axiomatic that they have struggled at their craft for years before landing their big break.

Expecting to succeed without losing is a recipe for failure. As has been pointed out, shame is on the underside of the coin of perfection. When you fail to attain perfection, as we all do, you feel shame, and this adds to your bitter sense of defeat.

Champions are not born; they are made. And what creates them are the losses they absorb and how they respond. If they do not respond, if the losses defeat and ultimately define them, they cannot call themselves champions.

It's a lie that winning begets winning. Losing begets winning. Only by enduring a loss, and another, and another, and another, and another, and another, can you ever hope to succeed. You reach the light at the end of the tunnel only after passing through darkness.

Never be discouraged by losing. It is an essential ingredient of success. Your first loss is your first step on the road to victory.

Resolved: I accept losing as part of the game and never get discouraged by it.

March 10

"It's almost too cold to hold a pen this morning. I've lost a toe since breakfast, my nose is on its last nostril. Who was the French poet who had alphabetically lettered underpants, and wore every one up to H on a cold morning?"

—Dylan Thomas

If only that poet had been a runner, he wouldn't have needed so many underpants. He could have gone out in the morning and worked up a little body heat.

It's a cool, cool day in March. Wait a minute: it's passed beyond cool to downright cold, even frigid. What do you do? Work up a little body heat. Sex is good for that. So's running. If you can't have sex at this moment, what about a five-mile run? Both are good for working up a little body heat.

It's good for the brain, good for the bones, good for the heart and lungs, good for the indigestion. It gets the blood pumping, and it can knock a few cents off your heating bill besides. Do yourself a favor: work up a little body heat.

Running in its essence is not about stopwatches and T-shirts and air-cushion soles. It's about tending to our oft-neglected animal self. And what does every animal crave? Food and warmth. After you work up a little body heat, get something to eat. Then growl. You'll feel like a new person.

Listen. You're not working up any body heat reading this book. Nor will you produce any by staring at a computer. Quit piling on the sweaters and turning up the space heater. You can drink only so much hot tea. Baby, it's cold outside. Work up a little body heat, and feel better about it.

Resolved: I go for a run and work up a little body heat.

March 11

"The plain fact remains that men and women the world over possess amounts of resources that only exceptional individuals push to their extreme use. Compared to what we ought to be, we are only half awake."

—William James, philosopher

It is a scientific fact that only a tiny portion of the brain's capacity is ever used by its owner. It's probably also true that few of us use our bodies to the fullest extent possible.

Running is one of the ways that people seek to get more out of themselves. It is not the only way, but it is one of them. When you run on a steady basis, you are trying to get more from your body. On some level you think that it can be more useful to you, that there are resources there that are still untapped.

Additionally, running enlarges your capacity for thought. It's good for the brain. After you run, you can think clearer thoughts. Your ideas are sharper.

So, you've made the commitment, whether you're conscious of it or not. Through running, you have decided that you want to be fully awake. You want to engage all of yourself, or at least as much as you can muster, and you want to do it as often as possible. You want to expand your capacities.

Good for you. Never be ashamed of the fact that, unlike so many others, you don't want to sleepwalk through life or experience it only through a TV set or computer. You want to be fully alive, and you want to realize it every second that you are, and running is part of that.

Resolved: I keep my commitment going to stay fully awake as a runner.

March 12

*"The whole of what we know is a system of compensations.
Each suffering is rewarded; each sacrifice is made up; every
debt is paid."*

—Ralph Waldo Emerson

In those down days that every runner has, it can sometimes
feel as if all your effort is meaningless and without reward.

What's the point, you ask yourself in disgust after you accidentally step in a puddle left over from yesterday's rain. Why
run? Why keep doing it? Why try to get better? It's not fun
anymore. It all feels like such a grand waste of time.

The fact is, the greatest philosophers the world has known
disagree with you.

Nothing is lost, they say. Everything you do in this world
matters. It all comes back to you, though it may not feel that
way in your most discouraged moments.

It's an offshoot of the idea of karma. What goes around
comes around. Do good works, and at some point, somehow,
good works will come to you.

The reason people get discouraged is that it's not immediate, it's not an instant karmic payback. Indeed, it may take
time. If, say, your sights in running are set toward achieving
some high and lofty goal, you may not see the results of what
you're doing for years and years. But make no mistake: every
step you take in running matters. And they all add up.

Resolved: I keep putting one foot in front of the other,
because I know it will pay off.

March 13

"Break away in the middle. No one can follow you."

—John Chaplin, running coach

For the best runners, a race is a thinking contest as much as a physical one. They must plot their strategy to achieve the ends they desire.

One line of thinking says to take the lead from the start. Set the pace, and let the others stay with you if they can. But it's awesomely difficult to sustain this strategy over a long race such as a marathon, and the front-runners frequently take turns in the lead to share this burden.

Another line of thinking says to save your kick for the end, though most agree that this is better suited for short and middle distances than long ones. Runners who count on having a big kick at the end of 26 miles may resemble investors after the great stock market crash of '29: they may go to the bank and find nothing there.

Yet another possibility is to break away in the middle of a race. This offers many advantages, not the least of which is the element of surprise. The other runners do not expect it. What? He (or she) is going now? They may doubt your resolve, and yet they have no other choice but to meet your challenge.

One of the biggest advantages of this strategy is that it makes you approach a race in a different way. The thought alone breaks you out of a familiar pattern and challenges you to respond. "If I break in the middle," you ask yourself, "will I have enough to finish?" Just the fact that you are asking this question—that you are thinking new thoughts about your running and asking new questions—will be to your benefit.

Resolved: I entertain new thoughts about my running, including the possibility of breaking away in the middle.

March 14

"Reason may fail you. If you are going to do anything with life, you have sometimes to move away from it. You must follow sometimes visions and dreams."

—Bede Jarrett, writer

Let's say you're a three-times-a-week runner, who clocks in maybe two miles each time. That's about all your schedule allows, and that's fine with you. It works. You're happy with the amount you run and the way it makes you feel.

Then one night you go to bed and you're transported to Africa. You've never been there before, but you know it's Africa because there are gazelles and giraffes and elephants running alongside you.

You keep running, now up the side of Mount Kilimanjaro, the continent's highest peak. But it's more like flying than running, and when you look down at your shoes, there are wings attached. Your spirit soars along with your legs, and in an instant you're at the summit. The clouds have parted, and the sky is blue.

You wake up. Suddenly you know your life is changed forever. This wasn't just a case of indigestion affecting your sleep; you've never had a dream so vivid, so pure, so enthralling. Now you know what you must do: run up Kilimanjaro.

As crazy as this may sound, many runners have had similar dreams. Not Kilimanjaro perhaps, but some other seemingly daffy notion that vitalized them and changed their lives. If ever you have a dream like that, follow it. You owe it to yourself to pursue it with everything you have. In that pursuit lies happiness.

Resolved: I pursue every crazy, half-baked dream I have in running.

March 15

"The initial path can be repeated forever."

—Luisa Valenzuela, philosopher

Having trouble getting motivated to run? Take one stride. After you take one, take another. Before you know it, you will be running.

But it first starts with one. Weight lifters will tell you that. Doing one repetition is a standard motivational technique for them. After you do one curl or one bench press, then you can go to a second. You can get to two only by starting with one.

One is a motivator. If you can do one, then it's almost certain that you can do two. First do one, and see how you feel. Most certainly you will feel like doing another.

Want to run three or five or seven days a week? First run one day. That's not enough, say some people. Yes, but it is *one*. First you allocate one day for running, then two, and so on.

It's a building process like anything else. The construction of the Cheops pyramid began with the placement of a single block of stone. If that hadn't been laid down, none of the others would have either.

Longtime runners may use a variation of this technique. Not feeling like running today? Why not just run a mile? A mile's nothing, right? You can do that in your sleep. Chances are, after you get out there and run that one mile, you will want to run two.

Resolved: First I do one. After I do one, I'll think about doing another.

March 16

Energy is like love. The more you give, the more you receive.

Some people are Scrooges of energy. They think that, by hoarding their personal reserves, they can hang onto them longer. Nothing could be further from the truth.

Running shows you that. The more you run, the more you feel like running. The more energy you expend in running, the more energy you have. As you're expending energy, you are creating it at the same time. You may run out of it in the short term, say at the end of a hard day or a long run. But it will come back to you in full flower by the following morning or soon thereafter.

Scientists will tell you that the amount of energy in the universe is constant. There may be temporary local energy crises (such as with oil), but in terms of the cosmic picture, the total amount of energy remains the same.

It's not that great of a stretch to apply this on a personal level. You will certainly have periods of low energy and low motivation when you run. But the energy available to you is constant; it's always there. What changes from day to day is your willingness to tap into it. Sometimes all that's needed is a change of attitude. Many people find, to their delight and surprise, that when they drag themselves out to run on those low-motivation days, they have far more energy than they thought they did.

Resolved: I create energy by using it.

March 17

"I use exercise to help me unwind. On days of big events, I often run beforehand."

—Tom Brokaw, runner and broadcaster

It's Saint Patrick's Day, a big event if there ever was one. What about a run and a beer after?

And if you're in the mood (and it's on the menu), what about some corned beef and Irish pudding as well? Followed by another beer or two.

If you need a beer recommendation, try a pint of Irish-brewed Guinness. That will put meat on your bones, which some skinny runners could use. Runners cannot expect to consume all this—corned beef, Irish pudding, pints of Guinness—and then go for a run afterward. You need to do your duty prior to the evening's celebration, else your duty will likely not get done.

In the spirit of combining two pleasurable activities, you may want to run down to the pub where the festivities are taking place. In that case you'll most likely need a cab home.

Another possibility is to run with a bunch of friends after work, then go down to the pub together. You can all feel virtuous for having run even as you are drinking and chowing down.

Always look for ways to combine running with pleasure. A run on Saint Patrick's Day—followed by a beer—is a recipe for just that.

Resolved: I celebrate Saint Patrick's Day with a run and a beer.

March 18

"Adopting the right attitude can convert a negative stress into a positive stress."

—Dr. Hans Selye, stress expert

Negative things occur in everyone's life. You've got to find a way to turn those negatives into positives.

Say you're driving to meet some friends for a Sunday-morning run and brunch after. But traffic is horrible. There's been a wreck, and what is normally an easy drive turns into an hour-and-a-half nightmare.

What do you do? Well, you can rage and fume at events that are basically out of your control. Or you can slip Bach or Mozart into the cassette player and relax, using the time for meditative thinking about running and other aspects of your life.

Stresses are temporary. At some point, traffic will clear, and you will get to where you're going. You will run and have brunch with your friends, even if it occurs later than you planned.

Your attitude will determine how long this essentially minor crisis—although it seems major at the time—stays with you. Granted, you have to stretch your creativity at times to find silver linings in some of the dark clouds that hover over daily life. But they're there, if you're willing to turn the situation around and look at it in a different way.

Like it or not, the stresses aren't going away. But your attitude can make a huge difference in how you handle those stresses.

Resolved: I find ways to turn negative stresses into positive ones.

March 19

"Age is a case of mind over matter. If you don't mind, it doesn't matter."

—Satchel Paige

One of the joys of running is that it turns the aging process on its head.

A widespread view in this youth-obsessed society of ours is that growing old is a kind of slow, inexorable march to the grave. The older you get, the sadder it is, for each birthday brings a person one step closer to the terminus.

Older runners hardly share this view. Matter of fact, many of them look forward to celebrating a birthday if it puts them into a new age category.

A 59-year-old runner exults when she turns 60 because she will now compete against the 60-and-over age group. Being one of the younger ones in her group can represent a competitive advantage for her.

This is true up and down the line for runners. A 29-year-old may not relish the prospect of turning 30, except when it comes to running, while the 39-year-old may even look forward to the big four-oh because of the new age group he enters.

When you run, you look, feel, and act younger than your years. But ironically, you don't mind growing old because it often makes you more competitive in races. It's a great sport, isn't it?

Resolved: I never let age be an excuse for not running.

March 20

"We are happy, when however briefly, we become one with ourselves, others, and the world of nature."

—David Cole Gordon, writer and naturalist

Runners know things before other people—things about the weather, the seasons, the trees, and the flowers.

Runners don't need a weatherman to tell them what the weather's like. They already know, because they've been out there and immersed themselves in it.

They've seen with their own eyes the clouds drifting across the sky. They've felt the sharp edge in the air and the breeze blowing in from the west.

Nor do runners need a calendar to tell them when the seasons are turning. They conduct a personal informal survey every day, and they know that the seasons never turn when the calendar says, anyhow.

Runners are among the first to see the buds appearing on the buckeye trees. They are among the first to see the wildflowers blooming on the hillsides, buttercups and purple lupines. These signs of spring appeared weeks ago, long before the official designated start of the season.

Because of their close contact with nature, runners live in a better world than those pale, closeted souls who mostly spend their days indoors. Be sure to enjoy it.

Resolved: I go out for a run and see what flowers are blooming today.

March 21

"If you're standing still, you're going backwards."

—Maxim

Every runner, like every person, is in transition. Life is a process of transition.

You can see it most clearly with children. The changes they undergo are rapid and dramatic. They grow physically and emotionally. This is why children need stability, because their lives are in constant upheaval.

As we grow older, we tend to discount this process of change in ourselves or become less conscious of it. But the changes are continuing. At every stage of life, a person is moving on to the next stage, whether he or she is aware of it or not.

Though the changes are less dramatic than what happens to a child, our bodies are in transition, too. This is where running steps in. It cannot "stop" the aging process; rather it helps us endure more gracefully the physical transitions that occur as we grow older.

And these transitions are not just among the senior set. A 25-year-old's body does not respond in the same fashion as it did when he was 18, nor will it when he turns 30.

You're never standing still, in life or in running. The fact that your 10K PR hasn't changed in a while doesn't mean you're not in transition. Like every period of transition, this time is ripe with opportunity. It could mean that you fall backward, or that you go forward. It's up to you.

Resolved: I accept that this is a time of transition for me, and I make the best of it.

March 22

"Very often a change of self is needed more than a change of scene."

—A. C. Benson, writer

Change is hard. No one likes to change. But change is frequently necessary for growth to occur.

The 12-step programs deal with this issue all the time. They encounter people whose lives are not succeeding on some level. Their lack of success may be caused by alcohol, drugs, or other reasons.

An alcoholic believes that he can continue to act the way he always has—that is, drink—and produce a different outcome in his life, even though it's been proved to him again and again that he can't. This is madness. Doing the same thing will only produce the same result. A person must realize that in order to get a different (and more positive) outcome, his or her actions must change.

Unlike drinking, running is a "positive" addiction. Even so, changes may be in order. You may injure yourself while running. After a period of rest and recuperation, you may come back and hurt yourself again. Clearly your body is telling you that your actions must change.

There are many other ways in which change can contribute to growth in running. Recognition of the need to change is the first hurdle. Once you get over that one, you're halfway there.

Resolved: I make changes in my running if I need to make them.

March 23

"In every competition there's a point when somebody wins and somebody loses. The loser will always settle. He'll say, 'This is all I can do.' A winner always finds a way."

—Dan O'Brien

Dan O'Brien has always found a way. His parents gave him up at birth, and he spent two years in foster homes as a child. A couple finally adopted him, and he grew up in a family with six brothers and sisters.

In 1992 O'Brien entered the U.S. Olympic Trials as the clear favorite. Athletes in the decathlon compete in 10 events over two exhausting days.

But in the pole-vault competition, O'Brien failed utterly. He did not make the qualifying height and thus was eliminated from contention. The best decathlete in the world and the early favorite to win a gold medal was staying home.

O'Brien was stunned, as was the rest of the track world. Was he finished as an Olympic-caliber athlete? How would he respond to such a heartbreak? Could he ever come back?

O'Brien answered these questions resoundingly in the years that followed. He continued to train and compete in the decathlon, setting records in the process. In 1996, after qualifying first in the U.S. Olympic Trials (easily getting over his pole-vaulting roadblock), he won the gold medal in the decathlon at the Atlanta Games.

"The decathlon is like life," says O'Brien. "You have good events and bad events, good days and bad days, and you have to get through them all."

Resolved: I have good days and bad days as a runner, and I always find a way to get through them.

March 24

"Many people shy away from hills. They make it easy on themselves, but that limits their improvement. The more you repeat something, the stronger you get."

—Joe Catalano, running coach

There is a surefire way to get stronger as a runner, and that is to run hills.

The Kenyans and all the other great ones do it. They run all over the place, and if some of those places are hills, they run over them. They certainly do not avoid them.

You do not want to see a hill at the 25-mile mark of a marathon. But if you want to improve your fitness, a hill is your friend.

Start easy. Run an easy hill at first. Walk up it if you need to. Then skip a day or two. Don't suddenly introduce a new element such as a hill into your running and then push yourself.

But come back to it. Go up it, skip another day or two, then do it again. You may no longer need to walk the hill. Over time you will find that you go up it much more quickly and easily than you did at first. You will also find that you are stronger and more competitive on the flats.

Hills build both stamina and speed. You must be determined in order to run a hill, and so it can be argued that hills build determination and perseverance, too.

Whatever your goals as a runner, the rule applies to all: run hills and you will get stronger.

Resolved: I gradually incorporate hills into my runs.

March 25

"If you want to achieve a high goal, you're going to have to take some chances."

—Alberto Salazar, marathoner

Ever hiked (or run) to the top of a mountain? The weather is usually harsher at the peak than it is down below, isn't it?

It doesn't have to be a mountain; it can be a hill or a ridge top. In the flatlands it may be calm and serene, not a whisper of a breeze. Turn upward, and then see what happens. It may stay calm as you wend your way up the side. But when you crest the summit, almost always the climate changes. It's windier, colder, grimmer. You can't linger on the peak as much as you'd prefer. You take in the sights and quickly turn back down to the lower elevations, where it is more hospitable.

This is how it is for anyone who strives for a high goal. It can be beatifically calm and serene when you're in training. But as you move closer to reaching your goal, the wind kicks up and the climbing becomes steeper.

Conditions have grown tougher. You know you're getting closer to your goal, and yet success seems more elusive. What do you do? Do you turn back or keep pressing on?

The decision is up to you. But always remember that with every mountain you climb, the going gets harder at the top.

Resolved: I realize that the closer I get to achieving my goals, the harder it may be.

March 26

"The idea that the harder you work, the better you're going to be is just garbage. The greatest improvement is made by the man or woman who works most intelligently."

—Bill Bowerman, running coach

The hardest workers do not always succeed. This is one of the most painful unfairnesses of life.

You can put in more miles than another runner. You can get up earlier and stay later. You can be the most deserving runner in the world based on how hard you work.

And yet that other runner—you know, the slacker—can finish ahead of you on race day. This may be a terrible injustice, but it's life.

How hard you work does not necessarily equate with success—that is, lower times or higher finishes. The miles you put in are important, but in the end, they are not the sole determinant of who wins and loses.

On the other hand, this knowledge can be liberating because it allows you to be responsive to mood. You don't always have to kill yourself. You can still attain your goals by listening to your mood.

If you feel tired or bored or not into it for some reason, cut your run short. No harm done. It's a sign of intelligence. You're looking at the long term, not judging yourself based on today's results only. You know you're putting in the work, but you also know there's more to success than that. Sometimes putting your nose to the grindstone will only get you a skinned nose.

Resolved: I stay receptive to mood. When I feel like cutting my run short, I cut it short.

March 27

"If I get tired, I'll slack off exercising. I do get worn out. It's from the children; it's from work. I listen to my body, but I don't use that as a cop-out."

—Kim Alexis, model and runner

Part of running is planning. Most people have to make room in their schedules in order to find the time to run, and that takes planning, especially when you have children.

It is possible, though, to maintain an active running calendar while still raising kids. Lots of runners who are parents do exactly that. Here are a few of their tricks:

- Take the child with you. Those three-wheeled jog strollers allow you to exercise while getting your small child outside and giving him or her some fresh air.
- Hire a sitter for an hour or two, or drop the child at day care. When you come back after your run, you'll be refreshed.
- Trade with another parent. The other parent doesn't even have to be a runner. He or she can watch your child while you run, and you can return the favor.
- Take turns with your partner. This is a favorite tactic of running parents. On the weekends, leave the child with your partner. You run, while your partner watches the kid. When you come back, you can give your partner some free time.

When you have children, it's sometimes hard to find the time to do anything, much less run. But you can raise kids and still keep running. It just takes a little bit of planning.

Resolved: I keep running, even if I have children. I just may need to do a little more planning.

March 28

There are many reasons for allowing plenty of time when you run.

Time equates with possibility and relaxation. There is more time to stretch before and to warm down after. You're not as rushed. You're more able to enjoy the experience. When there's time, there is always the possibility that you can run longer than you planned.

One more advantage to leaving a little extra time is that after you're done, you can sit and enjoy the view. You don't have to hop immediately into a car and get on the road. You can sit quietly on a bench and look across at the water and the hills beyond.

When you're running, you're focused. The attitude of many runners is: Scenery, what scenery? Their sense of their surroundings extends as far as the tips of their running shoes.

That's why it is nice to take a moment to see what you may have missed while on the run. Now that the work is over, be sure to enjoy some of its perks, drinking in your surroundings with a feeling of contentment and openness. Opening yourself to the world around you, you open yourself to what's inside you as well.

Resolved: I stop and admire the view after I run.

March 29

"Happiness is not a matter of events; it depends upon the tides of the mind."

—Alice Meynell, writer

One of the most frustrating things about an injury is that it forces you to slow down.

You may have a couple of running partners in which a rough equality exists. All of you run at about the same speed. But when an injury occurs, you can't run as you normally do, and you must drop off the pace.

That's aggravating, to say the least. You want to run with your pals, the way you always do. You don't want to hang back because your knee is bothering you.

But what else can you do? Pushing the knee at this point is tantamount to running suicide. It's going to make a bad thing worse. Drop off the pace, and take some pressure off that knee. A slower pace is not ideal perhaps, but it's better than not running, right?

It's imperative to find some sort of contentment in this slower pace, if only for a while. If you do not, you will try to come back too fast. You will push the knee more quickly and harder than you should, and it may not heal completely.

Find contentment in where you are, even if it's not where you want to be at that moment. That is one of the keys to happiness in running—and in life, for that matter.

Resolved: I take satisfaction in a slower pace, for as long as it's necessary.

March 30

"Being carefree is of the essence in this world."

—Anton Chekhov, playwright

Car people think of a dead-end road as a road that leads nowhere. Runners know different. A dead-end road—a good one—is only the beginning.

Runners like dead-end roads because car people generally do not. What's the point of going down a road on which you must turn around and come back the same way you drove in? That's the thinking of many car people. They prefer circular roads or roads that connect with other roads where they can espy new scenery from behind their tinted windows.

God bless 'em, say runners. That leaves the dead-end roads free for runners.

A good dead-end road is typically a country road. It winds lazily through the trees, which provide blessed shade on disagreeably warm days. Cars are few and far between. Without their foul-smelling sputterings, you become aware of how quiet it is and can ease gently into the run.

There's plenty of company on the road, though. Besides the other runners, deer, squirrels, turkey vultures, kestrels, robins, jays, and other creatures hang out and make the scene with you.

Parking is at the entry point. Runners get out, run to the end of the road, turn around, and come back. What better way to spend a carefree morning or afternoon?

Resolved: I find a good dead-end road nearby and work it.

March 31

"A hundred times a day I remind myself that my inner and outer life are based on the labors of other men and women, living and dead, and that I must exert myself in order to give in the same measure as I have received and am still receiving."

—Albert Einstein

Feeling a little snakebit these days? A little down on yourself? Give. Not money, but yourself.

Volunteer at a school. Help out at the local food bank. Put in some time at your church or temple. Or perhaps just sit and listen to a friend who's going through a hard time. In these ways, you will lift yourself out of your current dilemma or depressed state of mind and see that things are not so bad after all.

The running equivalent of this might be to volunteer at a race. Race organizers will almost certainly be able to put your services to use. Most are desperate for bodies to fill in at aid stations, direct runners and traffic, transport equipment, and assist in a hundred other ways.

Instead of being absorbed with yourself as you normally are when you compete, you direct your energies toward helping other runners. You see them having fun, struggling against long odds, making valiant efforts, laughing and talking and relishing the day, and in the process, you will perhaps remember why you got into running in the first place and why you think it's such a grand idea.

Whatever the motivation, volunteering at a race is a good idea. It's a form of payback to all the charitable anonymous souls who've assisted in the races you've run.

Resolved: I do a good deed. I volunteer at an upcoming race.

April 1

"Man is never more human than when he plays."

—Friedrich von Schiller, poet and dramatist

Never in Olympic history has there been another runner like Sidney Dahl, whose story begins in the small Norwegian fishing village where he was born. His father was a carpenter and his mother a seamstress, and they noticed immediately that their son was different from the other children. He was gifted. He could run like the wind.

As a 17-year-old wunderkind, Dahl won the 1944 Olympic Games Marathon in Buenos Aires, Argentina. Though he was the youngest runner ever to win an Olympic marathon, critics nevertheless scoffed at his triumph because many of the best runners of the time were away at war.

Stung by the criticism, Dahl retreated into isolation in his adopted home of Copenhagen, Denmark. No one in the international running community saw him for years. When he finally emerged in public, he was a new man. Well, no, actually, he was a woman. Realizing a lifelong dream, Sidney had undergone a sex change operation that allowed him to compete as a female.

Sidney entered the women's marathon in the 1956 Olympic Games in Melbourne, Australia, and remarkably, she won. Dahl became not only the first person to win the Olympic marathon twice, but also the first man and woman to do so.

Not really. April Fool!

Resolved: I go out for a run and forget this ridiculous prank.

April 2

*"Be truly motivated to train for a marathon. Do it for yourself—
not on a bet or a dare or because 'everyone else does.'"*

—Grete Waitz, champion runner

Nobody is forcing you to run. That is something to always keep in mind.

Running is not a job. It is not an assignment that is required of you, like homework for students. You do not have to do it at a certain time. You do not have to do it at all, in fact.

Some runners have voices inside their heads telling them, "You must . . . you should . . . or else!" These voices are of their own making. There is nothing obligatory about running. It's not like paying taxes; you can avoid running and no one will toss you in jail.

You run because you choose to run. There's no other reason. And if it's not your choice, why are you running?

Because of a bet? Because someone dared you? Because everyone else is doing it? You're not going to stay with it for long if these remain your motivations. There has to be something else, some other reason for doing it.

And there is: you choose to. Running is an expression of freedom. Never turn it in your mind into anything else. Because that will stop you dead in your tracks.

Resolved: I run because I choose to, and I see it as an expression of personal freedom.

April 3

"Everything I see and feel is more extreme when I'm in training. If I'm happy, I'm happier. If I'm sad, I'm sadder. I once ran 31 miles and after that there was nothing in the world I thought I couldn't do."

—Katherine Switzer, marathoner

Running opens you up as a human being. It makes your senses come alive. When you run, in the words of runner Kathryn Staines, it's like a "smellfest." You suddenly develop the nose of a canine. You can smell everything.

You smell the flowers in bloom. You smell the new grasses springing up from the recent rains. Stopping to smell the roses is no longer just an expression. Their fragrance fills your nostrils like opium.

This awakening of the senses is a metaphor for an awakening of self. Running lifts you out of the mundane middle and pushes you out toward the edges. In those extremes lies a world of possibility. Maybe nothing about your life is outwardly different from your neighbor's. But your attitude is markedly different from his, and that means everything.

Want to expand your senses? Renew your appreciation of what life has to offer? Get a fresh outlook on the day? Awaken to the possibilities inherent in your life?

Well, then. Just lace up the shoes and go outside and see what you can smell.

Resolved: I engage in a smellfest today. I run.

April 4

"To drink in the spirit of a place you should be not only alone, but not hurried."

—George Santayana, philosopher and poet

Travel is broadening, as they say, and never more so than when you combine it with running. When you run in a new town or city, you get to know it in ways that you otherwise would not. It's a more intimate connection; you're not just seeing it from behind the wheel of a rental car.

Travel by car is destination oriented; travel on foot is about the connections between places, not just the places themselves. Furthermore, when you run, you usually run alone, and that allows you an even richer sense of the place.

Perhaps the only thing that can compare to running in a new city or town is walking. But with running, you can cover far more ground and see more sights, though you're not really focused on the sights per se. You're in more of an exploratory mode. You get to see places off the beaten track, the places where people really work and live and play.

When you run in a new city or town, there is always the possibility that you will discover something entirely unexpected. You may hook up with other inspired souls who share your love for bipedal travel. Certainly on a business trip, a morning run will sharpen your thoughts and put you in a better frame of mind for the day to come. At day's end a run will build a wall between you and work and give you the space to relax.

All that's needed, then, are directions or perhaps a map. Your feet will take it from there.

Resolved: Whenever I travel, whether it's for business or pleasure, I make sure to build in some time for running.

April 5

"The only thing that's important in your training program is motivation. I've developed a set of motivational tricks that I'm constantly reviewing and refining. They have only one purpose: to keep me running."

—Amby Burfoot, marathoner

There are morning runners and evening runners, just as there are morning people and night people. Morning runners like to run before work, evening runners like to run after. (Granted, some people like to run at lunchtime or in the afternoon. They tend to use running as a means to break up the day.)

Morning runners like to do it early because it sets the tone for the rest of their day. It gives them energy for work or whatever else comes up.

Evening runners prefer the later approach because it lets them unwind from the events of the day. (Either that, or they just can't get up in the morning.) Their job responsibilities over, they can relax and devote themselves to something they enjoy, namely, running.

Whatever type of runner you are, here's a modest proposal: Why not try a different time of day for a change?

It's a way to break up the routine. You get to see the landmarks of your regular route at a different time of day. A different time means a change in the quality of light. You may see activities along the way that you don't see at your usual time. Running is play. Anything you can do to keep it that way is worth trying. And you can always go back to your regular time if the change in schedule is too hard on your system.

Resolved: Just for the heck of it, I run in the evening if I'm normally a morning runner, and vice versa.

April 6

"If people are physically fit, they are better adjusted for life. Running is the greatest anodyne. It's mental therapy. While running, one develops a rhythm. The mind becomes detached."
—Al Gordon, runner

Sometimes all of life seems to be in a conspiracy to put you in a bad mood.

The leg of your chair breaks, sending you sprawling to the floor. Your car stops running, requiring a $600 repair. Your screenplay—the one you've been working on without pay for years—gets rejected without comment. A tree falls across the roof of your house, and the bathroom toilet backs up.

In the face of such misfortune, there is a simple therapy: run. Running won't change a thing—not ultimately, anyhow. But it will change your mood, and that counts for a lot.

After a run, you will be spurred into fixing that chair or buying a new one. You will have the fortitude to call your plumber, insurance agent, and car repair shop, knowing that these things happen and that it's only money after all. And you'll tell yourself that even the greatest writers must endure years of rejections, resolving to store that script in the closet and start a new one after the sting goes away.

One way to cope with a bad mood is to change it. Next time you feel like punching a hole in the wall, go for a run instead. Good for you, good for your wall.

Resolved: I change a bad frame of mind by running.

April 7

"Today, as never before, one must love the body, be gently patient with it."

—Francis Thompson, therapist

Every body needs TLC from time to time. Your body is no different.

Running takes its toll on joints, muscles, ligaments, and bones. Your body takes a pounding from running, and after a while, all that pounding tends to add up.

Running is a thing you do for your body. Massage will help you do the thing you do for your body.

Is running your only form of exercise? Therapists and body workers say that single-sport athletes are more prone to injuries than athletes who play a variety of sports and use different muscle groups rather than the same ones all the time. Runners are particularly notorious for pushing themselves, with shinsplints often the result.

Taking care of your body is a form of motivation. When you feel good, you will want to feel even better. A massage is another way to associate running with pleasure. Running is about more than discipline and pushing yourself; it can be a sensual, body-healing, body-delighting ritual, too. Treat yourself to a massage today, and feel good about yourself.

Resolved: I treat myself to a massage today (and maybe even start doing it on a regular basis).

April 8

"When you run in the morning, you gain time in a sense. It's like stretching 24 hours into 25. You may need to sleep less and get up earlier, but if you can get by that, running early seems to expand the day."

—Fred Lebow, runner and marathon director

One of the nice things about running is that you can do it on your own timetable.

You don't have to run with anyone else (although it's sometimes nice) or fit it into any schedule other than your own. You can run when it suits you: morning, noon, or night.

Even so, there are days when you have lots of time to run and days when you have almost no time at all. Here are three ways to expand time when you're running short of it:

1. Get up earlier. As Fred Lebow says, it's like stretching time. An early start gives you more time for everything in the day, including running.
2. Shorten your workout. Running a little less is better than not at all.
3. Cut something else out of your schedule. Don't bump running; bump TV or some other less important activity.

A person who doesn't want to do something can never find the time to do it, while a person who wants to do it will always find the time. Longtime runners seldom complain that they can't find the time to run (although some say they can't find *enough* time). They want to run, so they make the time, even when time is tight. You can do it, too.

Resolved: I still try to get a run in even if I'm short on time.

April 9

"The body and soul are one for the purpose of all real evolution, and regrettable is any term suggestive of divorce between them."

—John Galsworthy, writer

Running is athletics in its purest form, a union of body and soul. You need almost no equipment. Abebe Bikila, one of the greatest marathoners of all time, ran in his bare feet through the streets of Rome and Tokyo, becoming the first person to win consecutive Olympic Games Marathons.

The rest of us, however, are probably going to need shoes.

Good shoes. Not necessarily expensive, but good. Some runners know it's time for new shoes when they feel a slight tugging in their knees or lower back. That's a sign their shoes are not giving them the support they need.

Having good shoes is vital for both physical and mental reasons. The physical reasons are obvious, but the mental ones are no less important. A new pair of shoes almost always picks up the spirits. You feel lighter and seem to run easier, at least for the first few days.

Furthermore, buying new shoes means that you are taking care of yourself. Your actions demonstrate that running is an activity of value to you, one that you are going to continue to do.

Tend to your feet, tend to your body. Tend to your body, tend to your soul. Now how about a foot massage while you're at it?

Resolved: I buy a new pair of running shoes.

April 10

"Start easy. Run a mile a day for a week. Run two miles a day the next week. But be comfortable. Take it easy. You're not in a race."

—Wilson Waigwa, miler

Grab for the gusto. Seize the day. Be present. Live for the moment.

But hey, if it doesn't work out, don't sweat it. In running, there's always tomorrow.

Carpe diem may be a good strategy for life, but it's not for running. Today's run will not be your last. You can run tomorrow and the next day and the day after that, if you choose. Relax and enjoy yourself. There's enough time.

If you're running as if today is your last day, you're running way too hard. You can't cram it all into one day, anyway, so why try?

The effect of running is cumulative. You simply cannot build a durable training base in a day or week or month. It takes time, oceans of time. An attitude of haste and hurry is not conducive to success in long-distance running. Besides, no one gives awards for a fast workout.

So yes, go out today and run. But do it with the idea that you'll be running tomorrow, too.

Resolved: I run with the idea that there's always tomorrow.

April 11

"Keep varying the program. Your body will tell you what to do."
—Joan Benoit, marathoner

Variety is the spice of life—and running. You've got to vary your running to keep your enthusiasm up.

Benoit and other great runners who must put in 100-mile weeks will vouch for that. Here are a few of the things she does to keep the spice in her running:

- Runs a mile hard (after suitable warm-up).
- Runs intervals (repeat quarter miles).
- Runs against a clock once in a while.
- Runs a set distance at a comfortable pace, say five miles in 40 minutes. The next time, she covers the same distance at a slightly faster pace, say 38 or 39 minutes.

There are many other ways to vary your routine. If you run on the track all the time, get off the track. If you run only on pavement, try the trails or even the beach. Vary the distances and the places you run, even the time of day. Run some hills; do some speed work (easy at first).

The idea is to keep yourself mentally fresh. But it will also keep your body fresher. Runners tend to use the same set of muscles in the same way over and over again. Putting variety into your workouts will lessen that tendency and reduce the chance of overuse injuries.

Resolved: I time myself over a set distance then run it again later at a slightly faster pace.

April 12

*"Don't let yourself be concerned by what other runners are
doing. By trial and error, find out what works for you."*

—Gayle Barron, marathoner

Suppose you did this: suppose you took some of the well-intentioned advice you've heard from other runners and tried to incorporate it into your running program. How do you think it would turn out?

You may have tried this once or twice before, so you already know the answer. You know that it's almost certainly bound to fail, and the reason is simple: what works for someone else may not work for you.

The experiences of other runners have taught them certain lessons that apply meaningfully to them. But those lessons do not apply to you. You must learn different lessons, and you must learn them on your own.

Sure, you can learn from other people. Other runners may give you tips from time to time that really do seem to help. But their wisdom can be of service to you only after you change and shape and mold it to fit your unique identity and circumstances. Although it'd be nice, someone cannot give you a wisdom pill that immediately tells you all you need to know. Different people must learn different things at different times.

Trial and error, it's the only way. And through that, you will find *your* way.

Resolved: I'm never afraid to experiment because, in doing that, I'll find out what works for me.

April 13

"There's always the feeling of getting stronger. I think that's what keeps me going."

—Frank Shorter, marathoner

Your body is responding to what you're doing. You can feel it. You don't need an outside party to confirm that fact for you. You see evidence of it every day.

You saw it yesterday when you walked up five flights of stairs to get to your car parked on the roof of a parking garage. You were barely winded when you reached the top.

You saw it the other day when you ran with a friend of yours. He hadn't been running in a while. You were so much stronger than he and clearly holding back so that he could keep up with you.

You see it every time you run. The course seems shorter somehow. What used to seem like a chore is now a pleasure. Your running is smoother and easier. You want to run longer because you're more able to handle it.

You see it in your diet. You're more sensitive to what you eat and far less interested in pigging out on junk.

You see it in your eagerness to run. The motivation is almost always there. You want to take your running further, get more fit, keep it going.

The body is an amazing organism. It responds well to positive stimuli, and it will keep answering to the challenges you give it.

Resolved: I'm getting stronger and I know it. I keep after it.

April 14

"Sustained motivation is essential to achieving your potential."

—Grete Waitz, champion runner

Motivation comes in many forms, and it doesn't necessarily have to come through running.

Waitz uses what she calls "mental stimuli" to help motivate her. These may include posters, inspirational sayings, books, magazines, and videos. "The more you see it," she says, "the more you remember it."

One proven motivational technique is to write down your goals on a piece of paper and post it in a prominent place, such as next to a bathroom mirror or on a bulletin board. Waitz does that, too.

Some runners may think about running only when they're running or just before and after. There's nothing wrong with that. Running has a place in their lives, and that's all the time they can or will commit to it.

Runners like Waitz possess a higher degree of commitment. By watching videos or reading *Running Times* or whatever, they make running part of their daily lives. When it's time to go out and do it, they're ready.

The more you run, the more it will become part of your nonrunning life. The more you make it part of your nonrunning life, the more you will run. It's a lovely circle to be caught up in.

Resolved: I let running become part of my daily life, even when I'm not running.

April 15

"Running long and hard is an ideal antidepressant, since it's hard to run and feel sorry for yourself at the same time. Also, there are those hours of clearheadedness that follow a long run."

—Monte Davis, runner

It's all over: the world has come to an end. At the start of this day you had a certain financial worth. At the end of this day that sum will be reduced to the equivalent of a couple of paper clips and a box of staples.

It's called income taxes, and today is the day they're due.

When faced with dire circumstances, the statesman Cato fell upon his sword, Ernest Hemingway unlocked his gun cabinet, and in 1929, after discovering they were ruined, Wall Street financiers jumped out of windows (or so the legend goes).

Fortunately there are other alternatives today to combat depression, such as running. Running puts things such as income taxes into perspective. You realize, first, that although you no longer have any money, you do have your health, and that counts for something. It'd be nice to have both your health *and* money (money being a vital ingredient in actually enjoying your health), but the federal government won't allow that, and so that's the way it is.

Still, you're not completely finished, you realize. You've got your family, and as long as you've got them, you've got everything. And you've got hope, even if it is crushed annually on this date.

Running won't change your tax picture, but it can improve the way you look at it, and on a day like today, that's plenty.

Resolved: I go for a run and plot strategies on how I can reduce my tax burden for next year.

April 16

"Why are there trees I never walk under but large and melodious thoughts descend upon me?"

—Walt Whitman

You almost don't notice at first. In fact you realize later that you may have run for two or three days in a row without noticing.

Later in spring it becomes dramatic, and everyone notices. There are pictures in the paper, and even people who don't spend much time outdoors notice it and talk about it.

You've gotten used to the bareness: the browns and grays and muted colors of winter. There is a certain stark beauty to winter, and you've come to accept and appreciate it for what it is.

Then you notice it. And once you notice it, you see it everywhere.

The trees are beginning to leaf and turn green. It's an amazing sight. It happens every year around this time, and yet it always catches you off guard. Though completely in the normal course of existence, the verdant beauty of this seasonal transformation defies credulity. It's a miracle of sorts.

The trees are turning green. Not only green, but pink and white and purple, too. Even in your runner's "trance" you cannot fail to notice, and as you run, you secretly rejoice. How great it is to be outside, how lucky I am!

Resolved: I run amid the green trees of spring.

April 17

"The truth dawns on me that all our 'incomprehensible moods' are logical and that they must have a secret psychic motivation."

—Dr. Wilhelm Stekhel, writer

OK, so you ran yesterday, and it wasn't so hot. You were in a bad mood, and running didn't seem to help.

Still, you went out. That's something right there. You have a dutiful nature. Even when you were feeling rotten, you made the effort. That's positive.

Consider how you would have felt if you hadn't run. Probably worse, it's true. Running may have stopped a foul mood from sinking even lower. Furthermore, even if your mind was not into it, you did a favor for your body. You unkinked the kinks and unscrewed the tightness, and that's something.

And there's a strong likelihood that because of who you are, you're going to go out again today. You'll put in your miles and see how it goes.

There's nothing wrong with having an off day. We all do. Nor do you need to argue yourself out of a bad mood. Let it unfold in all its foul splendor. Perhaps there's a reason for it that has nothing to do with running.

But even on our worst days, positive things occur if we're open to receive them.

Resolved: I find something positive even after a less-than-sterling run.

April 18

"It doesn't mean being one point or one run ahead at the end of a game. It means that you have given everything you have in the effort at that moment, and no matter what, that makes you a winner."

—Dot Richardson, Olympic softball player, on the meaning of success in sports

You can never be sure how you will finish in a race. All you can be sure about is the effort you give.

If you give everything you have, you can be content on some level, even if you finish dead last. There's no shame in finishing in the back of the pack if you give everything you have. Because you can't give any more than that.

Some days are going to be a struggle. But if you give everything you have, you'll find a way to get through them. What endures throughout all the winning and losing is your effort and commitment.

If at the end of a race you can look in the mirror and say, "Yeah, I gave it my best shot. I left it all on the course. No regrets"—if you can do that, you've got the world licked.

And really, what are you saving it for anyway? A better opportunity down the road? You must realize that this may be your golden opportunity right now. Your waiting may be over. But you will know that for sure only if you give it everything you have.

Resolved: I give everything I have in the moment I'm engaged in it.

April 19

"We are what we repeatedly do. Excellence, then, is not an act, but a habit."

—Aristotle

When you make running a habit, the hard part isn't running. It's *not* running.

Runners who have made running a habit generally do not have trouble finding the time to run. They have structured their lives in such a way that running has become part of the daily routine.

If they've built it into their schedule to, say, run at two o'clock every day, and they've done that for weeks and months and possibly even years, it's very difficult for them not to follow the dictates of their routine.

Running is what they do, and this is the time they do it. They don't even think about it anymore. The only time they really think about it is when they don't run at two P.M., for whatever reason. It throws their whole world off.

Running is still a choice for them, but on a daily basis, they've taken the choice out of it. It's just what they do, like taking a shower when they get up in the morning or breaking for lunch around noon.

It's a good goal to strive for and a good habit to maintain if you've already achieved it: taking running out of the realm of choice. Not deciding from one day to the next whether or not to do it, just strapping on the shoes and doing it.

Resolved: I don't think about whether I run or not. I just do it.

April 20

"I've never known what it is to be tired. I've never known what it was not to run everywhere. I leap out of bed in the morning with the disposition that something perfectly wonderful is going to happen to me that day."

—Brendan Gill, writer

It's January, a time of snow and cold and rain and dreary gray skies. At this time of year, it's hard to jump out of bed with the conviction that perfectly wonderful things are going to happen to you.

Wonderful things happen when you run. But what do you do when it's miserable outside?

Here's a thought: walk up the stairs to your office rather than take the elevator. Heck, if you're feeling frisky, you can take the stairs two at a time or even *run* up them.

It's been said that each step you walk up adds a minute to your life. In addition to quantity, there's the idea of quality. You feel better when you're fit, and that makes your life run more smoothly.

Obviously there will be times when stairs aren't practical. You may work on the 57th floor, and there may not be access to the stairwell. Still, there are things you can do for yourself to keep the blood circulating and the lungs pumping on days you can't run.

The weather will do what the weather will do. You can't control that. But you *can* control yourself and your own attitudes.

Resolved: I skip the elevator and walk up the steps to my office.

April 21

"What running did for me was, first, build my confidence and then help me come to grips with the unnecessary limitations under which I existed. My self-confidence has risen to a level where I can set goals that were previously unthinkable."

—Edward Epstein, runner

You can work to define yourself, recognizing your strengths and weaknesses to become a better runner. Here's another way to do it: turn your weaknesses into strengths.

Every weakness is a potential source of strength. Do you lack stamina? Do you wish you had more of a finishing kick? Would you like to run faster? Identifying an area of weakness is the first step in turning it into a strength.

Many people have psychological blocks about facing their weaknesses. But if a situation occurs again and again—say, you're running out of gas at the end of a race—then, clearly, that's an area of weakness. If you want a remedy for it, you're going to have to do something about it.

Realize that this isn't a mystical process, and it isn't personal. You weren't born with this limitation, whatever it is. It's not congenital. If you've picked up a bad habit over time, you can unlearn it. And if you were never taught how to do this thing that you're lacking, find somebody to teach you.

You may never have as strong a finishing kick as you'd like, but if you devote some time to improving this area, it will get better. And you can turn what was once a weakness into a strength.

Resolved: I turn my weaknesses in running into strengths.

April 22

"Train, don't strain."

—Running maxim

"Running within yourself"—that is, not straining—is a great concept, but what does it exactly mean?

It may be easiest to explain in terms of what it's not. It is *not* extending yourself to the maximum, at least not in recreational running and almost never in a race as well.

But it does not necessarily mean doing the minimum either. Doing the minimum is an excellent strategy for most runners, especially beginning ones. But a runner who does only the minimum, and nothing more, may not be happy with his or her progress over time.

Running within yourself probably falls somewhere in between minimum and maximum exertion, tilting to the one or the other, depending on your mood on a given day. As a rule it should trend more toward the minimum, because then you will be less prone to injury and can keep running.

Running within yourself—here's a positive expression of it—means listening to your body. Some days your body will feel as expansive as your mind, and you'll want to run into the next county and beyond. Other days your body will resemble a creaky old hinge in need of oil, and you'll want to take it easy.

You can run within yourself and still go fast. And you can run within yourself and take it slow. When you stay within yourself, you'll know which is the right choice.

Resolved: I avoid maximum exertion as a runner and stay within myself.

April 23

*"Too many people run a fast first half, then have to slow down.
An even pace almost always works best."*

—Jerry Nason, road racer, on how to run a marathon

It's a curious phenomenon how your good running days are
not that much different from your bad days in terms of time.

Some days you feel as if you're burning up the roads. Then
you check your watch and see that your time is about the
same as it always is.

It's true even when you feel rotten. You drag yourself out
to run, barely able to lift a leg without a Herculean labor. But
your time, even on a draggy day, is not so far off from what
you usually run. What's going on?

The answer is pace, which does not vary much from day to
day. Each person has a pace of his or her own. Obviously
some runners have a quicker pace than others. When you find
someone whose pace roughly matches yours, you've found a
running companion.

Pace can seem intractable at times. Even when you're consciously trying to push it, you often run close to your regular
pace. If your regular pace is slower than you like, that can be
frustrating.

On the other hand, pace is a reassuring thing. How you run
is not dependent on mood. Even when your mind drifts aim-
lessly, your body knows the way. It's going to follow a certain
rhythm and move at a certain pace. All you need to do is settle into the rhythm of your body that day and go with it.

Resolved: I settle into the rhythm of my body and go with it.

April 24

"Take your mind, throw it up the mountain, and then follow it."

—Breast cancer survivor, on how to achieve a hard goal

Runners use different motivational techniques at different times.

One technique is to focus on this moment, this stride, and not worry about what comes later. If you always take care of this moment and this stride, the thinking goes, you will end up where you want to be.

Another technique is to mentally jump to the end of the race and work backward from there. You see the race as a thing that's already been accomplished. Your steps then merely fulfill the vision you've laid out in your mind.

Yet another technique is to take your mind, throw it to the end of the race, and follow it.

As you struggle to keep going, you see yourself at the finish line. A volunteer wraps a blanket around you and steers you into the appropriate finishing chute. You imagine how good it will feel when you can finally stop.

Because of this vision, this promise of things to come, you're willing to absorb the hardships and indignities that occur along the way. When you're in the middle of the struggle, it seems as if nothing can ever justify the misery you're enduring. But a magical transformation occurs at journey's end. That surge you feel inside, that incredible feeling of accomplishment and joy—amazingly, it is all worth it at the end.

Resolved: I take my mind, I throw it to the end of a race, and then I follow it.

April 25

"Recognize the slightest change, the smallest try."

—Tom Dorrance, horse trainer

Tom Dorrance is a California riding teacher and horse trainer. He teaches men and women how to move with ease and grace on and off a horse, how to make one's body sensitive to the horse's, and how to become more balanced and relaxed in the saddle.

Runners do not generally have much to do with horses. But they can still learn a lot from a guy like Dorrance.

Runners need to become sensitive to their animal side, too. They need to tune in to what their feet, legs, and back are telling them. You can't just abuse your body and ride it into the ground. If you do, it will rear up and buck you off.

When dealing with your body, don't make big, dramatic movements. Small, slight movements are better.

When the movements are small, the body can better adjust to them. It's not such a shock to the system. Even small, seemingly insignificant movements can be extremely meaningful. You're teaching your body to move in a different way. Just *thinking* about the movement—even before your body learns how to do it—can have a positive effect.

The body is a highly teachable organism. Give it time, make small, incremental movements, and it will respond in the way you want.

Resolved: I make small, slight movements when I introduce changes in the way I move my body.

April 26

"Only he who does nothing makes a mistake."

—French proverb

A skier who never falls is a skier who never ventures into steep terrain. A pole-vaulter who's never missed her height is one who hasn't set the bar high enough yet. A runner who's never lost a race is a runner who's never entered one.

Mistakes are an essential ingredient of learning. You cannot learn what you need to learn unless you are willing to make mistakes. Adventurers exploring a new land are always lost before they find themselves. They must go down many wrong paths before locating the right one. Usually when they find it, it is not by design. They have stumbled onto it by accident, after many wrong turns, through trial and error.

Mistakes, then, are not the obstacles a person must overcome to reach his or her goal. They are the signposts that point the way to the goal. The trick, of course, is accurately reading those signposts and interpreting what they say.

If you keep making a mistake over and over, you're probably not reading the signpost accurately. You may need to go in a different direction.

The only direction *not* to go is in the direction of not trying. That way leads nowhere.

Resolved: I never not try in running, though I know I will make mistakes.

April 27

"Hold back for the first seven miles. Use it as a warm-up and then gradually increase your rate but never strain."

—Adolph Gruber, long-distance runner, on how to run a
marathon

It's always possible to pick up the pace. Never forget that. Although, after picking up the pace, you still may not get where you want to go as quickly as you'd like. That's important to remember, too.

Circumstances invariably change, in life as in a running race. You may find yourself in a position that you did not expect. It may be awkward, embarrassing, or even uncomfortable. But by readjusting your pace, you can get back to where you want to be.

Do not expect dramatic immediate results. You won't suddenly jump from 190th place to 19th. But you can gain small, incremental advantages that matter to you.

Picking up the pace is not simply a matter of willpower. You can't suddenly produce five-minute miles if they're not in you to do. You have to know your abilities and limits. Otherwise you may move to pick up the pace, and it won't be there. That happens sometimes.

It's not a good idea to rely too often on your ability to pick up the pace. You may unconsciously get into the habit of digging yourself a hole and then forever trying to scramble out of it. That's frustrating.

Still, there are times when a change of pace is in order. Know that you have the capability to adapt to altered circumstances, and that you can catch up and move forward.

Resolved: If I find myself falling behind a little, I pick up the pace and get back to where I want to be.

April 28

"I have examined myself thoroughly and come to the conclusion that I don't need to change much."

—Sigmund Freud

Change, change, change. The world is filled with grand ideas on how to make you a better person. Ask your mother how you can improve your relationship with her, and she'll tell you. Ask your spouse the same, and no doubt he or she will have plenty of ideas, too. Ask your boss, coworkers, and friends how you can improve, and they'll supply you with a list.

Flip on *Oprah* or any of the talk shows. Their stock-in-trade is self-improvement: how to become a better listener, how to have a sunnier outlook, how to talk to your manic-depressive children, how to quit quarreling with your inner self. It's the same story at the bookstore. The shelves are stocked with the scribblings of authors who think about nothing more than how to make a better you out of you.

Running is no different. Much of the talk centers on new and more sophisticated shoes, vitamin and diet fads, the latest training techniques, all with the idea of helping you set a new PR in the race of the moment.

For today, at least, let's take a break from all that worthy and well-intentioned advice. Let's not think about the butterflies we'd like to become; instead let's appreciate the larvae that we are.

Well, perhaps that isn't the right image. But you get the idea. Enough change, already. Let's do a bold thing and admit that we're fine just the way we are.

Resolved: I accept and exalt the runner (and person) I am. Tomorrow I'll think about changing.

April 29

"Nearly all the best things that came to me in life have been unexpected, unplanned by me."

—Carl Sandburg

It's amazing what good things can happen when you're not paying attention.

You may not consider yourself a runner, but you want to keep fit, and so you go to the gym a few times a week. When you're there, you like to work up a little sweat on the treadmill. Fast walking on a treadmill is not as boring as you thought it'd be, and before long you're up to four miles on it.

Then you think, "Hey, four miles. I'm doing four miles on a treadmill," and it occurs to you that you could be exercising *outside*. It's such a great day—the sun is springtime lovely and warm; why not go for a run?

And that's how it starts. You go for an easy run, and it's such a pleasant experience, you go for another . . . and another . . . and you're hooked.

What's the old saying? Life is what happens to you while you're making other plans. Sometimes you can plan and plan and plan and plan for a certain thing to happen, and it never does. But then something else will occur—the last thing in the world you expected, in fact—and it turns out to be a most surprising, and wonderful, discovery.

Stay open to the possibilities inherent in your life, and you will make lots of happy, surprising discoveries.

Resolved: I stay open to the possibility of making surprising discoveries in running—and life.

April 30

"It's best to approach your break point without breaking it. You advance in steps. Go up two or three steps, drop back one or two steps, then hop back to where you were and start stepping again."

—Lee Fidler, running coach

Making progress as a runner is never a uniform, uninterrupted movement forward.

Progress comes in stops and starts—two steps up, one step back. You may make a breakthrough in your 10K time, only to follow it inexplicably by weeks and weeks of sloggy, uninspired workouts.

The reverse could happen. You could have a series of fast, inspired workouts and feel on the verge of something truly great. Then on race day your legs turn into dead weights, and you struggle through a miserable performance that leaves you gasping for answers. It's as if you're going backward, not forward, and you don't know why.

You may indeed be making progress. It just wasn't evident that day. That's the way it is sometimes. You may be making progress without any evidence to show for it. Conversely, you may be retreating even as you think you're going forward.

What to do? Be consistent. Lee Fidler adds, "If you build constantly week after week, you get stronger, but you also find your break point." Build consistently week after week, while not pushing past your break point, and you will make progress.

Resolved: I maintain consistency as a runner, even as I sometimes take two steps forward and one step back.

May 1

"Think of taking a shower. That's just the point. It's so natural. It's the same with running. Just like a shower, running is part of my daily life."

—Nina Kuscik, marathoner

It's the first day of the month. What better reason than that to go for a run?

First things first on the first of the month. Before work, before family or personal responsibilities, before the demands of the day set in, first go running. Then you will be able to handle all those other things so much better.

It's not every day that you can put running first. But what could be more fitting today? You could make running the last thing you do, of course. That's always an option: end your day on a high note and all that.

But sometimes when you set things aside to take care of them later, they don't get done at all. When you put running first, you make sure it gets done. It becomes the way you start your day.

Who knows? Maybe it could become a habit. Make the first day of every month a kind of mental cue for you. That's the day, rain or shine, you put running first. Write it in your Day-timer for the remaining months of the year. Once you put running first on the first day, it will be so much easier to do it on the second day of the month, the third, the fourth, and so on.

Resolved: I make running the first thing I do today.

May 2

"I'm willing to accept any kind of pain to win a race."

—Rick Wohlhutter, former U.S. Olympic
1,500-meter runner

Every runner must toe a fine line when it comes to pain. There are those—such as top Olympic athletes like Wohlhutter, ultramarathoners, and others—who are willing to cross well beyond the normal thresholds. That's probably not where most of us want to go.

But it's unrealistic to run and not expect to experience some pain. The question is, how much?

Nobody can answer that except you. Nobody can make that judgment except you. It's something that you must monitor every day you run.

Certainly when you run a marathon or any other kind of race, you are generally willing to endure more pain than you would on a casual Sunday-afternoon run.

Willingness to endure pain is related to goal setting. If you have a goal you're striving for, and you're close to achieving it, you're probably willing to endure more pain than if you were far away from completion. A mother in the last stages of childbirth will tell you that.

And if you achieve that goal, you will have a far different view of the pain you endured from what you'd have if you somehow fell short of the goal. Pain with reward is far easier to take than pain without it.

There's an objective physical reality to pain that cannot be denied. But you can learn to manage it to some degree to your benefit.

Resolved: I'm willing to accept a little pain when I run, even as I monitor it every day.

May 3

"If I ever stopped running, I'd feel terrible, as if I were slowly decomposing. I enjoy being fit. There's a feeling of independence to it."

—Bill Rodgers, marathoner

For many people, "fitness" means working out. A person must work out in order to be fit, they believe.

Working out for them means going to a gym or aerobics studio, where they participate in a series of activities for a certain amount of time. Upon the conclusion of their workout, they resume the rest of their daily schedule.

Many runners see running in a similar way. When it's over, it's over. There's a boundary between running and the rest of their lives.

Top runners and other well-conditioned athletes do not see fitness as distinct from the rest of their lives. They do it all the time. It's part of who they are. They look for ways to incorporate fitness into their everyday routines.

Have you ever thought about running to where you run? Instead of driving or taking the subway or however you go, run (or walk) to where you run. Then, if possible, run back. This will add to your mileage in a gentle way and break down the thinking that when it's over, it's over.

When you run to where you run, you may have to reconsider old habits and familiar ways of doing things. But maybe it's time for that, too.

Resolved: If possible, I run to where I run.

May 4

"Every day I walk myself into a state of well-being and walk away from every illness. I have walked myself into my best thoughts, and I know of no thought so burdensome that I cannot walk away from it."

—Søren Kierkegaard

Though Kierkegaard was a mere walker, every runner knows what he was talking about.

Running produces good thoughts. You can be undecided about something, then go for a run and know exactly what to do by the time you return. It's a kind of daily spring cleaning for the mind.

There are times, though, when you go for a run and all you do is think. You go through your usual paces and cover your usual distance, but you hardly notice at all because your thoughts are focused so intently on the new assignment you've received at work, or the softball team you're coaching, or the party you're planning, or whatever.

This hard thinking may be necessary and is not to be discouraged. But you can be so intent on what's inside your head that you can forget to notice what you're doing and where you are.

Even if for a moment, even if only at the beginning or end of a run, never fail to appreciate what a great gift life is and how wonderful it is to have the strength and health to run.

Resolved: I never fail to notice: "Hey, I'm running! It's beautiful outside! I'm lucky to be alive!"

May 5

"The single most horrible thing that can happen to a runner is to be beaten in the stretch when he's still fresh. No matter who I was racing or what the circumstances, I tried to force myself to the limit over the whole distance."

—Ron Clarke, champion runner

Want to see how fit you truly are? Give yourself a real challenge? Take a genuine risk in a race and see what you are made of?

Well, then, force yourself to the limit over the whole distance.

This is not for the weak of heart or frail of limb. You must be in good shape, very good shape. You must be willing to leave your guts on the course and have nothing left at the end.

Anyone can force him- or herself to the limit for the stretch run. We are talking here about the whole race, the entire 5K or 10K or 26-mile, 385-yard distance—not an inch or centimeter less. That doesn't mean a dead sprint from start to finish; it only means testing the limits of what you can do, every step of the way.

There is, to be sure, a kind of recklessness to this tactic. It strikes at the heart of the long, slow distance philosophy. And you may find that you're not as fit as you thought you were. Then again, there is the undeniable possibility that you may force yourself to the limit over the entire distance, look back at the finish, and see no one else there.

Resolved: Some day when I feel ready, I will force myself to the limit over the whole distance.

May 6

Until you've run a marathon, you've never experienced it. But once you experience it, you realize it's there: the lure of the finish.

People who have never run a marathon are often overwhelmed by the experience—the doing of it. They think it's never going to end. All they know is what they are doing in the moment; they don't realize they're actually in transition. They don't know about the lure of the finish because they've never felt it.

The finish line in a marathon—in any race, really—works like a magnet, drawing runners to it. It possesses a kind of energy field. Almost no one ever quits a race once he or she enters this field of attraction.

This field is not precisely defined. It's different for everyone. Some elite runners feel it virtually from the start of the race, as if they're Labradors sniffing for rabbit, sensing a presence in the area that no one else does.

The lure of the finish applies to workouts as well. You may be tired as you near the end of a run, but once you get within that energy field, it pulls you in. Keep your sights set on the finish, knowing that as you come closer and closer to it, your energy will increase.

Resolved: I know that as I get closer to the finish my energy will increase.

May 7

"Health is the mystical and mysterious balance of all things by which we stand up straight and endure."

—G. K. Chesterton, writer

You always have more left, even when you think you don't. You may be in the middle of a race or workout and be absolutely dog tired. You may think to yourself, "I'm not going to make it."

But, somehow, you do. You're running along, nearly dead to the world, and another runner offers a word of encouragement. Or you pass an elderly woman in a walker, and it makes you think, "Maybe I'm not so beat after all." Or you see a squirrel nibbling on a nut, and, for some inexplicable reason, this glimpse of nature revitalizes you.

Or perhaps nothing *outside* you occurs. Something inside you just seems to turn over, and you gather more energy for what you need to do. You even pick up the pace on your way to the finish.

A "second wind" may be mysterious in origin, but its effects are real and undeniable. You can be struggling as a runner and then not. Reserves that you didn't know you had come to the fore, and these reserves carry you to the finish and sometimes on to a real breakthrough.

Believe in your capacity for a second wind. Believe that if you need it, you always have more energy to call upon.

Resolved: I know I have the capacity for a second wind, for getting more energy when I need it.

May 8

"I like finding out what my body can do."

—Charles Steinmetz, ultramarathoner

Funny thing about goal setting. Even before you achieve one goal, you start looking ahead to the next one.

Prior to embarking on a major project, you may look at it in its entirety and think how difficult it will be to achieve. So, you start. Once you get going and make the inevitable early mistakes, you find a way to do things that works for you, and you make progress. After a while you make such rapid progress that you can see the end of the project.

Once that happens, if you are like most people, your dreams and ambitions do not suddenly stop. You begin to look past the goal at hand—a goal that once seemed so difficult—and onto new, more adventurous goals for the future.

This must be what motivates ultramarathoners. Once upon a time a marathon was tough for them to do. Then, after achieving that near-impossible goal, they began to look ahead to even greater challenges that would test what their bodies could do.

You may not want to run ultramarathons. But the longer you run, the more your goals will inevitably expand. This is a sign of progress, perhaps even a sign that you can test your body more.

Resolved: As I achieve my early goals, I look ahead to setting other, possibly more challenging, goals.

May 9

"I've been running for over 20 years. I read all the books and articles, yet I need a coach. Why? I still have to be told, to be encouraged."

—Fred Lebow, runner and marathon director

Coaches can refine techniques, suggest improvements, and help runners adhere to a training regimen. Another important coaching responsibility, as Lebow suggests, is to encourage and motivate.

Every runner can benefit from a coach's wisdom from time to time. But for the most part, recreational runners are on their own.

If something is wrong with your technique, you're going to have to figure it out yourself. You're going to have to keep up-to-date on the latest nutritional and vitamin advice, just as you have to figure out a running regime that works for you.

As for encouraging and motivating, that's your baby, too.

Sooner or later even a runner who hires a coach must learn to motivate him- or herself. Coaches don't work for free, and inevitably there will come a time when you're back on your own, trying to figure things out in a way that works for you.

So, the questions of motivation and encouragement are always present. A coach is only a temporary fix. But every runner should feel heartened. Since the answers always come from within, that means they are always present, too.

Resolved: I realize I am my own best coach and motivator.

May 10

"O God, creator of our land. We drink in your creation with our eyes. We listen to the birds' jubilee with our ears."

—From an Ashanti prayer

Some runners (they're joggers, really) listen to canned music on their Walkmans. They don't know what they're missing. There's a symphony playing all around them, and they're not hearing a note of it.

This symphony is available to all, free of charge, assuming you're willing to prick up your ears and listen. Fortunately most runners *are* willing, and since they're frequently outdoors, they tune in to this symphony on a regular basis.

They hear the wind blowing through the trees and the leaves rustling. They hear the red-winged blackbirds calling to one another in the tule reeds. They hear scrub jays making sounds in the underbrush. They hear dogs (thankfully, behind fences) barking at them as they pass on the street. They hear crickets chirping. When they draw close, they notice that the crickets stop, resuming their chirpings only after they've passed.

Some runners concentrate so intently that they don't hear anything except the sound of their own breathing. If you're one of those, be sure to take note of the symphony after you run or before. It will make the experience infinitely more pleasant and rewarding.

Resolved: I tune in to the music of the outdoors when I run.

May 11

"The body loves variety. The body is the same as the seasons—it likes change."

—Priscilla Welch, runner

Pop quiz: What is a "fartlek"? Choose one of the following:

- (a) a lewd sound made by third-grade boys who want to disrupt class
- (b) a jump in ice-skating, named after its originator, Hyman Fartlek of Finland
- (c) a small rodent
- (d) a training technique for cross-country runners

If you answered (d), you are—not surprisingly—correct. *Fartlek* is the Swedish word for "speed play," and you would do well to make it part of your personal running vocabulary (if you haven't already).

Fartleks are for cross-country running—never on a track. You can run fartleks on the beach, in the mountains, over park trails, spontaneously varying your speeds, depending on mood and terrain. You may run easy your first mile, medium-hard for five minutes, then back to easy. You inject short bursts of speed into a long, slow distance run, perhaps even sprinting up a hill when you come to it. The idea is to avoid runner's disease: plodding along at the same pace the whole time.

Fartleking puts variety into your workout. It is not as dogmatic as interval training on a track, and yet it accomplishes many of the same goals, providing a stirring physical challenge and, not least, injecting some fun into your run.

Resolved: A-fartleking we go, we go, a-fartleking we go!

May 12

It's spring, and the butterflies are out, providing excellent training opportunities for runners.

As you're running along the trail and you see a butterfly pass by, go after it. Chase it up the hillside and down, across the creek and into the trees. When it alights on a flower, use that time to rest. When it sets off again, set off with it.

What's that, you say? Chasing butterflies is a frivolous pastime, hardly befitting the serious runner? When Bill Rodgers was a boy, he chased squirrels and rabbit in the woods around his home. That's how he came to love running and develop his great gift for it as well. He was a serious runner, wasn't he?

Besides, have you ever tried to catch a butterfly? They're fast, man. People who are serious about catching butterflies use nets; otherwise they don't have a chance. A person who catches a butterfly without a net is doing something.

Granted, it's hard to run while keeping your eyes open for butterflies. But one might appear some day, and when it does, you must be ready. How better to spend a day of running than chasing butterflies?

Resolved: I give chase to any butterflies that cross my path today.

May 13

"The quality of our expectations determines the quality of our actions."

—Andre Godin, philosopher

Some runners argue that it's better to have low expectations. Then you're happily surprised if you do better than you expected. Others think that approach is too negative. If you're always selling yourself short, you'll never realize your potential. Maintain high dreams and goals, and strive mightily to achieve them.

Still others say that it's better to have no expectations at all. Form no preconceptions, and be content with what happens, whether it's good, bad, or indifferent. Unless you're Buddha, though, that's a hard attitude to maintain. Everyone has certain expectations before entering a race or doing something big. This nervous anticipation, in fact, is part of the fun.

One thing is certain: to do more in life, you need to create the space to do more. This may mean devoting more time to whatever it is you're doing, although it may also mean other things.

Runners need to have proper shoes. They need to prioritize running in their lives. They need to eat the right kinds of foods. They need to be careful about injury and not overdo it. All of these things might be defined as creating the space to do more.

Giving yourself the space to do more does not necessarily mean that you will do more. But at least you are giving yourself the chance, and over time you will eventually do more—and exceed your expectations in the process.

Resolved: I create the space in my life to do more in running.

May 14

"The body is the mystery we know nothing of; it works its own will and goes its own way, like a cat or a god. . . . We can only do our best to keep it in good humor."

—Stephen Mackenna, philosopher

You know what Mondays are like in the workweek. Hard to wake up, hard to get going, hard to drum up either interest or enthusiasm. The best thing about a Monday usually is that it ends.

Tuesdays are different. You are in the groove by then (although, maybe not). You have more energy, you're more involved in your work, your attitude is much improved. So, why the change? Well, it's Tuesday, not Monday. That seems the only explanation.

This phenomenon occurs in running, too. There will always be Mondays when you run, days when you're not into it, days when you're tired or bored or both, days when you wonder why you beat your feet against the pavement at all.

If you've laid off from running for a while, expect to experience several Mondays in a row. You may feel stiff and awkward and even mechanical before your body adjusts.

For everyday runners, when it feels like a Monday to your body, back off a little. Realize that it's a down day and there's no need to press, for you must always know that after Monday comes Tuesday, when you are going to run with a far lighter step and feel like a different person.

Resolved: I pay attention to how my body is feeling, and if it feels like a Monday, I take it easy.

May 15

"You have to be determined. You'll probably make great progress at first, but then you'll reach a plateau. You think you're going to stay there forever. When that happens, just be patient."

—Ian Pyka, shot-putter, on how athletes progress

In spring, the hillsides are full of wildflowers in bloom: purple lupines, buttercups, the irislike blue-eyed grass, scarlet larkspurs, shooting stars, the radiantly red Indian paintbrush, broad-leaved mule ears, cow parsnips, and the orange monkey plant, to name a few.

But this amazing show of color does not occur all at once. Some flowers bloom early, to be followed by others, in stages. It is not a simultaneous unfolding, but rather a progressive one. Some flowers are only starting to bloom in May while others, having shown their colors early, are already wilting.

You can learn a lot from the wildflowers that light up the hillsides in spring. Do you expect to achieve success as a runner all at once? And once you do achieve it, assuming you do, do you expect it to last forever?

Runners bloom in stages, just as flowers do. Success won't happen all at once. Nor can you expect to run at a high level all the time. You're going to have periods in which you're up, really up, followed by periods in which it feels as if you're not making any progress at all. Then will come periods of renewal, when you feel up again.

You go past the wildflowers every day you run. Sometimes you notice them, sometimes you don't. But they teach wonderful lessons when we stop to pay attention.

Resolved: As a runner I realize I will progress in stages, with periods of "bloom" to be followed by periods of dormancy.

May 16

"If you hear a voice within you saying, 'You are not a painter,' then by all means paint . . . and that voice will be silenced."
—Vincent van Gogh

Listen to the voices inside you. What are they saying?

If the negative voices are saying, "You are not a runner," or "You will never be able to make the Olympic Trials Marathon," then by all means, set your sights on your goal, and go for it. Only through action will these voices be stilled.

The negative voices inside you possess only the power that you give them. Act against these voices, and you will rob them of their might. These voices are insistent, to be sure. They will not go away easily. As you set your sights on the qualifying time for the Trials Marathon, there will still be niggling little voices within you saying, "You call that running? You're nothing." Only by continuing to run will you shut them up.

No doubt there are competing voices warring for dominance inside your skull. Some are telling you, "Go for it. You can do it," while others are saying, "Forget it. It's hopeless."

Never give in to the negative voices. If you give in, you're lost. It's true that you may not become the runner that your most optimistic self thinks you can be, but you will never become that runner—or anything close to it—if you let the negative voices have sway.

The positive voices inside you speak to your higher self. Follow that higher self, and see where it leads.

Resolved: If I hear a voice inside me saying that I can't do something in running, then by all means, I do it.

May 17

"The secret of getting ahead is getting started. The secret of getting started is breaking your complex overwhelming tasks into small manageable tasks, and then starting on the first one."

—Mark Twain

OK, you've set a big goal in running. Whatever it is—running New York in less than three hours, finishing the 100-mile Ride and Tie, breaking 30 minutes in the 10K—you realize you've got your work cut out for you.

There's so much to do, in fact, that you don't know what to do. The project is so vast that you feel almost lost, and as a result, you do nothing.

A big task is often seen as full of obstacles, seemingly impossible to do. But almost everyone feels competent to handle a small task. Once you finish one small task, you move on to the next. Pretty soon these small tasks add up to one big one, and you're passing under the finish-line banner at New York in 2:59:59.

It's like with a person who can't find the time to run. Start with 5 minutes. Anyone can find 5 minutes, right? Well, once you find 5 minutes, you can probably find 10, then 15 and 20. Before you know it, you've carved out time in your schedule to run.

When you break a big task into smaller ones, your motivation stays high because you're constantly achieving goals as you go. You're not delaying your satisfaction for the big pay-off at the end; you're achieving small but meaningful victories every step of the way.

Resolved: I break my big running goal down to small manageable tasks, and I start.

May 18

"Beyond the very extreme of fatigue and distress, we may find amounts of ease and power we never dreamed ourselves to own, sources of strength never taxed at all because we never push through the obstruction."

—William James, philosopher

There comes a point in running when you simply cannot go one more step. You're so tired, so utterly tired. You've used up every ounce of energy you have, and there's nothing left to give. You're completely spent, and all you want to do is sit down on a curb and cry.

We all have our personal "walls," where we seemingly reach the limits of our endurance or desire or both. But how often have we reached one of these walls, only to find that it wasn't the end, that we had capabilities beyond what we previously thought?

This is one of the most inspiring elements of running. People break through walls all the time. What they thought was solid as concrete was only a mirage.

What's your personal wall? What are your limits as a runner? You'll never know how much you have or what you can do until you run smack-dab into a personal wall. That's the limit, you think, beyond which you cannot travel.

It's not true. Keep after it, and you will see. Like so many others, you will find that your personal wall has the consistency of air, and when you finally pass through it, your limits as a runner and a human being will expand.

Resolved: I never accept a wall as final in running.

May 19

"If you want to be successful in anything, it requires practice."
—Bill Wenmark, on running a marathon

There's a wonderful story about the violinist Fritz Kreisler. One of his fans came up to him after a concert and gushed about what he had just heard. "I'd give my whole life to play as beautifully as you do," said the fan.

To which Kreisler smiled and said, "I did."

If you want to be good at running, really good, you're going to have to make a commitment to it, the kind of commitment Kreisler made to his violin. Of course, it's intimidating to think about making a lifetime commitment to anything. A lifetime is a long time. You're talking about flipping lots and lots of calendar pages.

So, don't think in terms of that. Think in terms of today.

Kreisler played and practiced his violin every day. He made a daily commitment to it, and in the final tabulation the days added up to a lifetime. But his commitment was to each day.

Who knows what the future will bring? All you know about is today, and that's all you need to think about when you run. The best way to measure commitment is not in years or decades; it's in days. Run every day (or every other day, or as much as you can), and the years will take care of themselves.

Resolved: I make a daily commitment to running and let the years take care of themselves.

May 20

"My plan is to just wing it, and have a good time."

—Mary Hearn, bike racer, on her racing strategy

There are many racing strategies available to runners. Some runners may want to take it out fast at the start and see who can keep up. Others may want to hang back and preserve their energies for a big closing burst. Hardier souls may want to go all out over the entire distance, à la Ron Clarke.

Then again, you may just want to wing it and have a good time. Winging it has some distinct advantages. For one, runners who wing it will probably be happy finishing 5th, or 500th, or 5,000th. Where they place matters less than having a good time, although people often wing it and finish very high.

Runners who wing it may have a general sense of what they want to do, but they're open to change. Winging it means being flexible and adapting to how you feel at any moment based on the conditions.

Even runners with a definite prerace strategy must learn to wing it if the race takes on a different shape from what they anticipated, reducing their precious plans to rubble. A runner who cannot wing it will never be as successful as one who can.

Winging it is a good strategy, not just for racing, but for running in general. How much are you going to run today? Aw, who knows. Just see how you feel, and have a good time.

Resolved: I plan to wing it and have a good time.

May 21

"As long as I can remember, I've been absolutely hagridden with ambition. If I could wish to have anything in the world it would be to be free of that ambition."

—Tallulah Bankhead, actor

Ambition causes frustration. Every runner knows that.

You may be happy running, say, a few times a week. You run a couple of miles each time, and it feels so good that you decide to do a little more. You start running every day or at least every day you can. In the past you were satisfied with a rough estimate of how much you ran. No more. You measure the course and make sure you cover the requisite 2.5 miles each time you run.

With greater ambition comes greater expectations. You start timing yourself, and you get serious about it. If you don't cover the distance under a certain time, you become unhappy and frustrated. You begin to push to make sure you hit your mark and avoid those feelings of frustration.

But the pushing does not relieve the unhappiness; it only causes more of it. And suddenly you feel a twinge in your knee that you've never felt before.

Ambition has its place in the world, and it may even have a place in your running. But not every day, not all the time. You show plenty of ambition in your job and career. Let running be a break from all that, and some days, just go out and enjoy yourself.

Resolved: I forsake ambition for a while and just run.

May 22

"I still love those long, easy runs on Sunday. They're the mainstay of any training program. It's like saving pennies: put them in a jar and over a year you accumulate 50 or 60 dollars."

—Robert Wallace, marathoner

Weekends are the best for those long, slow runs. There's no rush; you can spend as much time as you want. That may be the loveliest thing: being able to spend as much time as you want, without being harassed by the demands of the clock.

On a Saturday or Sunday, you can take your time about stretching. That's something you often rush through during the week.

Since there's no pressure to be somewhere else, you can really cover some miles. You run farther than normal and not once think about doing anything else but running or being anywhere but where you are.

Afterward you don't have to pop into the car and drive off. You warm down nice 'n' easy and maybe even spend a little time chatting with the other runners. You sit on a bench and close your eyes and feel the soothing warmth of the sun on your face.

You're so often pressed for time when you run. Be sure to indulge yourself on the weekends and spend as much time as you want.

Resolved: I spend as much time running as I want on the weekends.

May 23

"See everything. Overlook a great deal. Improve a little."

—Pope John XXIII

When you improve a little in running, you improve a lot.

Success for you may be winning races, or building health of body and mind, or having a good time, or all three combined. However you define it, success comes only a little at a time.

Dramatic breakthroughs are a fiction, the stuff of movies or novels. For most runners, success is achieved through small, gradual, incremental, almost imperceptible improvements. But that is a lot. Get it out of your head that only big improvements are worthy of praise or attention. Little improvements add up to big improvements over time.

How do you improve as a runner? By running, mainly, but also by reading about it, talking to other runners, listening to coaches, watching top runners, running against the clock, running intervals and hills, putting variety into your workouts, watching your diet, and a hundred other ways.

Every improvement you make, no matter how tiny, is potentially significant. One microscopically small improvement can trigger a chain reaction of equally small improvements that combine to push you into a new level as a runner.

Set your sights on big, showy success, and you are setting yourself up for disappointment. Be patient instead. Take the long view. Take a little at a time, and be satisfied with that, for in running, a little is a lot.

Resolved: I improve a little over time.

May 24

"Running should be a lifelong activity. Approach it patiently and intelligently, and it will reward you for a long, long time."
—Michael Sargent, M.D.

The day you graduate from college, run. Take a nice easy jog around campus, reflect on what is past, passing, and to come, and then put on the cap and gown.

The morning of your wedding day, run. You'll need a run to calm the jitters. Afterward you'll be ready to get dressed and get hitched.

For men, the day after your first child is born, run. You won't be able to run the day of the birth because you'll be busy acting as labor coach. But once Mom and Baby are safe and sound, celebrate your good fortune with a run. (Moms are going to have to wait a while before they can do the same.)

The day before you buy your first house, run. Buying a house is a big decision, and a run will help you determine if you're making the right move.

The day your child enters kindergarten, run. Your child's first day at school is a big day for the child and you, and a run will show you that you're not so old after all.

The day your child graduates from college, run. It's unavoidable now: you *are* getting old. But maybe you and your child can run together.

The day after you retire, run. Take a nice easy jog around the park, reflect on what is past, passing, and to come, and then take a long, hot shower.

Resolved: I run today, as I run through all the major passages of my life.

May 25

That time of year is approaching. Who knows, it may already have arrived in your case. You know what we're talking about: that annual rite that strikes fear in people's hearts, when they must go shopping for a new swimsuit for summer. The horror, the horror!

Is anything more depressing than trying on a new bathing suit? You have this perception of yourself—a perception, it is true, based on your view of yourself with your clothes on. When you take your clothes off, the naked truth is revealed.

It's not enough to be standing in a changing closet in your birthday suit in front of a mirror that does not lie or even fudge the truth a little. No, you've got to pile indignity upon insult by actually trying to squeeze into some itsy-bitsy nylon loincloth that was apparently designed not for a living, breathing adult human being who has actual flesh attached to his or her skeletal structure, but for a Gumbylike stick figure (and a prepubescent one at that).

Such is life—and the fashion industry. But it's not too late, you know; in fact, summer hasn't even begun. There's still time before that big trip to the Caribbean or Hawaii. If you're unhappy with your shape, all you need to do is . . . *do* something about it. Why not start today?

Resolved: I put off buying that new swimsuit for a little while and get started on a summer fitness program.

May 26

"I have two doctors: my left leg and my right."

—George M. Trevelyan, historian and runner

Better than therapy (and cheaper, too).

Better than liquor.

Better than drugs.

Better than coffee.

Better than caffeinated tea.

Better than chocolate.

Better than Cherry Garcia ice cream.

Better than sex. (Well, maybe not better than sex. But without doubt, it helps the sex drive.)

Better than shopping.

Better than TV.

Better than vitamin supplements.

Better than the Zone.

Better than hospitals or doctors.

Better than Prozac.

Better than sleeping pills.

Better than cigarettes.

What's better for you than running? What's better to do right now than run?

Resolved: Nothing's better for me. I go for a run.

May 27

"I do better thinking when I run. If I'm stuck in the middle of a column, I'll go running and after a while it'll hit me. Either that, or a car will."

—Dave Barry, columnist and runner

Everybody has those times when the mind ceases to function. You're going along fine; all the cerebral connections are oiled up and revving. Then the mind goes bleary, and you can no longer spell "cat" even though they've spotted you the *c* and the *t*.

There's a simple answer when this happens: run.

Running changes the subject. More precisely, the subject stays the same, but running gives you a different view of it. If you're struggling with a problem and can think of it only in a certain way, take a break in the form of a run. When you come back, your struggling will be over, and you'll have the answer you've been looking for.

The problem itself hasn't changed, only your perception of it. And that makes all the difference.

Running is not a panacea. If you're struggling with a quantum physics equation, but you're not a physicist, chances are you're not going to find the answer even if you run to Djakarta and back. But if you have the goods to deal with what you're working on, running will put you in the frame of mind to do it.

Objective reality is one thing, but you *can* shape and alter your subjective reality. Running will break you out of whatever rut you happen to be in.

Resolved: When I get stuck, or in a rut, I take a run.

May 28

"After a week of the contained chaos that is my job, I need some solitary running time. On Sundays, I can unwind and reconnect with the natural world."

—Linda Jones, runner

Think of the unique nature of running. With the possible exception of bicycling and hiking, what other physical activity or sport takes you to all the places that it does?

Other sports take place in controlled settings. You play basketball in a gym or on a blacktop schoolyard. Baseball or softball is played on a ball field. Aerobics and weight training are done indoors. In swimming all you see are the walls of the pool.

When you run, however, you go on a journey. You run across a park, over a hill, down one street and along another, across a busy intersection, down a quiet lane, along a river, over a bridge, and then you turn around and come back.

Running puts you in touch with the broader outside world. Running indoors is practically an oxymoron. There is no established diamond or playground in which you run. The route you run is your own personal creation. You decide where you go and for how long. There's no clock telling you when to go and when to stop. You run as long as you feel like it.

Running is a means of connection with the natural world. Never lose sight of that fact. It's not just something you do for your own personal gain. See it as one of the ways you connect with the world around you.

Resolved: I see running as one of my connections to the natural world.

May 29

Count on it: there will be obstacles between you and the attainment of your goals as a runner.

There will be times when you think, "No way. Absolutely no way in the world can I do it. It's impossible. It can't be done. Maybe by others, but not by me."

There will be times when you come so close to achieving your goals that you can almost taste it. "Just a little more," you think, "and I'll be there." Then something unforeseen happens, and the end of your striving is even farther away than before.

This is discouraging. Even scary sometimes. You feel as if you're never going to get there, no matter how hard you try, no matter what you do. Fate seems to conspire against you.

Be fearless. That's all you can do in the face of these continuing obstacles. Accept your emotions. Don't deny your fears or disappointment or whatever you're feeling. It's OK to feel these things; everyone does.

The attainment of your goals won't come easy; it never does. You may have to cross a line of fire to get there. If that's the case, seal yourself into an asbestos suit, and do it. But always, be fearless.

Resolved: I am fearless in my pursuit of my goals as a runner.

May 30

*"Dreams pass into the reality of action. From the action stems
the dream again; and this interdependence produces the highest
form of living."*

—Anaïs Nin

You can't achieve your dreams in a single day. That's impossible. Dreams take time and planning and hard work and even
a little luck to achieve. You can't do all that today. There are
other matters to attend to as well. So, what do you do?

Take a step—one single step—today. That's all you need to
do. You don't have to achieve the dream today—we already
know that's impossible—just take one step toward it.

You may have only formed the dream and not yet started on
it. Well, then, take one step and get started today.

You may already be well on the way to achieving your
dream. Well, then, take another step today. Then another
tomorrow.

A magical thing occurs when you take action on a dream.
More dreams form. It's a regenerative cycle. You know what
needs to be done. You know the step that needs to be taken.
Take the step, and you're on your way.

Resolved: I take one step today on my way toward actualizing my dreams.

May 31

"When unhappy, one doubts everything; when happy, one doubts nothing."

—Joseph Roux, writer

The golfer Nancy Lopez has a simple philosophy: "Play happy." Her father taught it to her when she was young, and she has put it to good use during a long and storied Hall of Fame career.

What does it mean? First, it's a recognition of how lucky we are. If you're a runner, you probably have some leisure time in which to run, at least on weekends. You clearly appreciate good books. You probably have a job and food on your table. You may run in a nice pair of Nike or Brooks running shoes. When the shoes wear out, you buy a new pair. You probably are in pretty good health, although you feel you could always do better.

All those are blessings. All those facts speak to how lucky you are and why "running happy" may be a workable philosophy for you, too. Your heart and lungs are pumping? You're among friends? You have your health and freedom, and it's sunny and beautiful outside? What's not to be happy about?

Running happy keeps the inevitable disappointments of running (and everybody has them) in perspective. You recognize that although you may suffer setbacks, you have lots of blessings for which to be thankful. When you're happy, you're not under the oppressive thrall of doubt. You are more sure of yourself, and this surety in turn leads to more feelings of happiness.

Resolved: I run happy. And count my blessings.

June 1

"No yesterdays are ever wasted for those who give themselves to today."

—Brendan Francis, writer

It is the first of the month. What better way to celebrate it than with a run?

Last month you celebrated the first with a run, too. How'd it work out? Excellent, then. That gives you all the more reason to run today.

But you try to run every day, you say. What's so special about the first of the month?

Nothing, really. Or everything. Depends on your point of view. One person could regard this day like any other and find that fact boring or even depressing. But another person could see this same day as absolutely marvelous, a miracle of astounding proportions.

Which prompts the question: How do *you* regard today? Do you see it as typical, banal, inconsequential? Another day, another dollar? Are you bored? If so, why?

This is a day unlike any other. You will never have a June 1 like this again in your entire life. It is a day ripe with possibility, a day to celebrate. Waiting for you in this day is something you've never known before. But will you be able to recognize it when you see it? Or will you be yawning and miss it?

Resolved: It's the first of the month. I see today as a miracle of astounding proportions, and I run.

June 2

The time has come. Circumstances have changed, and now you must react. You know you can. You know you have what it takes; it is within your powers. Now it's simply a matter of doing it.

Oĸ, maybe not so simple. That's overstating a little bit. It's going to require more from you—more effort, more desire, more time, more hard work. And none of that will be simple. But you *can* do it. You can set the bar higher as a runner and achieve those loftier goals.

Setting the bar higher is the wrong metaphor for running— the bar belongs in the pole vault or high jump, which are field events—but you get the idea. You can do more than you are currently doing.

That doesn't mean push. It certainly doesn't mean risking injury. It just means . . . *doing more*. You had a certain idea of how things were going to work. And that idea worked fairly well. You were going along at what you thought was a reasonable pace and getting things done.

But now you know better. Maybe you ran a race and found out you weren't as far along as you thought you were. To get to where you want to go as a runner, set the bar higher.

Resolved: I set the bar higher as a runner—and find out more about myself.

June 3

"There is no evidence that speed protects, but mileage does."

—Running truism

To get what you want faster, go more slowly. It's one of the supreme ironies of life and running.

Some people go their entire lives and never figure it out. They rush and rush and rush in service to some larger ambition, and yet the more they hurry, the faster their goal recedes from them.

If they slowed down, they'd reach their goal more quickly and with less effort.

Runners must figure this out the hard way. But once they do, they never forget it. Here's a classic scenario. A runner thinks, "I want to break three hours in the marathon," and throws all his energies into the effort. He puts himself on a rigorous training program in which he quickly increases the number of miles he runs each day.

Boom. We all know what happens next. The runner is side-lined with painful shinsplints or worse. Or, if he's lucky enough to avoid injury, he soon loses interest because his results can't keep pace with his expectations. And he drops out without achieving his goal.

Slow down. Not only will you avoid injury, but you will also avoid burnout. There's wisdom in the phrase "slow but sure." Go slow, and be sure.

Resolved: I slow down as a runner and make sure.

June 4

"Rock and ice and wind and the great blue canopy of the sky are not all that a person finds upon the mountain-tops. He discovers things about his body and mind that he had almost forgotten in the day-to-day routine of living. He learns what his legs are for, what his lungs are for."

—James Ramsey Ullman, naturalist

Here's another idea to put variety into your workouts: why not altitude running? Many top runners train, at least part of the time, at altitudes from 1,000 to 5,000 feet above sea level or even higher. They travel up into the mountains and hills where the air is thinner. This requires their blood-delivery system—heart, lungs, blood vessels—to work harder yet more efficiently. When they return to sea level, they run stronger and faster.

There's no reason why you can't do this, too. Now, obviously, booking a flight to the highlands of Tibet is not the way to go, at least not at first. You want to take it slow and easy (and maybe talk to your doctor first).

If you live in the flatlands, running at altitude is going to hit you like a ton of bricks. Your legs will be dead. You'll be winded almost immediately. You'll think, "What is wrong with me?" before adapting to the fact that there is indeed a lot less oxygen at these altitudes. But gradually your strength and endurance will improve.

The mountains offer so many things to a runner: wide-open spaces, big sky, fewer people, a place to get away from the rat race. Yet another attribute is a chance to train at altitude.

Resolved: On my next trip to the mountains, I make sure to include time for some easy high-altitude running.

June 5

There is a simple way to become a better runner: run. Run every day if you can. If you can't do that, run every other day. Over time you will become stronger, faster, and more fit.

Write it down on the calendar, starting today. Jot down "I run," and think about a time in your schedule when you can make it happen. Skip a day and jot it down again, continuing on an every-other-day basis through the rest of the month and into July.

A first step in running regularly is getting it into your schedule. This creates a place for it in your mind, and body follows mind.

Don't say you don't have time. You can make room for it. Suppose you're a single man and you meet a really terrific lady. You may have the schedule of the president of the United States, but you know you'll make room for her in a minute (especially if you're the president). It's the same for women when they meet a new guy. When the desire's there, you find the time.

So, maybe see running, at least initially, as the new hot flame in your life. Once you start seeing her regularly, you won't believe what great days and nights you'll have together.

Resolved: I never go two days without running.

June 6

"Give up TV, and you'll be amazed at how much time you have to run."

—Kees Tuinzing, runner and publisher

Want to create more time to run? Here's one way: shut off the tube. It's not exactly a motivational technique, but it works. As Tuinzing says, it's amazing how much time we waste sitting in front of that box. And it's equally amazing how much time we gain when we shut it off.

But you can't just shut the TV off cold turkey. You've got to replace it with something. Let that something be running.

Sure, there are occasionally some good programs on. But inevitably you let the TV stay on after you're done watching the program you tuned in to see. Invariably what follows is dreck. So, you end up watching a bunch of garbage and wasting your time.

Then again, you may be saying, that's the point. You get enough brain work during the day. In the evening you just want to space out for a while and relax.

That's reasonable enough. But if you're having trouble finding time to run, something has to give. Why not try this: shut off the TV this weekend, and see what happens. Instead of camping out on the couch, go for a run. You may find that it's a trade worth making.

Resolved: If I'm having trouble finding time to run, I turn off the TV and see what happens.

June 7

"You didn't beat me. You merely finished in front of me."

—Hal Higdon, runner and writer

It's hard keeping up with the Joneses, in running or in any other area of life.

You may think you're not progressing as fast as you should. You may want to run better times. So, you force the pace in your eagerness to keep up with other, faster runners. Unfortunately this kind of pressure only makes you tie up. It works against you and all that you've accomplished.

People often put pressure on themselves trying to keep up with what others are doing. An eight-minute-a-mile runner sees a flock of six-minute milers pass by and thinks, "I should be going faster. I should be doing better."

Her perception is not based on how much she runs, or on how long she's been running, or on her aptitude for it. It is based on a vague sense that she is falling behind and that she should be doing better relative to these others. When her performance doesn't fulfill her unrealistic expectations, she gets discouraged.

Forget about keeping up with the Joneses. Keep running, at least, free from this type of worry. Ease up on yourself—today, tomorrow, and the next day. You're a human being. You're doing fine, the best you can. And you'll do even better without putting added pressure on yourself.

Resolved: I forget about the Joneses; I ease up on putting pressure on myself—and just run.

June 8

"Each of us makes his own weather, determines the color of the skies in the emotional universe which he inhabits."

—Fulton J. Sheen, religious leader

Consistency may be the hobgoblin of little minds, but it's also the hallmark of great runners.

It makes no sense to go all out one day and then be completely burned out the next. Better to even out the highs and lows into one steady groove. You have a running pace with which you feel comfortable. Every runner does. Get into that pace, and go with it. When you're tired, stop. The next day do it again.

Make running a kind of emotionally "neutral" activity. Of course, you will have highs and lows, days when you feel terrific and days when you feel lousy. But if you can even out the highs and lows, you'll tend to run more frequently.

Be a slow-burning candle when it comes to running, rather than a roaring fire. Make running a plain fact of your life, not subject to emotional upheavals. Do this, and you will run more and thus be able to ride out the occasional lows that you experience. You won't get so down when you're down. But you will still be able to experience those soaring highs.

Consistency in running is not just a matter of doing it every day. Let your emotions match the steadiness of your stride.

Resolved: I remain emotionally consistent as a runner, evening out the highs and lows.

June 9

"There's nothing quite like the feeling you get from knowing you're in good physical condition. I wake up alert and singing in the morning, ready to go."

—Stan Gerstein, runner

Being in good shape. That *is* a good feeling.

Your clothes fit better. You have more energy. You can not only work harder but also work better. You have less desire to drink alcohol. Junk food seems far less tempting.

Your skin looks healthier. Your eyes are clearer. Your internal plumbing is clog free. Your lungs are clear as a Montana sky, and you have the pulsing heart of an athlete. You don't huff and puff when you walk up steps. You enjoy walking up steps; in fact, you seek them out. When you see people you haven't seen in a while and they say, "You look good," you feel inwardly pleased because you know it's true.

You're even happier about your sex life. Morning, noon, and night, all systems are go.

You're less groggy and tired. You get going faster in the morning, and you're able to get more things done. You have fewer aches and pains. And when those aches and pains come, at least you know how to cope with them: by going outside and running.

Your parents or relatives may think you look too skinny, but you know the truth of it. You're as lean and hard as Kip Keino. That's the way you like it, and that's the way it's going to be.

Resolved: I keep this feeling going. I keep running and stay in shape.

June 10

"Pain may be caused by many things which, if their advantageous aspect had been considered, might have given rise to satisfaction."

—Baltasar Gracián, writer and philosopher

The most difficult aspect of pain is often not the pain itself but accepting the fact of it.

Life is going along fine, or so you believe, and then at the end of a long day you get it into your head to start moving furniture around to make a new arrangement in the living room. The next morning you wake up with a pain in your back.

Angry at the pain, and at yourself for being so stupid as to be moving furniture around late at night, you resolve that you're not going to let it affect you. You're going to do everything you normally do, including stepping out for your usual run.

The back loosens up some after your run (and the ensuing hot shower), and you think you've got it licked. Then later that day it stiffens up again, and you know you've got trouble.

What's so hard about accepting pain is that it demands change. It's inconvenient, among other things. You can't do all the things you normally do, so it forces you to change your usual routine. You're going to have to rest and take care of yourself. You may have to skip running for a few days.

The first step in getting out of pain is acceptance. Everything gets a lot easier when you do that. The sooner you accept, the sooner you recover.

Resolved: As hard as it is at times, I try to accept the fact of pain as the first step in my recovery.

June 11

"Running is my sunshine. Every morning before I run, I say a prayer—giving thanks to God."

—Joan Twine, runner

A person heals in many ways: through prayer, through service to others, through rest, through healthy living, through meditation, through therapy, through laughter and tears.

Let running be a form of healing, too.

When you are feeling down, take a run. You will feel much better after getting outdoors and experiencing nature.

When something bad happens to you or to a member of your family, take a run. The bad thing will not magically change to good because of running. But you will be better able to cope with it.

When your body is feeling cranky and out of sorts, take a run. A run will get your heart and lungs pumping, and that can only be good.

When the world is pressing on you and not giving you enough space to breathe, take a run. The world will take a few backward steps after that.

When you are feeling out of touch with yourself or what truly matters in this life, take a run. A run can set you straight if you've been knocked askew and start the process of healing.

Resolved: When I feel out of touch with myself, I take a run.

June 12

It's almost summer, time to think about entering a race. What's that you say? You just ran one? Good for you. Time to plan for another, then. Never run one, you say? Well, then, no better time than now.

But you need to get tactical, adopt a little strategy. Take down a calendar. How many days are there before the race? And how many of those days can you actually run? Look at it realistically, and build gradually. What do you need to do prior to the race to give yourself the opportunity to succeed?

Obviously a marathon requires a different training schedule from a 5K. You have to log more miles over a longer period to successfully negotiate 26 miles. Charting distances and days on a calendar will help you do that.

Plan for a race the way you'd plan for a vacation. It's always nice to know a little something about where you're going before you go. That way you avoid surprises or silly mistakes, like packing your heavy winter coat for a week on Maui.

Run this summer with a goal in mind. Pick out a race that you'd like to run, and gear your training schedule around it.

Resolved: I get tactical with my running. I pick out a race I'd like to run this summer and train with it in mind.

June 13

"There are as many ways to be successful as a distance runner as there are athletes. You have to develop a training schedule of your own."

—Craig Virgin, champion distance runner

Every runner nowadays may choose from a veritable smorgasbord of training philosophies and programs. Which one you select depends on your tastes and sensibilities.

A runner, such as Bill Rodgers or Frank Shorter, may be "hot" for a while and publish a book that includes a training program. If something in that program works for you, use it. But when it outlives its usefulness, drop it like a hot coal.

Philosophies come and go. They have their time, and their time passes. Philosophies also clash, like armies in the night. One prominent coach or runner believes one thing, while another prominent coach or runner advocates the exact opposite. In a few short years, everyone will forget both systems, which seem so important at the time.

New systems replace old systems. Then newer systems replace the systems that replaced the old systems. Often the system that replaces the current system reflects an older system which was itself replaced by a previous generation. And round and round it goes.

You can simplify all of this by asking one question of your current training philosophy or program: Are you enjoying yourself? If you're enjoying your running, if you're having fun with it, then you're on the right path.

Resolved: I eschew any running philosophy that does not have enjoyment at the heart of it.

June 14

"The first thing I had to do was learn that I could do it."

—Sue Stricklin, runner

This is the first step: learning you can do it. Once you make this step, all the other steps that need to be made will become clear.

You can run the New York Marathon. You can run a marathon under 2:50. You can put it all together and run New York in under 2:50. You can do that.

Name your goal in running, whatever it is. You can do *that*, too.

It won't be easy. It will require perseverance and hard work—those boring old verities. It won't happen overnight, and it may not happen until you've tried and failed several times. But you can do it; it's within your power.

Realize that only one person can get in your way, and that person is you. Granted that fate, time, luck, and other random forces may come into play. But you'll never overcome these forces if you continue to trip yourself up and pose an obstacle to yourself.

Other people will not get in your way, and if they do, you will simply outlast them. The same can be said for fate, time, and luck. You will outlast them all.

The person who can achieve your dreams is the same one who can stop them from occurring. So, which person are you going to be?

Resolved: I realize I can do it. I run New York in under 2:50, or whatever else I set my sights on.

June 15

*"Make running a habit. Set aside a time solely for running.
Running is more fun if you don't have to rush through it."*

—Jim Fixx

You look at your activity-crazy schedule and think, "No way can I run. There's just no time."

Yes there is. Squeeze it in.

Make a game of it. Have fun with it. There are cracks in every schedule, including yours. Squeeze your runs in between the cracks.

Sometimes a schedule can seem as hard as concrete. But by squeezing in a run here and there, you will find that the cracks gradually expand. Say you have an 8 o'clock meeting followed by an 11 o'clock. Between meetings, who will notice if you step out for a little while?

Ok, maybe lots of people will notice. Maybe that strategy won't work this time. But what about running at noon? You can squeeze it in on your lunch hour. No one will begrudge you that. If you can't run during work hours, squeeze it in after you punch out and before you go home.

Sure, running is more fun if you don't have to rush through it, but sometimes there's no other choice. In which case, squeeze it in.

Resolved: I squeeze in a run every chance I get.

June 16

"People get a relief from tension by running. One thing that almost always happens is that your sense of self-worth improves. You accept yourself a little better."

—Ted Corbitt, former U.S. Olympic marathoner

Saturdays and Sundays get all the publicity, but Friday evenings are pretty good for running, too. The workweek is over, and there's not as much pressure on you to get home. Since you don't have to go to work the next morning, you don't have to stick to such a strict evening schedule.

It's not always true, but if you're creative, you usually can swing some free time for yourself on Fridays after work. Of course, you may want to spend this time in a TGIF celebration with your coworkers. But why is it an either/or deal? Why not run before you meet your friends?

If you commute, instead of battling the always heavy Friday getaway traffic, you can run. Pull off the freeway, find a park with running trails or some other appropriate venue, and go crazy. Now, *that's* a trade-off most people would gladly make: instead of getting all stressed out stuck in traffic in your overheated vehicle, spend that time in a pleasurable and healthful way—that is, running. Then when you get back on the road after your run, the traffic has cleared out, and you can sail home.

Running on a Friday evening starts your weekend off right. You're in a good mood when you get home and ready to embrace the weekend.

Resolved: I end my workweek with a Friday-evening run.

June 17

"When you're young and just beginning, you have a dream, an unrealistic dream, of what you can achieve. Follow that dream, hold onto it. Don't let it disappear."

—Franklin Jacobs, former indoor world record holder in the high jump

There's a great scene in the 1989 movie *Field of Dreams*, in which Kevin Costner, playing a dreamer who builds a ballpark in the middle of an Iowa cornfield, stands with his wife looking at his creation. "I have just created something totally illogical," he says.

Totally illogical, but also very beautiful. Fields of corn surround the diamond, which is lit up in the night. Costner's wife in the movie, played by Amy Madigan, revels in this beauty as well as in the totally illogical nature of the enterprise. "That's what I like about it," she says with a soft smile.

Whatever your dream in running, there is going to be some illogic to it. Something about it just won't add up. It will be unrealistic on some level. You may not even know why you must do it.

When you examine your dream in the cold light of day, it will be found wanting. There will be questions about it, questions for which there are no ready answers. Its flaws will be clearly visible, to you and to others. Others will point out, and you may agree, how difficult it is going to be to achieve this dream.

Hang onto your dream, in all of its unrealistic, illogical, doesn't-add-up beauty. Sometimes a dream makes sense only after it comes true.

Resolved: I pursue my dreams, always taking pleasure in the illogical.

June 18

"I know a lot of women want to beat me. I'm not going to let them."

—Lynn Jennings, racer

Take it from the turtle: slow and steady wins the race. Starting too fast and not maintaining an even pace will usually leave you, like the hare, gasping and beaten.

Equally foolhardy is the idea that a big kick at the end will enable you to fly by the other competitors and win. Save yourself for the finish, and you will likely be far out of contention long before then. Also, if you have a lot of energy left over at the end, you may not be running hard enough throughout the race.

Nevertheless, there will be times when you need to put on a finishing kick, especially in shorter races. Even middle- and back-of-the-pack runners occasionally find themselves in duels to the finish with other runners. You feel (or see) someone breathing hard on your shoulder, and you rise to meet his or her challenge.

The next time that happens, know that you *can* respond. In athletics and in life, belief in yourself is a powerful tool. It takes a certain amount of arrogance to finish strong. All the great kickers have it. They've done the training, put in the work. And they simply refuse to be beaten down the stretch.

Barbra Streisand once said that singing is 80 percent attitude and 20 percent vocal ability. It's the same with a strong finishing kick. Have the attitude that you can outkick your competition, and it may spur you on to do exactly that.

Resolved: I always outkick 'em.

June 19

"Strenuousness is the open foe of attainment. The strength that wins is calm and has an exhaustless source in its passive depth."

—Rabindranath Tagore, philosopher

As has been discussed, counting on a big finishing kick is hardly the best racing strategy. Being steady and resolute—ah, that's how you obtain the keys to the kingdom of running.

Here's another way to get a set of keys made: run a faster last mile than a first mile.

If you start a race fast but slowly die on the vine, you will surely be disappointed. You will naturally focus not on how well you started but on how poorly you finished, and your confidence may flag as a result.

But if you start slow and finish strong—running the last mile faster than the first—your view of the race will be entirely different, even though your time could be exactly the same. Having finished on an up note, you will feel good about yourself. You will be optimistic that you can do much better because of how strong you felt at the end.

A runner who finishes strong is a smart runner, unlike the misguided creatures who take off like wild horses at the start of a race. As your strength and speed increase, theirs inevitably falter, and you pass them easily as the race progresses.

Take pride in the fact that you are stronger at the end of a race than at the beginning. Let it govern your race strategy, and make it a goal in your everyday running, too.

Resolved: I run a faster last mile than a first mile.

June 20

"The panic of what to do next never goes away. I might be in line at a movie theater, and somebody's slip is hanging the wrong way, and it looks good. But you have to be smart about what inspiration you use. It has to be the right time."

—Betsey Johnson, clothing designer

What inspires you today may not inspire you tomorrow.

What motivated you last week may not do so this week.

What spurred you on to greater heights last year may seem sadly lacking this year.

Just as you change from day to day, and year to year, your sources of inspiration change, too. And arise in unexpected ways. Someone may give you a tip about running that makes no sense at all when you first hear it. But a month, or a year, or five years later, you remember what was said, and it seems the perfect advice.

Inspiration for running will not always come from the world of running. It may come from other athletes, businesspeople, musicians, artists, politicians—you name it. The ingredients for success—hard work, perseverance, desire, a little luck—are basically the same in every field of activity.

Inspiration can be found in the unlikeliest of places, at the unlikeliest of times. Something that doesn't seem useful now may seem a divine spark of wisdom later. The important thing is, stay open—both to yourself and to the world around you. Do that, and sources of inspiration will be present everywhere.

Resolved: I stay open and know that sources of inspiration can be found wherever I look.

June 21

"The suggestiveness of summer!—a word that is so weighted with the fullness of existence. It means more to me than any other word in the language."

—Edward Martin Taber, writer

Every season is a good season for running, but summer may be the best. The days are warmer and longer. It's not so hard to drag yourself out of the rack in the morning. And if you can't run in the morning, there's plenty of daylight after work.

Summer has a feel to it that the other seasons do not. Fall is cooler and more reflective. Spring bristles with manic energy; it can go from hot to cold to hot in a single day. Winter is frequently cold, wet, and snowy, turning a Sunday-afternoon jog into a battle with the elements.

Summer, on the other hand, is as lazy as you want to make it. It is a time for being outside, inviting friends over for a barbecue, and popping open some cold ones. A ball game plays softly on the radio, and later someone falls asleep in the grass.

And of course, there's running. On a hot day in summer, you're warmed up almost as soon as you start. This can cause problems, too, so watch out for overheating. But if you run in the early morning, before the heat takes hold, or in the early evening, after it's loosened its grip on the day, it can be positively blissful.

Whatever you do this summer, run. Get out of the house, feel the warmth of the sun on your body, and run.

Resolved: I make sure I run—a lot—this summer.

June 22

"Risk! Risk anything! Do the hardest thing on earth for you. Act for yourself."

—Katherine Mansfield, author

Motivation comes in many forms, and one form is the approval of others. Every runner knows how thrilling it is to hear the applause of spectators along a racecourse. Their support and enthusiasm lift your spirits and buoy you along to the finish.

Here's another way to receive motivation from others: call up your local newspaper and see if they want to do a story on you.

At first blush, you may think, "Me? Why would anyone want to do a story on me?" You may be surprised. You may be more interesting than you think.

Perhaps you recently won your age group in a local race. Perhaps you're one of the oldest or one of the youngest runners around. Perhaps you're training for a 50-mile ultramarathon. There are any number of possible story angles about you, even if you don't race at all. What motivates someone like yourself to get up at five A.M. every day and run seven miles? Perhaps you run with a group, and the writer can do a feature on all of you.

Seeing your name in print or your picture in the paper can be very motivating. It shows that your efforts and hard work are being recognized and appreciated.

Resolved: I call up the local newspaper to see if they're interested in doing a story about me.

June 23

"It is a universal maxim worthy of all acceptation that a man may have that allowance which he takes. Take the place and attitude to which you see your unquestionable right, and all men acquiesce."

—Ralph Waldo Emerson

They say you'll never stick at running, that you don't have the dedication. Prove 'em wrong.

They say you'll never make the team. Prove 'em wrong.

They say you'll never work hard enough to be any good. Prove 'em wrong.

They say you're too scared to enter a race, that you're "not the competitive type." Prove 'em wrong.

They say you're a quitter, that your attitude needs improvement. Prove 'em wrong.

They say you'll never win the race. Prove 'em wrong.

They say you'll never complete a marathon. Prove 'em wrong.

They say you'll never run a marathon under 2 hours and 50 minutes. Prove 'em wrong.

They say you'll never run Boston and New York in the same year. Prove 'em wrong.

They say that's the fastest you can go, that you can't go any faster. Prove 'em wrong.

They say you're not good enough to run with the very best. Prove 'em wrong.

They say you're this or you're that, always wanting to pin labels on you. Rebel against all that. Prove 'em wrong.

Resolved: I prove 'em wrong; I always prove 'em wrong.

June 24

"Winning is nice, but you savor that victory for an evening and it's gone. Competing well is just not to be equated with winning."

—Bill Bowerman, running coach

There is only one winner. Everybody else is an also-ran.

That's the conventional view of athletic competition, anyhow. But it's not the case in running. For one, there is always a men's and a women's winner in every running race. Also, because of age-group divisions, there are many winners according to their age.

Additionally, in running, the person who finishes last can feel just as happy and satisfied as the person who finishes first. Where you finish in a race does not necessarily equate with feeling good about yourself afterward.

When you enter a race, assuming you do, put the emphasis on competing well, rather than winning. This will provide far more lasting rewards in the end.

Even in running, only a select few walk away with the ribbons and awards. Satisfaction must be found elsewhere.

Give your all. Play fair. Bask in the camaraderie of racing, the sheer animal pleasure of being around so many other bodies. Make sure to have fun even as you compete. Keep your perspective. Remember how lucky you are to be doing what you're doing (and to be healthy and alive!). Keep these elements in mind, and you will compete well.

Resolved: When I compete, I compete well.

June 25

"People today tend to overdo. This applies especially, I think, to distance runners and the training they do. What you should do is develop a training program that suits your physical makeup, your stamina, and your ability as a runner."

—Gayle Barron, marathoner

Fitness is its own reward. When you get fit, you want to become more fit. You feel good; you look good. You want to keep it all going. You want to keep improving.

With this goal in mind, you may want to take your training up a notch higher. Maybe you increase the distance you run each day. Maybe you go from running three days a week to five days a week. Maybe you add some speed work on a track to your regular routine.

Take a go-slow approach on this. Stabilize and sustain your workout at these higher levels before you attempt to do more.

For example, if you decide to increase your mileage, do so gradually. Sudden jumps in mileage cause injuries. Further, avoid running that increased new mileage every day. Run three miles (or whatever it is) one day, then fall back to your typical two miles. Remember: stabilize and sustain. Give your body time to grow accustomed to the changes that you are introducing.

Be satisfied with the improvements you see (and feel), and go slowly when you institute changes. Although it's sometimes hard to hold back, your body needs that time. Building fitness is like building a housing development. It must be done in phases.

Resolved: When I reach a higher level of fitness, I stabilize and sustain it before attempting to do more.

June 26

An old man once asked a young college student what his major was. The student sheepishly replied, "English."

"What's wrong with that?" said the old man, puzzled by the youngster's attitude.

"I don't know," said the student. "It's just that whenever I tell people that I'm an English major, they always say, 'Are you going to be a teacher?' And no, I don't want to be a teacher. But I don't really know what I want to do. So, I almost feel as if I'm wasting my time in English."

The old man smiled. "No," he said with the patience of his years, "you're not wasting your time. English and mathematics are the two best subjects to study. Do you know why?" The student shook his head. "Because you will always use them. Whatever career you pursue, you will always use English." The young man felt much better after that.

What is true for English and math is also true for running. It is the base of every physical activity. Whatever sport you play, whatever activity you pursue, you will be better at it because you run.

Resolved: I keep running, knowing that it helps me in all my other activities.

June 27

"What you intuitively desire, that is possible to you. Whereas what you mentally or consciously desire is nine times out of ten impossible; hitch your wagon to a star, and you'll just stay where you are."

—D. H. Lawrence

When you first start running, personal bests seem to fall over like dominoes, one after another. It seems as if every time you go out, you set a new one.

That gets a little harder to do after you've run for a while.

Nobody can tell you how to set a personal best. But here's how *not* to: run with the idea of setting one. You cannot order up a personal best as if it were a turkey on rye, hold the onions. It's not a conscious act. A personal best is a kind of gift bestowed upon you. You're not sure where it came from or how.

It's very hard to achieve a personal best after you've run for a while and brought your times down. It takes training and hard work. But remarkably, those who achieve personal bests all say the same thing: how easy it felt. They weren't straining, they weren't pushing; it just seemed to come to them.

If you run with the idea that you are going to set a personal best, you will almost certainly tie up and run an average or less-than-average time. But if you run instead with the idea that you're just going to enjoy yourself, that you're going to relax and have a good time, that whatever happens, happens—well, those are the days when personal bests occur.

Resolved: I do not consciously seek a personal best, although I always stay open to the possibility that one will occur.

June 28

What's the best thing that could happen to you in running?

Maybe you've got a plan in mind, a vision of things to come. But you're not sure if you can trust it. You're an upbeat person generally, but over the years you've taken your share of knocks. Not everything has worked out the way you'd like—in running or in life.

Still, you've got your hopes and dreams. Projecting ahead a few months (or longer), you can see that if you can get through this rough stretch, and your running continues to progress, and things happen for you in a certain way, then you're going to be all right. Better than all right; in fact, you'll be sitting pretty.

Well, what's wrong with hoping for that outcome? Seeing it in your mind, and helping to make it come true in fact? It would be too depressing to think that our futures are cast in concrete already. We must be able to shape our ends to some degree. Not totally, perhaps, as there are many forces—internal and external—at work upon us. But to the extent that we can make a difference, why not pursue the optimistic scenario?

It *can* happen. It *is* possible. Great things can happen for us and to us. But first we must allow for that possibility in our minds. See a positive outcome for yourself, and do everything you can to make it a reality.

Resolved: I pursue the optimistic scenario in running.

June 29

"At bottom no one in life can help anyone else in life. But that isn't as bad as it may at first appear. It is the best thing in life that each should have everything in himself: his fate, his future, his world."

—Rainer Maria Rilke, poet

You've put it off and put it off and put it off, hoping it would go away. It hasn't. It's still hanging around, still undone.

You hoped someone else would do it for you, or at least tell you how to do it. Neither hope has borne fruit. No one has stepped forward.

You're familiar with the saying "If you want something done well, do it yourself," but you were hoping it wouldn't apply in this case. You're also well acquainted with the saying "God helps those who help themselves," but again, you didn't think it applied in this case, and besides, what's God have to do with this?

There's really no avoiding it anymore. It's been bugging you for too long. Clearly no one else is coming forward. This is your life, your world, your future. It's up to you to get this thing done or not.

Get it done. Today. Take this thing that is bugging you and won't leave you alone, and do it. Turn your thoughts into deeds. No more putting it off till tomorrow, no more waiting around for someone else to come up with the answer for you. The only answer that will work for certain is the one you find yourself and have the force of personality to put into action.

Resolved: Whatever I need to do in running, I get it done.

June 30

"The need for laziness becomes overpowering in all of us from time to time. There are a few sensible people. They go off into a corner somewhere and are as lazy as can be."

—Dr. Wilhelm Stekhel, writer

Yesterday was a day of action and purpose. You resolved to get things done, and you did. You took care of what needed to be taken care of, you addressed what needed to be addressed, you solved what needed solving.

Enough of that.

It feels good to get things done. It also feels good to occasionally let things go. Today, if you can, let things go.

It's important to see this in the proper light. When you take it easy, when you take a day off, you're not "doing nothing." Don't look at it in those terms. Fact is, a body cannot be in motion constantly. It needs to rest periodically. Both states of being—rest and activity—are crucial to its survival.

This is certainly true for runners. You can't go after it every day as if you're Michael Johnson training for the 2000 Olympics. Even Michael Johnson has off days. They're built into his training schedule; he plans for them.

Ambition is fine, but not every day. Make this an ambition-free day. Those things that absolutely need to get done? They can wait. Forget about running, forget about duty, forget about getting things done. There'll be time enough for all that tomorrow.

Resolved: Whatever I need to do in running, I let it slide.

July 1

"My life is so much more exciting, much more fun, as a result of running. Life is so richer as a result of running. Running gives me more than I have ever given to it."

—Unidentified runner

At the start of this year you resolved to make this the best year of your running life. How's it going so far?

What's that? You say there's been some ups and downs? Well, that's to be expected. The important thing is not to get discouraged.

Every runner will tell you there are times when he or she feels like a million bucks. Then there are times when your shoes have holes and you don't have a quarter for a phone call. That's the way it goes.

Amid the inevitable ups and downs, remember to enjoy yourself. Keep the focus on that, and everything will work out. If you don't enjoy running, you're not going to do it. It's as simple as that. If you keep doing it—if you keep running—you will see the benefits. And the more you see the benefits—a stronger heart, clearer lungs, a trimmer figure, to name three—the more motivated you will be to run.

In some ways it's silly to evaluate a person's progress after only six months. That's hardly time enough. Running is a lifetime activity. Longtime runners view it not in terms of days or months but in terms of years. Or even decades.

Then again, that may be too intimidating for some people. Don't worry about years. Just think about today. What are you doing today? Wanna go for a run?

Resolved: I run today—and rededicate myself to making this the best year of my running life.

July 2

"When it's pouring rain and you're bowling along through the wet, there's satisfaction in knowing you're out there and the others aren't."

—Peter Snell, distance runner

Blue skies are overhead, though there's an angry fist of dark clouds moving in from the north. You take off anyway, thinking you can get your run in before the storm hits. But clouds can move faster than even you, and before long you're feeling big, juicy drops on your head.

So what? you say. A little water never hurt anyone. And you keep running. There *is* a kind of virtue in knowing that you're the only one out there. The rain feels good, cooling the world off and rinsing it down.

But the longer you run, the more it rains. It's a real gully washer. Thunder sounds; you see a spike of lightning. You begin to wonder, "Should I keep going or turn around?"

In a matter of minutes you're soaked. You duck into a doorway and wait for it to let up. The rain keeps coming and coming, harder and harder. If you had taken off a half hour earlier, you probably would've been able to get your run in. The desire is there, but not the timing.

It happens. Sometimes you can run through a storm, and other times you're better off just turning around. So, that's what you do, retreating into the dry warmth of your home with the certain knowledge that tomorrow is another day.

Resolved: I run through a summer storm, though I can always turn back if it gets to be too much.

July 3

"I swam, and what is more delicious than swimming? It is exercise and luxury at once."

—Richard Jefferies, writer

It's summer; it's warm outside. It's time to get in the pool.

Running and swimming go together like ice cream and cake. Few physical activities can match the pleasures inherent in going for a run and taking a swim after. You work up a nice, easy sweat when you run. Then you cool off in the pool with a nice, easy swim. Follow that with a steam bath and rubdown, and you've attained physical-fitness nirvana.

The benefits and pleasures of swimming hardly need elucidation here. Swimming may be the best all-around body conditioner, providing excellent aerobic exercise while putting the arms and upper body to work as well.

Running puts a lot of pressure on the lower extremities. Swimming eases that pressure. It lengthens the muscles and ligaments and causes little impact on your feet and shins.

If it's possible, it might be fun to run to the community pool, do a gentle workout, and run back. If you live in the country, you may prefer swimming in a lake or river to a chlorinated pool.

Swimming, like bicycling, fits nicely into the runner's life. Pick out a local body of water, and go for it.

Resolved: I take a run and go for a swim after.

July 4

It's the Fourth of July. What better reason do you need to go for a run?

There may be a party in the afternoon and fireworks tonight. Better to get the run in this morning before the festivities start.

There's time. For once, there's time. You can have a dawdling sort of run and not feel guilty about it. Running on a holiday is like running on a Sunday. It feels like a free day. There's no pressing work that needs to be done, and you can relax about things.

Nice feeling, isn't it? Not having to be somewhere at a certain time, you stretch out and maybe run a little farther than usual. Afterward, feeling virtuous and fit, you're in the mood to spend time with your family and celebrate.

There may be guests coming over later in the day, and you need to get some chores done. OK, but put the run at the top of the priority list. Running will give you more energy to do the chores.

But today is not a day of work. It's a day for rest and pleasure, barbecues and friends, fireworks and watching *Yankee Doodle Dandy* starring Jimmy Cagney on video. And oh yes, a bracing run in the morning.

Resolved: I celebrate the Fourth of July by going for a run.

July 5

"Mountains should be climbed with as little effort as possible and without desire. The reality of your own nature should determine the speed."

—Robert Pirsig, writer

Throw away the calendar; quit looking at your watch. You're right where you should be.

How can that be, you ask? You want to be ready for New York in October, and you feel as if you're falling behind.

Relax; you're right on schedule. There is no other place for you to be than right where you are. In any case, fretting about it won't help. That may only cause you to fall behind more.

If you have the perception that you are falling behind on your training schedule, treat it as useful information. You may need to adjust your training accordingly—run more distances or run more intervals.

But it may be that your expectations are off, not you. Perhaps your training regime was too ambitious in the first place and needs to be brought back into line with where you are as a runner.

Quit judging your progress by external measures; look to yourself. Ask yourself how you are faring, and trust the answer you receive.

Resolved: I relax about my running and feel confident about the progress I'm making.

July 6

It's sunny and blue today. So, what are you up to? Although it may turn hot in the afternoon, it hasn't gotten there yet. Morning is sharp and even cool, perfect for a run.

Your usual daily pattern is to go for a run and come back. Makes sense, right? Run for a half hour or an hour (or whatever) as part of your normal schedule.

But it's too nice a day to be stuck indoors, or go to work, or do anything but play. That gentle, healing sun has chased all thoughts of normalcy away. Some days you must do your duty despite your most ardent desires to the contrary. But today is not one of those days. Today you must give in to your most ardent desires. That is your duty.

Call someone up. Round up your family. Grab a friend or, better yet, a lover, and make a day of it. Pack a picnic lunch, or if that seems to lack appropriate spontaneity, grab whatever else strikes your fancy at the corner deli, and just go. Drive to someplace out of the ordinary, and take a run. When you come back, sprawl languorously on the grass, and peel each other grapes. Later, when you're stuffed to contentment and the sun has gotten high and hot, crawl under a shade tree and fall deliciously asleep.

The best running days are the ones that aren't planned. Plan on having a few of those this summer.

Resolved: I suspend my normal daily schedule today. I go for a run and make a day of it.

July 7

"Live all you can. It doesn't so much matter what you do in particular, so long as you have had your life. If you haven't had that what have you had?"

—Henry James

There are days for the paved streets and the track, days when you must follow the normal course traveled by other runners.

Then there are days when you leave the beaten path behind and run cross-country across the top of a ridge.

Sure, there will be obstacles. The obstacles are part of the adventure. It's rough going in spots. You slog through high grass; there are holes. The hills are rolling and uneven, and at times you may have to walk.

But it's worth it, every moment is worth it, because you have this feeling of making your way across uncharted terrain. You know you won't see any other runners up *here*. The only creatures around are brown and black dairy cattle who stare at you stupidly before returning to their chewing.

You laugh as you run past them, trotting down one hill and up another.

What's so wonderful is this feeling of being on top of the world. Below you is your usual running trail. You can see down the hillside and across the strait and beyond the mountains to the north.

You feel fit—that's another part of it. You feel fit and ready, and with these feelings your confidence grows. You're ready for new challenges, for whatever life brings, and you run like a deer across the tops of the hills.

Resolved: I leave the beaten path and run cross-country over a ridge top.

July 8

"If we only knew the real value of a day, nothing would contribute more to put us in possession of ourselves. Once a person fully realizes that he can mold only the day he has, he will begin both to take things easily and do them well."

—Joseph Farrell, writer

Many runners regard the middle of the day much as a lion tamer regards the lion. They proceed with extreme caution, for it is truly a horrid thing to be pounced upon, and rendered helpless, by a high, hot sun in the middle of the afternoon. There are runners who've been trapped by such horrors and lived to tell the tale, but they are few and far between.

Actually, though, if you choose a cool, overcast afternoon, there is much to be said for running in the middle of the day. It represents a therapeutic change in routine. You're out at a different time of day, seeing people and sights you normally don't see. It's quieter, and there's less traffic (foot and car). It's as if you've discovered a brand-new world, even though you may be running in the same place you usually do.

While all the rest of the world is at work (assuming this is a weekday), you are bounding around in your running shoes, carefree as a teenager on summer recess. Though, it's true, the demands of your work may not permit that.

If you work at home, consider yourself lucky. Running is the perfect way to break up the day. After working hard in the morning and early afternoon, go for a run. Refreshed and reinvigorated, you can come back and squeeze in a little more work before evening settles in and it's dinnertime.

Resolved: The next chance I get, I take advantage of a mid-afternoon break and go for a run.

July 9

"Anything, everything, little or big, becomes an adventure when the right person shares it. Nothing, nothing, nothing is worthwhile when we have to do it all alone."

—Kathleen Norris, writer

Running is a thing you love to do alone. But always? You love your family. You love to run. Why not combine the two?

See that family on the trail. The boy, who must be 11 or 12, is sprinting to get ahead of his mother. They're playing a game. He's smiling, she's laughing. Meanwhile, the dad and husband jogs behind, watching the two of them with obvious love and affection.

What better way to model fitness for your children than taking them on a run? For that matter, how better to model it to your spouse?

Expect reluctance when you first suggest it. The child may think it's boring and resist. Well, then, let her ride her bike alongside you. The spouse may put up an even bigger stink. He can walk. The hard part will be getting them out there. Once they're out there, it's up to them. And if they continue to complain and make your life miserable, well, at least you tried.

Running is, as they say, great for the entire family. And lots of families—husbands, wives, children—do it together. You may not have your best workout when they're with you, but there are compensations. All of you are outside, enjoying one another's company, participating in a fun and healthful activity. What could be better than that?

Resolved: I give it a whirl. I take my family with me on a run this weekend.

July 10

"The beginning and the end reach out their hands to each other."

—Chinese proverb

Let the beginning of your run reach out its hands to the end.

You probably won't be too pleased if you start a race strong but falter at the end. Nor will you be completely happy if you start poorly but finish strong.

Go into each race with this mind-set: Start strong, finish strong. With the idea of a strong finish firmly tucked into your cranium, you will be cautious about flying off too quickly at the start. At that point there's a lot of race left to run, and you'll want to have something left at the end.

But you're not going to want to save it all for the finish, either. You'll want to get off the blocks in fine form. Because an auspicious start often augurs an auspicious ending.

Some people go crazy at the start. Some people save it all up for a big dramatic finale. You're going to avoid both of those traps. Finish your races—and why not your training runs as well?—the same as you started them: strong.

Start strong. Finish strong. Now all you have to worry about is the middle.

Resolved: I start strong; I finish strong.

July 11

"To work independently of results; this is perfect work."
—Augustus Dignam, philosopher

It's virtually impossible to run for any period of time without thinking of times and results.

We live in a competitive world. We measure our houses, our cars, our salaries against those of our neighbors and friends. We want to do better than they do or at least keep pace with them.

It's the same in running. Hours, minutes, and seconds are the coin of the realm, the measure of how we're faring. We compare our times with other runners, and mightily strive to outdo them. There's nothing wrong with competition. Indeed it's crucial to becoming a faster runner. It trims away what's unnecessary and helps set your gaze on achieving a better result. What do you need to do to improve as a runner? Enter a race. You'll find out fast.

Nevertheless, there are limits to what competition can teach you. When you're competing, you're letting others define your performance. You're measuring your results against theirs and using this to gauge your performance.

Look to yourself instead. Create your own definition of success. The running crowd defines success by results and times. Measure your results in your own way. Every mile you run, every mileage marker you pass, consider that a personal achievement. Why not? Progress is not solely defined by endings (that's the way the crowd does it); what matters even more is how you get there.

Resolved: I see every mile I run, every mileage marker I pass, as a personal achievement.

July 12

"One value of running is that it can serve as a simulation of life. It serves as an ideal learning experience in that it allows you to experiment, learn new skills, and to practice without suffering the real effects of less than goal achievement."

—James C. Brown, running researcher

Less than goal achievement? That's professor talk for falling flat on your face. And, in that regard, running is indeed an excellent simulation of life.

It happens to everyone. You have bad days, bad workouts, bad races. So, what do you do? What else can you do? You bounce back.

Ideally, you try not to get too down when you fall into a running slough of despond. But heck, there's no denying it. Occasionally you stink up the joint and feel miserable about it. You feel like tossing your Nikes into a trash can, dousing them with gasoline, and putting a torch to them.

Hey, put that match out.

You've had bad days before, right? And what did you do in the past? That's right: you came back. You rebounded. Give yourself credit for some resiliency.

Maybe yesterday was one of those light-the-shoes-on-fire days. OK, so today you rebound. Today, you come back.

And how do you do that? First of all, you let that bad day go. That was yesterday; it's over. Check the calendar if you don't believe it. Flip on the radio. Ask someone. They'll all confirm it: it's a new day. Time to let yesterday go and start fresh.

Resolved: I rebound from a bad day.

July 13

"Keeping workouts varied is one way to ensure success."

—Joe Catalano, running coach

Ain't running grand? You just step outside your door (home or office), and you're off to the races.

After a while, though, all that pounding on pavement can take a toll on body and mind. In which case, it may be time to leave the streets behind for a while and run on a dirt trail. Or at the very least, mix a little of both into your daily constitutional.

You may already do that. You may run on the street to get to a local park, where you make a circle route on dirt trails. Then, after you're done there, you return to the streets to go home.

However you do it, just be sure you do it. Get off the pavement. If you always run on pavement, running on the trails is a revelation. You don't have to breathe exhaust fumes. There are birds singing instead of cars honking. You run amid trees and flowers instead of overflowing trash cans. It's a wonder.

Another benefit to the dirt is that it puts some needed variety into your running. Running is something you do in lots of places, not just one place. If you live in the heart of the city, it may take some doing to find good dirt trails. You may have to get it in a car or ride a bus. But it's worth it once you get there.

Resolved: I get off the pavement for a while and run on a dirt trail.

July 14

"The more joy we have, the more nearly perfect we are."
—Benedict de Spinoza, philosopher

Upon turning 40, the writer Rick Reilly envisioned "a perfect day" for himself. So, what would be your perfect day? Here's one of my possible scenarios:

7 A.M. Alarm clock rings. Throw clock out window. No work today, all play.

7:30 A.M. Step into hot shower.

8:30 A.M. Leave shower.

9 A.M. Go for morning run and decide to enter local marathon in progress.

11:08 A.M. Set new world record in marathon.

Noon. Nike offers me $1 million a year to endorse its shoes.

12:30 P.M. Share spoonfuls of mayonnaise out of a jar with Bill Rodgers.

1:45 P.M. Marty Liquori interviews me for his show. Afterward challenges me to mile race. I run 3:55 flat, leaving poor Marty in the dust.

3:13 P.M. *Runner's World* announces that it is putting me on its cover.

5:30 P.M. Brooks ups Nike's offer, says it will pay me $2 million a year to wear its shoes.

6 P.M. *The Runner's Book of Daily Inspiration* appears at top of *New York Times* bestseller list.

8:30 P.M. Take long, hot shower. Then crawl into bed with my wife.

Resolved: I envision a perfect day of running for myself.

July 15

It's summer, and it's hot. Time to expose all those parts and tags of you.

No, really. Get naked. Liberate yourself from Victorian inhibitions. Strip off your clothes (except for your shoes and socks, of course), and go for a run.

Want your running to cause comments? Want to create a stir in the neighborhood? Go for a jog in the buff—that'll do it.

One of the traditions of the Stanford University cross-country team is called "the Freedom Run." Every year they shed their togs and run *au naturel* through the stately pines of Palo Alto. Hey, if they can do it, why not you?

Well, you reply, they're college kids. Firm young bodies. No responsibilities. What do they care if they run around like Lady Godiva? If you tried a stunt like that, you'd wind up in jail.

OK, maybe. But how about this for a compromise? Instead of shedding *all* your clothes, what about a few select pieces? It's not winter anymore; you don't have to cover up. You've worked hard on your body; be proud of it. Just changing from sweats to shorts, or taking off your shirt if you're a guy, can be an invigorating experience.

Resolved: I shed a few clothes when I run today.

July 16

"I've learned to read my body very well. By staying healthy I hope to run for the rest of my life. That's the big goal now."

—Anne Audain, masters runner

Here's how to stay healthy and enjoy running more: be nice to yourself.

Ridiculously simple, isn't it? But oh so hard to put into practice sometimes. If you're nice to yourself, good things will happen to you in running.

If you're nice to yourself, you will be able to run for a long, long time. You will be healthier and less prone to injury. You will know when to quit and be unwilling to push yourself to extremes.

Being nice to yourself means taking the long view. You won't be quite as fixated by ribbons and trophies. Building health and fitness over the long term will seem more important than the quest for temporary glory. You will always know what to do next in running if you're nice to yourself. You will know when to put out the effort and when to pull it back. And you will enjoy it far more than those other people you see who seem to equate running more with torture than pleasure.

You don't need a running coach or guru to tell you what it means to be nice to yourself. You know; everybody knows. It means being gentle with yourself, taking it easy, not beating yourself up. Be nice to yourself—and you will stay healthy and run for a long, long time.

Resolved: It seems a little silly, but OK, I give it a try: I'm nice to myself when I run today.

July 17

"Of course what he most intensely dreams of is being taken out on walks, and the more you are able to indulge him the more he will adore you and the more all the latent beauty of his nature will come out."

—Henry James, on his dog Max

Many runners have dogs but do not run with them. This is understandable. A dog can be a worry and a bother when you run.

Nevertheless, there are people who do run with their dogs. This is equally understandable, for a dog can be a pleasant running companion at times.

Also, an extremely irritating one. If you are the type who sometimes forgets (or ignores) when it's time to run, get a dog. A dog never forgets. He knows when it is time for you to run because that's when he gets outside.

A dog is more reliable than an alarm clock. At the appropriate time—don't ask me how he knows, for it's well known that dogs do not carry watches—he will begin to stir and pace. He will look up at you with wounded eyes. When you stand up, he will stand up, too, as if to say, "I'm ready. Is it time? Can we go? Is it time?"

It's no use trying to ignore him. He won't give up until you relent. He'll whimper and continue pacing. "C'mon, it's time; you know it's time. What's wrong with you? Let's go. . . ."

You may lack motivation and not feel like running on a given day. But when the appointed time rolls around, there will be your dog, staring at you expectantly with those big brown eyes. How can you possibly say no?

Resolved: When my dog tells me it's time for a run, I listen to him.

July 18

"There are three goals in marathon running: to finish, to improve, and to win. Which goal you strive for depends on what level of running you're at."

—Hal Higdon, runner and writer

The artist Pablo Picasso used to say that first you make a thing. Then someone comes along and makes it beautiful.

It's the same with running marathons. You must first finish a marathon. After you do that, you can think about making it pretty—that is, running under a certain time.

The first marathon is almost always the hardest, for you must surmount great psychological barriers as well as physical ones. You have to prove that you can do it. Once you do that, the process becomes somewhat easier (although running a marathon is never easy).

Marathon running is like mountain climbing. First ascents are always more difficult than second and third ascents. The men and women who make first ascents are the ones who get their names in the mountaineering journals. They've led the way for the others.

In a sense, when you enter a marathon for the first time, you're leading the way for yourself. You're making a first ascent. After that first ascent will come second and third ascents—and better times. But first you must do it. You must do what you set out to do. You must finish.

Resolved: First I finish a marathon. Then I think about improving my time.

July 19

"If you want to win a race, you have to go a little berserk."

—Bill Rodgers, marathoner

Today's entry is not for everybody, which makes sense because not everybody wins races. In fact, only a precious few runners win races—the lunatic fringe, one might say.

The winners of races are the ones who run and run and run and run and run. They plan and prepare and think. They've got to Einstein their way around a track or racecourse in order to win.

All this is true, but so is this: you've got to go a little berserk to win. You're coming down the homestretch, neck and neck with another runner on the final sprint. You can go to the bank on it: the one who goes a little berserk is the one who will win.

They've just flown in an elite group of Kenyans, Tanzanians, and Australians for your local hometown race. As you check them out at the starting line, one thing is clear: you're going to have to go a little berserk to have any chance at all.

Winning is not simply a triumph of logic. The best runner does not always win. The best runner who goes a little berserk—that's the one to put your money on.

If you go a little berserk and you haven't done your training, you're headed for a fall. If you go a little berserk too early, you may run out of steam before the finish. If you go a little berserk too late, you may miss your opportunity. But if you use your head and go a little berserk at the right time—well, wave to us all from the victory stand.

Resolved: I go a little berserk the next time I enter a race.

July 20

"Usually I prefer to do my fast running at a track where something is going on, even if it's only soccer practice and nobody's watching me. It's often hard to run when nobody's around."

—Doug Kurtis, marathoner

Even veteran runners occasionally have trouble with the solitary nature of their sport. They want to run, and yet they don't want to be alone. So, what to do?

Go to a track. You can work on your fast running (or slow running). You can run intervals or even sprints if you choose. Afterward you can sit in the bleachers or lounge on the grass and people watch.

Although you can be alone at a track, it is not primarily a solitary place. It is a meeting ground for runners and other athletes. You will see both sexes working out there. You will find long-distance runners as well as sprinters.

Sometimes while you're running, there will be a soccer or football team practicing on the field. You may only watch them out of the corner of your eye, but their presence can make you feel less alone and your workout more tolerable.

Some people get bored with running on a track. It's just round and round, they say. They'd rather run on the roads and see the sights. Still, a track can be inspiring in its own way. You see and perhaps meet other people who are involved in the same struggle as you are. There is a community of runners out there, and you're a part of it. That lifts your spirits, and without your noticing it, your pace picks up a little.

Resolved: From time to time, I do my fast running (or slow running) on a track.

July 21

"Just be consistent. This is what older runners learn, because the secret of endurance is to stay uninjured. All you need to do is run steadily every day."

—Tom Cross, running coach

Not fast, not slow. But: steady.

Not up, not down. But: consistent.

Not tomorrow, not next week. But: every day.

Not in the A.M. one day and the P.M. the next. But: the same time every day (if you can).

Not pushing, yet not holding back. But: your pace.

Not testing the limits, yet not selling yourself short. But: within your capacity.

Not pushing it every day, nor going easy every day. But: alternating easy days with hard.

Not looking for immediate gains, nor always staying the same. But: gradual improvements.

Not this month, nor even this year. But: over time.

Not this year, nor even next year. But: over a lifetime.

Not deadened by routine, and not leaving it to whim. But: running as a regular, enjoyable habit.

Not being either optimistic or pessimistic. But: a positive attitude.

Not raising your expectations, nor lowering them. But: being open to possibility.

Resolved: Not tomorrow, not next week: I run steadily every day.

July 22

"I run as I feel."

—Henry Rono, champion runner

If you are running and think, "I want to turn back," even if it's before your usual turnaround, then turn back.

Conversely, if you think, "I want to keep running," even though you'll be going farther than you normally do, then follow your thoughts and run some more.

Try this simple lesson: Heed your thoughts, whatever they tell you. Tune in to your thinking, and use it as your guide for your running.

Of course, your thoughts will tell you different things on different days. Some days they will tell you to go fast, other days to slow down. Sometimes they will tell you to run steps or intervals, while the next morning they may ask you to give your achy muscles the day off.

Some runners follow the dictates of a coach. Others follow a training program that they read about in a magazine or book. Slower runners sometimes try to duplicate the success of faster runners by copying what they do. None of these methods works as well as the one available inside your head. Following your thoughts will teach you to trust your instincts, which can only aid your progress as a runner.

Resolved: I follow my thoughts when I run.

July 23

"Life is simple, however complex the organism may be; and everything goes to pieces when the living truth of the central simplicity is lost."

—Rabindranath Tagore, philosopher

If you want lots of things in this life (or you have lots of dreams and ambitions), chances are you are not going to get most of them. But if you narrow your wants, you will give yourself a much better chance of success.

What you want may be hard to get. But if it's strictly defined, and you know what it is you're looking for, you may get it even though it is difficult to obtain. For example, the New York Marathon. You may not be able to win it, but you *can* enter it and finish it. Thus, by narrowing your wants, you expand the range of what you can do.

Time is on your side when you know what you want. You're less inclined to hurry. You are looking for a specific thing, and you're willing to wait until you get it.

Some people are unhappy when they don't get what they want. But these same people are often unclear about what they want. They really don't know what they want; they just want. Narrowing your wants will help you "learn the market." You can't know everything there is to know. But you can know a lot about a little, and that can help you achieve your aims.

It is the folly of youth to have desires that are all over the map. But it is the folly of the old to have been thwarted in desire and thus to cease desiring. You can get what you want, whatever your age, as long as you define your desires narrowly.

Resolved: I narrow my wants as a runner.

July 24

"It's all very well to talk of being unhurt, keeping yourself clear, triumphant. To give your faith, that is the risk."

—Katharine Butler Hathaway, writer

A famous man once said, "God is in the details." That may be true, but you know what else is in the details? Distraction, delay, avoidance.

Face it. You're not going to know everything you need to know about a marathon (or a half-marathon or an ultra or a 10K or even a 5K) prior to running it. No way can you anticipate everything that you will do or feel.

You can think you'll know. You can imagine what it will feel like. You can prepare for all the possible contingencies. You can talk to other people to hear what happened to them. You can read about it or watch it. But you won't know until you actually *do* it.

Which points to a truism: while sometimes useful, research is of limited value. It will help you only so far—and no more. Frequently the need for further research is merely an excuse to delay and avoid. A person is afraid. Research is a place to hide.

Know this: the details will work themselves out once the commitment is there. That's your job: supplying the commitment. That means sticking with it, regardless of the details, regardless of the obstacles. Even a 5K walk can be a meaningful event. What makes it meaningful is your commitment to it.

Resolved: I make a commitment to run (pick the event) then take care of the details as I go along.

July 25

"Life's most persistent and urgent question is: what are you doing for others?"

—Martin Luther King Jr.

Running is a solitary activity, but there are ways to make it less so. Joining a running club, volunteering at a race, running with a partner—these are a few.

Another way is to run for a good cause. You're not just running for yourself; you're running for something. There's a difference. And as you're helping people, you'll meet people.

Some charitable nonprofit organizations sponsor individual runners. They even provide partial funding and airfare in some cases. In exchange, the runner agrees to raise a certain amount of money by participating in a race. He or she does this by collecting financial pledges from family, friends, coworkers, neighbors, and others.

Everybody wins: the organization, the cause, the race, and the runner. Not only are you helping yourself, but you're also helping others as you run. Every step you take is on behalf of other people. There are plenty of good causes out there: Alzheimer's, heart research, breast cancer, abused children, diabetes, homeless people, and rehabilitating injured wildlife, among others. Pick an organization, and give it a call.

Need a reason to run? Looking for clear motivation? Attach yourself to a worthy cause, and run for it.

Resolved: I give it some thought. Maybe at some point I'll run for a cause.

July 26

"Ultimately the bond of all companionship, whether in marriage or in friendship, is conversation."

—Oscar Wilde

Usually, when you run, you see other runners. But mostly you keep your thoughts to yourself, saying little except perhaps for an occasional hello to people passing in the opposite direction.

The other day, though, you were out jogging, and you noticed a woman on the trail ahead of you. Looking back, she seemed to speed up when she saw you. No problem. Because it was an isolated section of the trail, you could understand why she'd be cautious with a man behind her. Women runners need to be careful in ways that men do not.

That was the last you thought about it until you saw the woman again at the end of the trail. Strangely, she was now behind you. You couldn't help but ask, "How did you get behind me? You were ahead of me on the trail."

She smiled, explaining that she had tried to take a shortcut, but that it had led nowhere. She ran halfway down a steep hillside until she realized she had to turn back. By the time she reached the main trail again, she had fallen behind. You nodded, not saying another word. No more words were necessary. Both of you are runners; you understand each other on some level. Two people, engaged in a similar pastime, exchanging a few brief pleasantries. That's all it was.

But sometimes that's pretty cool—and all you need at the end of a run. Why take a vow of silence when you run? Just a brief exchange of pleasantries can be uplifting.

Resolved: After my next run, if it seems appropriate, I strike up a brief conversation with another runner.

July 27

"Reality is for people who lack imagination."

—Popular bumper sticker

The late, great baseball announcer Harry Caray had a signature phrase. Actually he had several of them. His most popular one (later appropriated by Phil Rizzuto) was "Holy cow!" which he would shout after witnessing some astonishing feat on the field.

Another Caray signature phrase occurred whenever a Cubs player—although he broadcast for other clubs in his career, his last team, before his death in 1998, was the Chicago Cubs—hit a home run. As the ball flew off the bat, Caray would utter, "It might be! It could be! It IS!"—this last sentence coming as the ball landed in the seats and the friendly confines of Wrigley Field erupted in cheers.

It might be. It could be. It is. Is there any finer motto for a runner?

Whatever you want to do, whatever goal you'd like to pursue in this crazy sport, approach it with the attitude of: it might be. It could be. Then—after it becomes true, after it becomes a reality—it is!

But achieving a goal takes time, lots of time. That's too much to consider today. Instead, just think about making the phrase relevant to your life *now*. Make it a motto for today, this moment. Think about what you'd like to get done, how far you'd like to run, and for how long. Today, turn a "might be" or a "could be" into an "is." Do that, and make old Harry Caray proud.

Resolved: Today I turn a might be in running into a what is.

July 28

"I often solved problems as I ran. The kind of thinking I most like to do while I run, though, is just to let my thoughts wander wherever they wish."

—Jim Fixx

Funny thing about running: you can be thinking hard about one thing before you start to run. Indeed that may be why you want to go out: to see if you can come to grips with your thoughts and arrive at some sort of an understanding.

But when you start running, rather than focus on the subject you intend to, your mind drifts to other fancies. It's as if your subconscious is telling you that you've worried about that subject long enough. Now you're going to think about something else for a while.

So, you get into your run and follow your thoughts where they lead. You notice what a beautiful day it is. You see a dark-shouldered hawk hovering in a field, looking for prey. You notice that the shapes of the clouds resemble big doughy marshmallows. You wave at a carload of teenagers passing by.

This is one of the loveliest aspects of running: it takes you out of yourself and away from your usual preoccupations. The thoughts that seem so important when you're in a business suit seem considerably less so when you're wearing shorts and running shoes.

Then another interesting thing happens. After not thinking about that one subject that obsessed you earlier, you come to the end of your run and know precisely what to do about it. You've arrived at the place where you wanted to be without consciously seeking it. And running helped get you there.

Resolved: When I go for a run, I let my thoughts lead wherever they want to.

July 29

"If you believe you have an edge, even if it's razor-thin, that's a very powerful force."

—Deane Beman, golfer

All athletes—whether they're runners or basketball players or gymnasts or bikers or shot-putters or whatever—are looking for the same thing: an edge over their competition.

An edge can be physical or mental (or a combination of both). You may have trained harder and put in more miles than the other runners and simply be more fit. But in the penthouses of sport, where the best athletes train year-round, the edge often exists only in the mind. If it feels like an edge to you, then it's an edge.

Even if you're not in the hunt to win a race, getting an edge can help you to perform better. You may have a lucky T-shirt. Whenever you wear it, you always run well. If it gives you an edge, put it on.

One way to get an edge before a race is to drive (or walk or jog) the course beforehand. The elite runners almost always do this. Race organizers take them on a private tour, allowing them to get the lay of the land and a feel for the course so that when they run it for real, it's not entirely foreign to them; they're familiar with it to some degree.

Why not you, too? If it's good enough for the best runners, it's good enough for you. Check out the course before you run. Or put on that cherished T-shirt. Anything for an edge.

Resolved: I get an edge. If getting an edge means driving the course beforehand, I drive the course.

July 30

"To ask that one's own higher self should forgive one's own trespasses is the hardest prayer to answer that we ever offer up. We cannot forgive others unless we have first learnt how to forgive ourselves."

—Havelock Ellis, writer

One of the finest qualities that you can cultivate as a runner (and as a human being) is forgiveness. Forgive yourself, and you will be more likely to forgive your perceived inadequacies as a runner or athlete. Be less judgmental. Be less critical.

These are hard things. They're not done in a day. Other people may mock them as being unessential to success as a runner.

They're wrong. Forgiving yourself allows you to define success in your own way: not your parents' way, not your spouse's way, not society's way—your way. Flip it around. What makes people tense and freeze under pressure? What makes them tie up and not give their best performance?

Here are some reasons: The sense of always being judged. The sense that if they do one thing wrong, even if it's tiny and insignificant, they'll be criticized for it. The sense that no matter what they do, no matter how hard they try, it's never good enough.

You can't control what other people say and do. Some people—such as your parents, perhaps—may never find it in their hearts to forgive. But you can forgive yourself or at least begin the process, and if you can do that, you will obtain comfort in all the elements of your life, including running.

Resolved: I forgive myself and my perceived inadequacies as a runner.

July 31

"If you take up distance running and you're not successful right away, don't be disappointed. Don't give up trying; it takes time. You have to realize this."

—Grete Waitz, champion runner

How many times have you "failed" as a runner, using the term in the conventional sense? Well, however many times it is, it's not enough. You must fail more.

Grete Waitz began running at 13. But she was hardly an instant success. "I went a long time without ever winning anything," she admits. Only gradually did she begin to see results in what became one of the greatest careers in the history of running.

Grete will tell you: failing once just won't do. If you accept defeat after only one failure, that's hardly even trying. Once is not enough.

Nor is twice. Or three times. Or four times. Or five times. You must keep failing. When you're failing, you're learning. When you're learning, you're getting better. And if you're learning and getting better while you're at it, how can that be considered failing?

Still, you may decide that it is. You may not be satisfied by personal victories or internal rewards. You may want to be declared a winner through objective measures—that is, by beating the pants off other runners, by bringing down your times, by winning awards. The answer, then, is the same. You must fail 10 more times. No, 20 more times. Thirty more times, 40 more times if you have to. As long as you're failing, you have a chance to win.

Resolved: I fail 10 times—no, 20 times—before I accept defeat as a runner.

August I

*"He who is outside the door has already a good part of his
journey behind him."*

—Dutch proverb

It's the first of the month, and by now you must know what
happens today. Whatever your schedule says, whatever the
demands on your time, whatever stresses you are dealing with
at the moment, you run.

The first is a perfect time to start over, if starting over is
what you need to do. Flip the calendar page, and make a new
beginning. Go outside the door. Go on. One step outside, and
you'll be on your way. It always happens that way: reluctance
at first, lots of voices telling you why not. Somehow you overcome the voices, and off you go, quieting the voices until the
next time.

Forget what happened last year or last month or even last
week, if you need to. The past no longer applies, unless it's
useful to you. Keep it around, in that case. In any event, step
outside. Think positive; lift your thoughts to the future. Perhaps this month you'll make the breakthrough you've been
looking for. Perhaps this month you'll run a personal best in
the 10K.

If running is a big thing in your life, you have no need to
be convinced. You're probably already out there, pounding the
pavement. But even if running is a small thing to you, is that
any reason to neglect it? Small things need tending, too, sometimes even more than big things.

The day is calling to you. Heck, it's shouting. Step outside,
and answer it.

Resolved: It's the first of the month: I make a fresh start. I
step outside and run.

August 2

*"Try and find your deepest issue in every confusion, and abide
by that."*

—D. H. Lawrence

When Tiger Woods was a young boy, his father asked him
what he thought about when he swung a golf club. "Where I
want the ball to go," Tiger replied.

He did not clutter his head with thoughts of golf-swing
mechanics nor ponder the well-meaning advice of others. All
he thought about was where he wanted the ball to go. Now in
his early 20s, Tiger still has an uncanny ability to hit the ball
to his target.

Runners may take some inspiration from his example.
There are always lots of distracting thoughts competing for
attention inside your head. Lots of noise and confusion. But all
you need to do, really, is ask yourself this essential question:
Where do you want to go as a runner?

All right, then. *Go there.*

If you can't see the path ahead of you, you're going to have
trouble getting there. One of the ways to obtain clarity is by
looking beneath the surface confusion, all those thoughts playing bumper cars inside your brain. What's permanent with
you? What stays? In that answer lies your direction.

Once you let go of some of those surface concerns, you'll
find they weren't so important after all. You'll wonder why
you hung on to them for so long. The confusion and clutter in
your mind will ease. You'll see more clearly what's important
to you and be more resolute about sticking with it.

Resolved: I ask myself where I want to go as a runner, and I
go there.

August 3

"Don't overwork; enjoy yourself. Be creative about what you do. The motivation for running has to come from inside. If you're not enjoying it, you won't be motivated."

—Martha Cooksey, marathoner

It's easy to overwork yourself when you run. To borrow from an old John Mellencamp song, running "hurts so good." It hurts so good that you want to do it all the time and keep pushing the pace.

If you feel as if you're beginning to overwork yourself, an easy solution is at hand: cut back. Cut back on your mileage. Even cut back on the days you run. It'll be good for your motivation and good for your body.

How do you know when you're overworking? You'll know. The signs—for example, chronic fatigue, listlessness, an increase in aches and pains—are always evident. But you don't have to stop outright. All you have to do is rein yourself in a little.

A little can mean a lot. It's a way of saying that you are in charge of your running, not the other way around. From a psychological as well as a physiological standpoint, a person who runs 2 miles a day gets as much benefit as a person who runs 10. A runner who amasses lots of mileage is not necessarily a happier runner, merely a tireder one.

Nor is cutting back a sign that you're taking a step backward as a runner. It's merely a form of reconnoitering, a temporary realignment of the troops. When you feel up to it, you can always up your miles again (gradually, of course).

Resolved: You're right. I'm overworking myself. I cut back on my mileage until my enthusiasm returns.

August 4

"Beyond a few tests and some prescriptive advice, there is really nothing I can do to you or for you. If anything happens, it will be because you do it to and for yourself."

—Dr. Art Mollen, advising runners

Here's something you can do for yourself: when things get rough, go back to the tried and true. When they begin to fall apart, go back to a time when they were all glued together.

Never be afraid to revisit a past success. How did you do it back then? And what are you doing now that's different and not as good? It's possible to fall into bad habits when you run. Everybody does from time to time. Think about how your habits have changed, and correct them.

Maybe you've gone on a new diet. Or you've switched around your workout schedule. Or increased the number of miles you run or the number of days. Maybe it's your attitude. Maybe you did better when you had a more carefree approach to running, when you didn't care as much. Now that you've become more serious about it, you're pushing too hard.

In a sense, going back to basics is a return to trusting your instincts. For one reason or another, you've gotten away from the principles and practices that are more natural to you, more comfortable. Most likely, you've layered on complications where before it was simple.

Whatever it was, go back to it. Other people do not have the answer for what ails you (assuming something does); you do. And the key to achieving success today may be buried in yesterday.

Resolved: If I start struggling, I go back to what worked for me in the past.

August 5

"Instead of seeing how fast you can go or how much pain your body can take, you're much better off training in a comfortable zone. This teaches your body to burn fat and spare glycogen, which will maintain your physiological health and reduce the risk of injury."

—Stu Mittleman, ultramarathoner

There is weekday energy, and there is weekend energy. Weekdays are for working and all that implies. On the weekends things slow down a little, and you can relax.

You know how good you feel on a Saturday or Sunday? How relaxed and easy? Run with that frame of mind *every day*.

You push yourself at work all week. You grind, you get things done. And when it comes time to run, you often attack it with the same buzz-saw attitude.

The weekends, however, are different. You have more time, and your running reflects it. You ease off the pedal. You feel less harried and frazzled, and that attitude frequently carries into easy, yet productive running.

What's your comfort zone? Very often it is the way you run on the weekend. Why not maintain this more relaxed attitude on Monday . . . and Tuesday . . . and Wednesday . . . and Thursday . . . and Friday?

When you run on the weekend, you're focused on pleasure. You've paid your dues all week long. Now you're going to relax, have fun, and stay in your comfort zone. Run with that same attitude during the week, and you will find that your workouts will continue to be easy, yet productive.

Resolved: I run with a weekend frame of mind every day.

August 6

Is there anything as lovely as taking a nap outside in the sun?

You've just gone for a run. You've done your work, put in your time. Yet, it's so lovely outside that you don't feel like hopping into your car and driving home right away. After you stretch, you spot an unoccupied park bench. When you started your run, there was an old lady on the bench feeding the seagulls, but she's gone now. You sit down and look around. It seems safe.

With the force of natural law, almost like Newton's apple, your head comes to rest on the bench. The bench is concrete, but it feels soft as a pillow. You didn't realize how tired you were. Not tired from running, but just tired from . . . *everything*.

You lie back and close your eyes, stretching out on your concrete bed. Your body feels limber and well taken care of. The sun on your face feels restorative, as if there are solar-powered batteries inside you and they're being recharged. And you fall gently asleep, like a baby.

Your nap takes place in the same place you did your work: outside. That seems right somehow. There's such a feeling of freedom when you fall asleep in the sun. And no better way to end a run.

Resolved: I lie down after my run and take a nap in the sun.

August 7

"Talking of pleasure, this moment I was holding to my mouth a nectarine—good God how fine. It went down soft, pulpy, slushy, oozy—all its delicious embodiment melted down my throat like a large, beautiful strawberry."

—John Keats

It's summer. Go down to your local farmers market and wander through the stands. Be indiscriminate in your purchases. Buy strawberries, peaches, one of Keats's juicy nectarines, apples, grapes, nuts, and berries of all kinds.

The farmers market may not carry everything you need. If that's the case, venture to the grocery store. Be equally indiscriminate. Buy kiwifruit, bananas, mangoes, papayas, and whatever else looks good. Unpack your overflowing bags when you get home, wash the fruit, and start chopping. Maybe you've got a recipe handed down by your grandmother. Not to worry, though, if you don't. It's pretty hard to blow a fruit salad when you've got fresh ingredients.

Throw it all together in a bowl, and let it chill in the refrigerator a while. Maybe you'll have it for dessert or as a side dish at dinner, or better still, eat it all on its own. How you eat it is up to you. Just eat it.

What's this got to do with running? Everything. Running is about health, and what's healthier than a fruit salad? Running is about having an appetite (and a thirst!) and satisfying it. Running is about pleasure, too, and what tastes better than fresh fruit? Feast on fresh fruit and running (though not at the same time), and a long, rewarding life will be yours.

Resolved: It's summer. I go for a run and afterward fix myself a big fresh fruit salad.

August 8

"Rest is an important part of a training program. There are times of the year when you should just go to the beach."

—Thom Hunt, distance runner

It is truly possible in life to have too much of a good thing, including running.

The need for rest is a frequent topic of discussion in these entries. Every runner needs reminders from time to time to let it go for a while. That's admittedly tough to do. Few things in life jazz you up as much as running. When you're doing it, you're happy. When you're not doing it, you're thinking about when you can get back on the roads again.

Learning to leave it alone is one of the hardest things that some runners have to do. But it's vital to clear the head and give the body a break. It's like being away from your lover. You truly learn to appreciate her more and realize how much you miss her.

Certainly, obsessing or worrying about your running isn't the way to go. By focusing so intently on it, you lose sight of the bigger picture. You become absorbed with minor details, details that drain away your energy and enthusiasm.

Getting away even for a day or two creates a space in your life and mind that allows other things to come in. While building a sand castle on the beach, you may have an insight into your running—or some other topic in your life. And if nothing else, you can at least work on your tan.

Resolved: I let running go for a while—and, what the heck, kick back at the beach while I'm at it.

August 9

"I can still remember quite vividly a time when as a child I ran barefoot along damp firm sand by the seashore. It was an intense moment of discovery of a source of power and beauty that one previously hardly dreamt existed."

—Roger Bannister, the first person to break four minutes in the mile

Now that you're resting comfortably at the beach (see yesterday's entry), at some point you're going to feel like moving your body again. Don't rush it. There's plenty of time. First roll onto your back and get some sun on your tummy. Then think about it.

Running on the beach is unlike running anywhere else. It's different from running on city streets or around a track, or even on a hard-packed dirt trail through trees. For one, no shoes. You can run in your bare feet.

When you run at the beach, you worry far less about such conventional nuisances as time—you left your watch back at the room anyhow—or distance. You're going to run down to the pier, turn around, and come back. All the while breathing that incredible fresh salt air. Can anything be better?

So much of running in our daily workaday lives is connected with duty. We must run because it is good for us, or so we tell ourselves. But at the beach we remember how emotionally satisfying running can be. It brings joy and feelings of freedom and youth.

Running in your bare feet. It's a thing you loved to do as a kid. Why not as an adult, too?

Resolved: I run barefoot along damp firm sand.

August 10

"Shoot for the moon—even if you miss you'll be among the stars."

—Saying

All summer long, you've been running every day and riding your bicycle almost as much. (Well, haven't you?) Lots of days you even hop into the pool and churn some laps.

So, why not try a triathlon? Maybe not the Hawaii Ironman to start, but there are no doubt less arduous triathlons being held in your area this summer and fall.

A triathlon is three events in one: swimming, bicycling, and road racing, usually in that order. The events are held back to back to back—you go from the water to the bicycle to running, with nary a break in between—so, the winner is invariably a superfit demigod who swims like Matt Biondi, rides like Greg Lemond, and runs like Grete Waitz (or a close approximation).

A worthwhile, and somewhat less taxing, alternative is a two-element biathlon. There are different types: swimming-biking, swimming-running, biking-running. Distances vary in biathlons, just as they do with triathlons.

You don't have to be a superstar athlete to enter a triathlon or biathlon and get something out of it. It's a great way to gauge your overall fitness, not just how fast you run. Swimming and biking regularly will only help your running. They reduce the likelihood of injury (you're using different muscles from when you run, thus giving your overworked running muscles a break) and build strength and endurance. Give it a whirl; you may like it.

Resolved: What the heck, I enter a triathlon or biathlon.

August 11

"Whatever the emotion, whether it ranges from annoyance to rage, from disquiet to terror, from guilt to remorse, one of the best remedies is vigorous action. Sport is the therapy best suited for the instant treatment of emotional distress."

—George Sheehan, philosopher-runner

It's August, the dreaded dog days of August. It's scorching hot outside. Not fit for mad dogs or Englishmen.

All you can do, all you have the energy to do, is sit in front of the fan. A fan is not a luxury; it's a necessity. There is no air-conditioning in the building. Sweat pours off your nose.

From your window you see two boys frying eggs on the sidewalk. The newspaper reports the story of a man who received third-degree burns on the soles of his feet when he walked outside without shoes. You put on a shirt. It's immediately soaked. You take it off, wring it out, and put it back on again. Clothing of any kind seems a horrible burden. Except for shoes.

A sparrow sits sadly on your windowsill, its feathers drooping, too worn out to fly. Its expression seems to say, "Shoot me. I'd be better off." You realize that you're beginning to talk to birds. It's getting that bad. You take a Heineken out of the freezer and press it against your forehead, hoping for relief.

You flip on the tube. The weatherman says, sorry, no break in the heat wave. What are you going to do? How do you shake this emotional and physical torpor? There's only one answer: run very early in the morning.

Resolved: On superhot days, I make myself get up and run early in the morning.

August 12

"I want my runners to run at a relatively even pace. Given this, they should view those who bolt out early as foolish people whom they will catch at the end."

—Tom Grogon, running coach

It's nice to have energy. It's better to be smart.

Some days, you get up, full of spit, feeling as if you can run with the wind. So, you go out and challenge the wind to a match race, and that's the day you feel a twinge in your leg. Or you enter a race. Primed for a new personal best, you roar out of the gates like Secretariat. You push the pace, but before long the pace begins to push you. As runner after runner passes you, you wonder how all that enthusiasm and energy could dry up so fast.

But it does. Energy waxes and wanes, like the tides. So does enthusiasm. Look at young runners. If energy alone won races, they'd be unstoppable. But just as the hottest fires often burn out the fastest, impulsively energetic runners are the ones who flame out come race time.

The best runners are a potent mix of energy and experience. They run smart, evening out the ups and downs, knowing that enthusiasm will carry them only so far. They may push the early pace, but only for tactical advantage. They know they're going to have to back off at some point or they won't be able to compete at the end.

You (like all runners) have a limited storehouse of energy. Learn to use what you have. Take advantage of early enthusiasm, to be sure. But know, too, that it won't last forever, and adapt your strategy accordingly.

Resolved: I use my resources wisely, and I always run smart.

August 13

"We awaken in others the same attitude of mind we hold toward them."

—Elbert Hubbard, philosopher-wit

There are lots of reasons why people run. Here is one of the most basic: you feel a certain way after you run that's different from how you felt before. You feel better about yourself and other people, more positive about your place in the world. You feel more connected to nature and to essential things. You feel healthier, more spontaneous, more energetic—more alive.

Bring that feeling home with you after you run, and put it into your daily life. Maybe you had a bad day at work, and you're feeling rotten. You're yelling at the kids and snippy with your spouse.

Then you start to run. That magical transformative thing that happens when you run happens again. Somehow at the end of your run you're different from when you started. Not different fundamentally, but different in terms of mood and attitude, which is still pretty big.

You open the door of your house. Your spouse, your kids, and your dog all look at you with nervous apprehension. "Uh-oh, look who's back," their silence seems to say.

You owe it to your family—and yourself—to share the benefits of running with them. Leave that old grumpy self outside, and let your new attitude—more relaxed, more forgiving, more loving—fill the air. You'll feel better about it. So will they. And the good feelings that come from running will spread into all the corners of your life.

Resolved: I bring a "better me" into the home after I run, and I share it with my family.

August 14

"You eat a hamburger, you run like a hamburger."

—Steve Riddick, sprinter

It's true: you've got to watch what you eat. Although you burn up lots of calories when you run, you can't just eat anything you want. You've got to have a balanced diet and all that.

Still, you can have an ice cream. Today, after you run. Maybe that's a good destination for your run: the ice-cream parlor. It's summer, after all. What better time for ice cream? On second thought, is there a bad time for ice cream?

What flavor do you like? Chocolate? Jamoca almond fudge? Cookies 'n' cream? Can't decide between lemon sherbet and raspberry? Why not have them both?

Cup or cone? Sometimes you have to eat faster with a cone because the ice cream melts. But when you get a cup, you miss out on the satisfying crunchy sweetness of a sugar cone. Some places will let you have it both ways: cup and cone.

You may not have an ice-cream parlor nearby. No matter. Go to the store and pick up a pint of Ben and Jerry's Cherry Garcia. That's paradise in a carton.

The main message is, treat yourself. Running is a form of self-discipline and denial. But you cannot deny yourself all the time. You must stay motivated and enthusiastic. From time to time, you must go for a run and have an ice cream. You can't do it every day. But why not today?

Resolved: I go for a run. Then I have an ice cream.

August 15

"That daily life is really good one appreciates when one wakes from a horrible dream, or when one takes the first outing after a sickness. Why not realize it now?"

—William Phelps, writer

Here's a sure cure for the running blues: take a forced holiday from it. That will cure your blues in a second.

It's one thing to choose not to run for a few days or a few weeks or even a few months. You know you can come back to it anytime you wish. There's a certain luxury in stepping away of your own free will. But if the choice is not your own—if you are forced to stop because of injury or other reasons—this feeling of luxury evaporates in an instant. You feel suddenly bereft. This thing you love has been taken away from you, and you feel the loss acutely.

After such a forced layoff, when you finally get a chance to run again, it's as if you're born again as a runner. You know what it's like not to be able to run. You know what it's like to lose something you love. And you appreciate it all the more when you return.

Obviously you want to avoid injuries when you run. If you take a break from the sport, you want it to be your choice. But if you've ever been laid off against your will, you can put that experience to use. Remember how bad it was not to be able to run, and how good you felt when you came back. That is certain to pick you up. And if you've been able to avoid forced layoffs altogether? Know that you're a blessed person indeed, and appreciate that each time you run.

Resolved: If I ever get the running blues, I remember what it was like when I couldn't run.

August 16

"We must recognize that our real duty is always found running in the direction of our worthiest desires. No duty that runs roughshod over the personality can have a legitimate claim upon us."

—Randolph Bourne, philosopher

Many people run because it gives them energy to do other things in life, such as work. It's a boost, like caffeine, only healthier.

But you can take it the other way, too. You can use running as a spur to do those other things in life, a motivator. Once you get them done, you can run.

For example: all you may want to do today is run. Running is fun. It gives you spirit food. The other things you are scheduled to do today are not nearly as much fun or rewarding. Nevertheless, they have to be done. Maybe it's a big project with a deadline looming over you. Maybe it's more mundane: you simply need to mow the lawn or weed the garden. Anyway, there's no getting around it or out of it. It's an obligation that must be done.

Do what you have to do. Then run. See running as the carrot, the reward, the treat after all that work. The sooner you fulfill your responsibilities, the sooner you can run. Because of the pleasure that awaits you when it's over, you will be focused on the tasks in front of you. You will dispatch them quickly and efficiently—no loitering, no tarrying, no wasted motion—for you know that after you've done your duty, you'll get your reward: a run.

Resolved: I do what I have to do. Then I run.

August 17

"Good enough never is."

—Debbi Fields, founder, Mrs. Fields Cookies

You may have been running a while and be quite proud of it. You're fit and healthy, and you enjoy the thrice-weekly habit you've developed. Then one day someone asks you if you've ever run a marathon, and it's like a slap in the face. "No," you respond, almost in shock, "I haven't. I don't think I could. Twenty-six miles. It's too much, don't you think?"

After a while, though, the question still bugs you. For some reason it really got under your skin, and you're not sure why. Then it dawns on you: running a marathon is a challenge, and you've been avoiding the challenge.

To be sure, you don't have to run a marathon to be a runner. Lots of runners never run marathons. But avoiding a challenge—ah, well, that's another story.

Maybe you're an experienced runner who's run marathons and other races. But you've always shied away from testing yourself at big races such as New York or Boston or Chicago. Or perhaps you've come close to breaking the three-hour mark but never quite managed it. You've always stepped back from the commitment it takes to break that magic barrier.

Challenges in running come in many shapes and forms. They're different for different people. But here's a rule: whatever stretches you, as a runner and a human being, is good. Never settle for good enough. When the time comes, answer the challenge.

Resolved: I never walk away from a challenge. If it stretches me, it's good.

August 18

The IRS has informed you that you will be the subject of an audit. Forget about it, and run.

The vet says that because you failed to give your dog regular teeth cleanings, he needs gum surgery. Forget about it, and run.

Your boss tells you that the company is not downsizing, but "rightsizing," and that you may be rightsized out of a job. Forget about it, and run.

The plumber says your toilet is backed up because of an underground pipe that will need to be excavated. Forget about it, and run.

Your teenage daughter's new boyfriend has tattoos on both biceps, wears gold hoop earrings, and drives a Harley. Forget about it, and run.

Your ex-wife wants breast-enhancement surgery and thinks that according to the terms of the divorce, you are obligated to pay for it. Forget about it, and run.

Your teenage son is driving too fast and smashes into a new 911 owned by a personal liability lawyer. Forget about it, and run.

A tree falls through the roof of your house. The tree contains a spotted owl nest, and environmentalists file suit against you for harming an endangered species. Forget about it, and run.

Resolved: I forget about it, and run. (Or, as they say in New York: fuhgeddaboutit.)

August 19

"Long distance running can give you a teenage cholesterol, remodel your lungs, lower your blood pressure, and slow your pulse."

—Dr. Richard Steiner, marathoner

You want motivation to run? Tonight, after your partner falls asleep, look at the face in bed next to you. This person needs you. And needs you to run.

Are you a parent? Go into your children's room and look at them asleep. The faces of angels, right? Well, they need you, too. What about your parents? Are they still alive? Despite your occasional problems with them (and vice versa), you love them and want them to stick around. They would no doubt say the same about you.

And what about your friends? You like being with them, right? Well, the feeling is mutual. You talk, you laugh, you trade stories. You are an important part of one another's lives. What would you do if something happened to one of them? Conversely, what would they do if something happened to you? They need you as surely as you need them.

Consider this: your health matters to other people. Your family loves you. Your spouse loves you. Your friends love you. They're all counting on you in some way. They need you to be healthy and well. Running will help keep you that way.

So, run for yourself, yes. That will always be the prime motivation. But keep in mind that there are lots of people who care about you, and that they want you to stay healthy and fit, too.

Resolved: I run for my health, and in so doing, I keep in mind that others want me to be healthy, too.

August 20

"This is a magic moment for me. It's something I've been dreaming of all my life."
—Lameck Aguta of Kenya, after winning the Boston Marathon

One of the most wonderful things about running is that magic moments are still available, and that they are available to all in the most ordinary of ways.

The phrase itself is sort of corny, the sugar-coated sentiment of a pop song. Little children who believe in fairy tales believe in such concepts as "magic moments." But not adults. Too sophisticated, too blasé.

Well, maybe some adults mock the idea, but not runners. They believe in magic moments because they've experienced them.

Only a rarefied few will ever break the tape at a world-class marathon, but magical sensations are hardly restricted to the elite. Just finishing a marathon, or even a 5K fun run, can produce one. But you can have a magic moment during an ordinary midweek run. You're running along, when suddenly a feeling of joy sweeps you up. You feel like shouting at the top of your lungs and, what the heck, you do just that.

Magic moments can happen anytime, often when you least expect it. You can be running at night, or early in the morning before the sun comes up, and see stars shoot across the sky like white flames. On an ordinary afternoon in August you can see a hawk hovering above water, drop down, and fly off with a fish in its talons. Who knows? Maybe today will hold a magic moment for you.

Resolved: When I run today, as corny as it may seem, I hold open the possibility of a magic moment.

August 21

"Never trust an idea you come upon sitting down."

—Friedrich Nietzsche

Ideas come to people in a variety of ways, places, and situations. Some of us (we won't mention names) do our best thinking—and reading—while seated in the porcelain library. Others find the solitude of a car stimulating. For them the commute to work is often the only time during the day that they're alone.

Solitude does seem to have a connection with the germination of ideas. It's not mandatory, but it helps. It's certainly true that very few good ideas are born while on the job. Work is too task oriented. To cultivate ideas, the mind must be allowed to drift, wherever it wishes, like a pleasure boat on a lake on a sunny summer's day.

Whatever idea you have, however you happen upon it, make sure you road test it with a run.

How will you know if it's any good if you don't road test it? Running is solitary for the most part, and it gives you time to think. While it is task oriented (the task of running), the physical act of exerting your body puts it into a different category from that of your normal activities at work, allowing the mind the freedom to ponder ideas and think new thoughts. Sometimes the ideas that spring out of your head when you run are wholly unanticipated and original.

Running will tell you whether your idea is a product of genius or . . . something less. If it's the latter, well, at least you still got in a good workout.

Resolved: I road test all my ideas with a run.

August 22

"One of the best things about running—if not the best—is running with a friend. . . . You've heard it before, but it's so true: there's nothing like good conversation to make a run fly by."

—Gail Kislevitz, runner

The benefits of partner running are well documented. It's safer. Having someone along to keep you company can serve as an antidote to boredom. He or she can pick up the pace and challenge you if your running grows flat and uninspired. Also, as has been noted, it's far more pleasant to chat with another human being as opposed to just yourself, although some grumpy solitary types may disagree.

Another benefit of partner running is that your partner can act as a tour guide and show you different places to run. You can meet your friend at his or her place and run that person's regular route. You get to see different scenery for a change, in addition to the conversational and other benefits of partnering.

Every runner needs a change of scenery from time to time, but sometimes it's hard to find a new running spot on your own. It takes more time than you can afford, and after all that effort you still may not end up with a satisfying place to run. Knowing someone who knows the area can help you short-circuit all of that. The two of you may also want to explore new terrain untouched by either set of feet. Sometimes it's easier to go adventuring with another person than by yourself.

Running in different places is stimulating. The same old places can get boring after a while. Get out of your rut, grab a friend or partner, and go run in someplace new for a change.

Resolved: I call up a friend and ask to go along on a tour of his or her regular running route.

August 23

"When action grows unprofitable, gather information. When information grows unprofitable, sleep."

—Ursula K. LeGuin, writer

The wonderful Greek actress Melina Mercouri was once asked, What is the secret to a happy life? "Do the work you love to do," she said. "Fill your life with love, and—" she added, "take naps."

This is not such bad advice for people in search of a happy running life. Running is an arduous physical activity. It can wear you out. But your body needs rest in combination with activity.

Naps are a most luxurious form of rest. As such they usually take place on the weekends, in the afternoon, although some fortunate souls manage to sneak them in during the week. A person who naps goes on hiatus for 15 or 30 minutes or more, calling a halt to the relentless march of events of the day and indulging in a short, sweet minivacation.

Some runners get so charged up by running that they cannot fathom the idea of a nap after a run. They are perfect candidates for a nap before. Others may feel drained after a run and want to check out for a while. These people may nap after. But naps are good for all runners, whatever time you choose to take one.

Some people are simply unable to close their eyes in the middle of the day. They still can have a quiet time, however, by lying on the bed and reading or meditating.

Give your body what it needs. Take a run and a nap. Both are gifts to the body and soul.

Resolved: Occasionally on the weekends, before or after a run, I take a long, indulgent nap.

August 24

"If you start thinking of the number of laps to go or the time or how tired you will be at the end, you will start getting tense and then you will lose the rhythm, and when that stops, you can't go anymore."

—Joshua Kimeto, runner

Running is like music. When you're running well, you're in a groove. There are no wrong notes; it's perfect and easy. Your arms and legs and eyes and feet and head are all in sync, like a jazz orchestra conducted by Wynton Marsalis.

Unfortunately, you can't order your body to move in a syncopated rhythm. It just doesn't work that way. In fact there's one surefire way to put pressure on yourself: tell yourself there's no pressure. Negative thoughts will come into your head; you can't keep them out. All you can do is keep your mind on the moment and concentrate on what you can control. Your body—and mind—will do what it will do. Trying to force negative thoughts out will only open the floodgates to them.

Accept the fact that you feel pressure. Acknowledge it. Convert those butterflies into energy. Those butterflies—the fact that you feel nervous—are a sign that you care. Caring is a good thing. Because you care, you will continue to improve and grow as a runner—regardless of what happens to you on any specific day or in any specific race.

Use pressure as a stimulant, if you can. The more you experience pressure, the better you will cope with it. You will come to recognize when the jaws of pressure are tightening down on you and learn not to fight, but to relax.

Resolved: I never try to fool myself about pressure. I accept the fact of it and convert my butterflies into energy.

August 25

*"It is in his pleasure that a man really lives; it is from his leisure
that he constructs the true fabric of self."*

—Agnes Repplier, writer

Accept these facts of life: The lawn always needs mowing.
There are always weeds to pull.

All right, perhaps you live in a building in the city and are
not troubled by such time-gobbling, bourgeois nuisances as
lawns and weeds. Thus amended, the rule reads this way:
There are always dishes that need to be done. There are always
clothes that need to be cleaned. There are always things—
papers, books, CDs, whatever—that need to be filed, or put
away, or dusted.

Moving away from boring domestic concerns and into the
realm of job and career, the rule still applies: There is always
work that needs to be done. There is always a call that should
be returned, a memo that needs to be read or prepared, a
meeting that must be scheduled. In other words, it's always
something. Whoever you are, whatever you do, there is always
something to keep you from running.

To heck with that. It's a better day to run than it is to do
any of those other things. Furthermore, you'll be able to do
whatever you need to do after you run. And if what you need
to do gets put off until tomorrow, because you're running
instead, what's the harm, really? Run now. The other stuff can
wait.

Resolved: Instead of mowing the lawn, I run. And hang the
consequences.

August 26

There is a cruel logic to running. Go to any race. The people who have spent lots of time running prior to the race will spend less time on the course. Those who have not run as much prior to the race will spend more time on the course. It's a brutal but fair system.

Success in running has almost the purity of a mathematical equation: the more you run, the faster you will go; the less you run, the slower you will go.

Here's a simple suggestion on how to run more and faster: When you have a lot of time, do more. When you have less time, do less. On those days when you've got a million things on your plate, accept that you are going to run a little less that day. A little running is better than no running. Once you're into it, you may find that you have more time than you anticipated.

But on the weekends or midweek days when your schedule is lighter, run a little bit more. It's not a matter of making up what you "lost" on those other days. That attitude only puts pressure on you and makes you push. It's more a matter of now having the time and taking advantage of it.

Running less when you have less time, and running a little more when you have more time, eases the pressure on you. It creates an attitude that allows you to relax while you run. And being relaxed is essential to spending less time on the course.

Resolved: When I have a lot of time, I do more. When I have less time, I do less.

August 27

"I'd phone in sick. I missed 13 days in 14 months and my boss finally sent me a letter pointing this out to me. Since taking up running, I've had only 2 sick days in the last 15 months."

—Martin Kraft, runner

Without question, you are a healthier person because you run. Look at your attendance record at work. You almost never miss a day due to illness, in part because you are a chronic exerciser. Think of how many days you would have missed if you weren't a runner and were therefore more susceptible to colds, the flu, and other ailments? It's hard to say exactly, but almost certainly you would have missed a lot more than you have.

So, the company owes you. That much is clear. It's profited from your near-spotless attendance record, not to mention your enhanced job performance. Now it's payback time.

Pick up the phone and call in sick. Are you sick? Of course not. You're healthy as an ox. But you need a day off, and the company owes you. It's only right.

Some people may have qualms about calling in sick when they're not. All right, then, call it a "well day." Say that you just feel too good to come into work and that you want to spend the day outside, taking an ultralong, sinfully slow distance run. Explain that since you took up running a few years ago, you've hardly had any sick days, and so the company shouldn't mind because it's coming out way ahead on that score. It's August anyway, you might even add, so who cares?

Or come up with your own excuse. It's just too nice a day to do anything but run. Your employer will understand.

Resolved: I phone in sick, take the day off, and run.

August 28

"People never believe in volcanoes until the lava actually overtakes them."

—George Santayana, philosopher and poet

You like to run in this lovely wooded area that winds through rolling open pasturelands. Cattle graze there, and in the early evenings, just before dark, you occasionally see deer come down from the hills to drink at the creek.

One day, after your run, a rust-bucket Chevy pulls up next to you on the road. The Chevy was probably a real fine vehicle in its day, but that day was about 40 years ago. There's a man and a beagle inside. The man rolls down his window and, with the engine idling, starts talking to you. "Hey," he says, "the other day I saw a mountain lion up there, did you know that?"

"No," you tell him, and he continues, "Oh yeah, a big one. It was close to dark like now. I see this deer by the creek all of a sudden take off. I don't know what spooks it until I see this big shadow moving across the hill above me.

"Turns out it's a mountain lion," he goes on, "checking me out. It walks along with me right past that deadfall you see at the start of the trail. With the deer gone, I seriously think it was considering taking me on. Luckily my dog was with me"—here, he pats the heroic beagle—"and I don't think it wanted to mess with him."

The man and the beagle peel out, leaving you standing by the side of the road. A mountain lion? In the place where you run? Hmmm.

Resolved: I stay safe when I run, and if I need to change my route to be or feel safe, I do it.

August 29

Runners are, by and large, a modest, highly intelligent lot. There are exceptions, though: people whose deeds, shall we say, do not match the loftiness of their rhetoric.

It is a most sublime sort of motivation to beat one of those bores in a race. To silence a big talker, if only for a while.

Oh, that's not a very evolved view, you say? Do your own thing, you say; don't worry about the next person. The true victories in running are always personal.

True enough, but there's only so much a person can take; don't you agree? You hear all this talk about PRS and how he's planning to run Boston next year and who he's training with and what Frank Shorter said the other day, and you just want to hit something.

Rather than resort to violence, there's a far healthier outlet: competition. Both of you enter the same race and run together the whole way. That is, until the end. Normally it's not good strategy to hold back for a big finishing kick, but in this case, you make an exception, turning on the afterburners with less than a mile to go. As you pull away, you say innocently that you'll see him again at the finish and leave him gasping in your wake.

What it lacks in enlightenment, it makes up for in satisfaction. You may want to try it some time.

Resolved: I put a running bore in his place by whipping him soundly in a race.

August 30

"Every time you live through something like this, you'll be tougher for the next time. You've just got to keep fighting and fighting and fighting until it breaks, and it will break."

—Dusty Baker, baseball manager, advising
a young, slumping player

Yesterday was bad. Today will be better. That's not Pollyannaish. That's cold, hard fact.

More facts: You've gotten through things like this before. You'll get through it again. Once you get through it, you'll be stronger for the next time.

You're having a down period. OK, it happens. Keep it in perspective. How's your health overall? Is your family well? Do you have enough to pay the rent, put food on the table? If you've got those things, you've got a lot more than some people.

There will be good times in running (and in life). There will be bad times. This has nothing to do with you personally. They're facts of nature, like thunder and lightning. "Good" and "bad" are relative concepts anyhow. You can find good things even in the worst of times. Similarly, nothing is ever completely good. There are always trade-offs. Although, granted, it sometimes takes the distance of years to see the good in certain events.

You may have great luck, or not. The breaks may fall your way, or not. Life is a struggle in any case. What you must do is fight and fight and fight and fight and ride through the inevitable bad times. Then enjoy the heck out of the good times when they come.

Resolved: I keep fighting and fighting and fighting until better times come my way. When they do, I make sure to appreciate them.

August 31

"How beautiful it is to do nothing, and then to rest afterward."

—Spanish proverb

It is the last day of August; the kids are getting ready to go back to school. Summer is nearly gone. There's even a little sharpness in the air. Autumn is knocking on the door, wanting to come in.

You're not sure why exactly, but for some reason you're uneasy about all of this. Maybe it's because you haven't done enough of nothing.

Summer is not—or rather, should not be—a time of grand ambition. So, what have you done? Seized every moment, pounced on every opportunity, grabbed for the golden ring every chance you got. What a waste of a summer.

But wait. Before this golden season passes away for another year, there's still time to salvage it. Today, do nothing. Have a resolution-free day. Abandon all projects; suspend all ambitions. Run if you feel like it. If you don't, don't. Instead, get to know the underside of an oak tree. Lie flat on your back in the grass, watching the leaves shimmer in the sunlight. Read or nap or make love to your partner on a blanket, or do none of those if any of them begins to resemble ambition or anything close. Let time gently meander along, like Old Man River, at least for a while.

Now, then. Ain't it beautiful?

Resolved: I have a resolution-free day and get to know the underside of an old oak tree.

September 1

"People who run find their lives so much more enjoyable.
Everything works better: their cardiovascular system, their
gastrointestinal system, even their ability to think."

—Dr. Ralph Paffenbarger, runner and scientist

When it comes to running, you can either get started or keep going. There are no other choices.

Wait, that's not true. You could rest. Every runner needs to make rest a habitual part of his or her running routine. But today? Rest on the first? No, no, rest on the *last* of the month or even tomorrow. But never the first. Today you run.

A few people might be thinking, "There is one other alternative he hasn't mentioned. I could stop altogether." You could . . . *what?* Why would you want to do that? What would be the point?

There are certain issues in life that you can never run from, and one of them is your health. Running promotes health. Can there be any doubt of that? Well, then, what is it? What would ever possess you to consider stopping?

Are you hurting? Well, then, take a break. Or mix in some easy walking with the running. Are you bored? Pump some variety into your workouts. Quit thinking of them as workouts. Don't associate running with work at all. Just go out and run around a little, as you did when you were a kid. If you do that—run around like a kid—you will find yourself running into a healthy old age.

Resolved: It's the first of the month. I get started, or I keep going. But I never stop.

September 2

"Sometimes the difficult thing is to hold back when things are going well, to remember that what you're doing is, after all, preparation."

—Sebastian Coe, runner

Hold back or push? It's a continuing question for people who run.

There are so many days when you feel like such a plodder. But every now and then, fueled by something you wish they would bottle and sell at grocery stores, it's as if you're running on air. And you're supposed to hold back on those days? That is indeed tough, very tough.

Some runners might argue that those are precisely the days to push it, that you are finally seeing the results of all your hard training, and that you are on the verge of a real break-through. If you always hold back, you may never fully realize your potential, never know what you can do. And what a waste that would be.

But there's a risk to pushing, especially in a workout. What are the stakes, really? When you push, you risk injury. Are you prepared to suffer the consequences if the risk doesn't work out the way you hoped?

Like so many other things in running and athletics, the answer may be to ask your body. Listen to it, and trust the answer it gives (even if it's not the one you wanted to hear). Almost always in running, it's best to hold back something. But you'll know what's best for yourself on any given day.

Resolved: I listen to my body and trust the answer I get.

September 3

"If you are patient in one moment of anger, you will escape a hundred days of sorrow."

—Chinese proverb

Let's face it: there are times when you're no good to anybody. You have no patience, no tolerance. It's not that you're a bad person—not at all. It's just that you're tired and fed up. It's as if you've got nothing left. Everybody's ragging on you—or it feels like it, anyway—and you're sick of it.

Do the world a favor. Go for a run and clear your head.

When you blow, what happens? Only bad things; you know that. To paraphrase a Jerry Jeff Walker line, you've been down that road once or twice before. You're smart enough not to want to keep repeating the same stupid mistakes.

Exercise is a proven stress manager. It's true for anger, too. If something continually bugs you and sets you off, you may have to look deeper to find the source of that anger and deal with it in a meaningful way. But if it's just a surface irritation—your kid accidentally spills her glass of milk at the table—you'll save yourself (and your family) a world of trouble by taking your anger out on the roads.

Resolved: When I get into one of those moods, I go for a run to clear my head.

September 4

"Every day is a god, each day is a god, and holiness holds forth in time."

—Annie Dillard, writer

Runners are like everyone else. They can have a good day on Monday. Then they'll go out on Tuesday and expect a repeat performance. When it doesn't happen, they're disappointed and troubled. What's wrong? they ask.

Nothing is wrong. Their expectations may be off, but other than that, the universe is operating just as it has for the past billion years or so.

Each day is different, with its own rhythms and energy. While appearing the same as every other day you have experienced so far in your life, this day is, in fact, unique. It's nothing at all like yesterday and a different beast entirely from how tomorrow will be.

Knowing this to be true, why, then, do you expect the same results as yesterday? And if today turns out well, why do you expect to duplicate it tomorrow?

Instead of judging each day on strict standards of "good" or "bad," it might be worthwhile to look at it in a different way. Is it possible that, even though you had a theoretically "bad" day, you got the most out of that day that you could possibly get? That you derived more benefit from that "bad" day than you did when things were so easy for you on the theoretically "good" day?

Be responsive to each day, for each day holds unique possibilities. Treat each day as the gift it is, and make the most out of what this gift allows you.

Resolved: I get the most out of what every day allows me.

September 5

"People are wrong about the motion of the future. The future stands still. It is we who are moving in infinite space."

—Rainer Maria Rilke, poet

The end of the year is a traditional time for taking stock, but it doesn't always have to occur then. A change of seasons is a good time for that, too.

At the start of the summer you thought about entering a race or even attempting a marathon. How'd you do? Or perhaps you decided, in the spirit of the warm months, to take it easy. To have no ambitions or grand plans but to take things as they come and enjoy yourself. Well, how'd that go?

Whatever your goals, this might be an appropriate time for review. Some runners (men particularly) tend to put their heads down and go for it. Whatever it is they're going for almost doesn't matter. Because as soon as they get it, they're off to the next thing and, when they get that, the next thing after that.

If this describes you, hold on for a moment. Ceaseless forward movement for its own sake is often a means of avoiding hard truths. It provides the illusion of progress and yet accomplishes nothing of value. In the end you may feel lost and betrayed.

Check in with yourself; see how you're faring. Evaluating where you've been will help you decide where to go next and how best to get there. After achieving one goal, but before going on to the next, you may want to ask yourself: Am I getting what I want from running? If not, why not? To know where you want to go, stop to see where you've been.

Resolved: I take stock of myself as a runner before I go on to the next thing.

September 6

"Running frees me from the monosyllabic inanities of my usual tongue-tied state. It removes me from the kind of talk which aims at concealing rather than revealing what is in my heart, and what I mean to do and be."

—George Sheehan, philosopher-runner

There are lots of ways to talk to someone—share "meaningful dialogue," if you will. You can call up and talk on the phone. You can meet at the coffee shop or over drinks at a bar. You can take a walk together on the beach. Here's another way: run together. Running and conversation go together like chocolate cake and vanilla ice cream. If you're running too fast to talk, you're running too fast. You've found the right pace when you can hold a conversation while running.

When you run, you're stripped down to bare essentials (well, almost). You're not in your street clothes; you're in shorts and running shoes.

You're also outdoors. Something about being outside frees the human spirit. People are not the same indoors as they are outdoors. In the best cases they become more open and relaxed, more responsive to others.

When you run, your body is in motion. This makes a difference in the conversation, too. It tends to pare away the unessential. You talk a lot about running, it's true. But you talk about lots of other things, too. You can start (and settle) a debate with a friend. You can have a heart-to-heart talk. Or you can just shoot the breeze. Somehow it all goes a little bit better when you run.

Resolved: When I run with a friend, I go at a conversational pace, shooting the breeze with him or her.

September 7

"The heart has its reasons which reason knows nothing of."
—Blaise Pascal, mathematician and philosopher

On the surface, at least, today seems to have a lot in common with yesterday.

Same bed, same spouse. Same alarm clock going off at 6:45 A.M., same time as yesterday.

Same dog barking next door at the neighbor's.

Same breakfast of eggs, toast, and coffee.

Same commute to work with the usual traffic tie-up at the same place in the highway.

And, oh yes, same job.

Same sun. Same earth.

Same life, after all.

Still, something is different. For some reason, it's a better day today than it was yesterday. Granted, a good night's sleep may have something to do with it, but that doesn't explain it entirely.

Don't think twice. Don't look for cosmic explanations. When extra energy surges through you like an electrical current, just go with it. Take advantage of it, and run. And after you run, you'll find you have even more.

Resolved: When a good day comes along, when I feel full of vim and vigor, I take advantage of it and run.

September 8

"Most of us don't wear out. We rust."

—Unidentified physician

One of the most inspiring things you can do as a runner is go to a race and check out the people. They're a good-looking bunch, aren't they?

Both the men and women are generally very fit and good looking. But perhaps even more impressive are the older runners who appear in greater numbers toward the rear of the pack. They have trim figures and healthy, clear skin. Their faces glow.

Some older runners run very fast for their age. Others would be hard-pressed to beat a snail across the street. Yet, all of them—fast and slow alike—obviously derive health benefits from running.

These older runners embody the truth of the "Use it or lose it" school of philosophy. They're using it, and they're not losing it (at least they're not losing it as fast as they would if they weren't exercising). They recognize, in the words of the U.S. Administration on Aging, that "disuse is the mortal enemy of the human body." They're not letting their bodies—or their lives—turn to rust.

Now, you may be 19 and think your body will always be the rock-hard object of desire that it is today. In which case you probably don't care what those old fogies are doing. But if you do have a sense that your body is changing as you age, you can learn a lot from older runners. They're modeling the way you could look in the future.

Resolved: I take a tip from my good-looking elders: as I get older, I keep running.

September 9

"The whole duty of man may be expressed in one line—make yourself a perfect body."

—Henry David Thoreau

Pardon me, Henry, but your thought needs to be amended slightly. A better way to put it would be, ". . . make a perfect body *for you.*"

For better or worse, you're stuck with your body. You can't have Dan O'Brien's body or Jackie Joyner Kersee's body. Your body is uniquely your own—and no one's is perfect. No doubt even specimens like O'Brien and Joyner Kersee find flaws in their physical form. Probably when you stand naked in front of a mirror, you find a few of your own.

But that's not really the point. What you're trying to do is develop a body that works for you. And if you achieve it, there is a kind of perfection to that.

People get discouraged when they work out because they feel they're not doing as much as some other people. Or perhaps they're not doing as much as they did when they were younger. They compare themselves with an abstract standard and find themselves lacking in some way.

If you insist on applying a standard, try this one: perfect for you. What works for your body at this time? Perfection is unattainable, but it is possible to get in better shape. When you get in better shape, you'll feel better and be able to do more.

Resolved: My conditioning goal is to develop a body that works for me.

September 10

Nah, not this morning; too tight. Packed with meetings. The afternoon doesn't look any better. You could wait till you get home, but by that time you're tired and you usually don't feel like going anywhere.

The solution? Run at lunch. It takes a little advance planning, but it's worth it. You need to pack a lunch because you probably won't have time to go out for anything. You'll have to eat at your desk. Assuming, of course, your employer doesn't mind. But if you're back on the job by the required time, what does the boss care? She or he should encourage it. Running makes you more alert, less prone to the afternoon blahs.

Then there's the shower issue, probably the biggest obstacle to running at lunch. You can change in the rest room, but after you run, then what? You're sweaty, your hair is messed up, and you smell like a pair of old gym socks.

Maybe there's a gym in the area with showers. You could change there. Or what if you toweled off in the rest room? Would that work? If you're looking for excuses not to run, you can find them anywhere. But if you want to run, you can overcome every obstacle, including messy hair and sweaty armpits.

Resolved: I run at lunch today (or start figuring out how to do it).

September 11

"I've had a wonderful time, and I've made so many wonderful friends in the sport. I just like to run."

—Elaine Pedersen, one of the first women to compete in the Boston Marathon

When you talk to runners who've been at it for a while, they use words such as *enjoy* and *fun* and *like*, as in: "I like to run. I enjoy it. It's fun."

They tend not to use ponderous polysyllabic words such as "commitment." People are committed to mental institutions. Runners, however, seldom confess to being "committed" to it. Nor do they run because it's "good for them." It is indeed good for them, but that's not why they do it. They run because they love it.

Running is a simple activity with simple pleasures. You run to be alone. But you also run to be with others. Running helps you feel good about yourself and your body. It helps your body systems work more efficiently. You don't have to be an expert to run. It's an outgrowth of walking, which you learn as a child. After you learn to walk, you start to run.

So, never speak of running in terms of "commitment" (although sometimes, it's true, this author makes that mistake). Let words such as *enjoy* and *fun* and *like* be the ones you use. For as long as you like to run, you'll be committed to it.

Resolved: I never "commit" to running; I just run.

September 12

"You don't know what pain is until you get up around 21 or 22 miles. You just hurt like hell. You'd give anything in the world to quit, but you just keep going."

—Dr. Fred Blanton, after running a marathon

You're almost done. Keep going. When you get to the end, you can quit. But you're not there yet.

You've come a long way. Some people would be content to stop now. But you're not some people, and you're not stopping. How long is a marathon? There is its actual distance—26 miles, 385 yards—and there is how much it feels like when you're running it. At about mile 20, it feels as if you've been dropped into a vat of boiling oil.

Painful? Bamboo shoots under the fingernails would be preferable. Even so, it's not passive pain, if that makes sense. It's not something being inflicted upon you that you are powerless to change. The pain is, in fact, a choice, and you are facing it head-on. You're not backing away: you're continuing on.

And look, you're almost there. The end is so close, you can almost taste it. Just think how painful it'd be if you quit now, after all that work. The thought of quitting is even more painful than all the pain you've absorbed to this point.

Then there's this: think of how good it's going to feel when you stop. O frabjous day! Callooh! Callay! Won't that be wonderful?

Resolved: I keep going. Despite the pain, I keep going.

September 13

"To run and leap, to dart about with sweat pouring from your body, to expend your last ounce of energy and afterward to stand beneath a hot shower—how few things in life can give such enjoyment."

—Yukio Mishima, novelist

Is anything more satisfying than working up a good, honest sweat?

Liquid pools in your belly button. Your hair is plastered against your head as if it's covered with grease, and sweat runs off your forehead. You wipe your face to keep the moisture out of your eyes. The back of your neck is sticky. Your whole body is dripping—hair, face, chest, arms, legs. You can even feel the sweat inside your socks. An unsuspecting person touches your unclothed back and immediately jerks his hand away. "Yuck," he says, "you're not getting in my car." You smile. You don't care.

Sweat is connected to work. You've done your work—or you're in the process—and that's why you're sweating. It feels good to put in a good day's work. Sweat is one of the things you have to show for it.

Corpses do not sweat; humans do. When you're sweating, you're alive. You're running, you're pushing, your heart is beating, you're stretching those legs, you're gulping in fresh air, you're smelling the flowers, you're seeing the sights, you're outside, the world is full, and life is good. Keep sweating.

Resolved: I work up a sopping good sweat today.

September 14

There is an element of power in being fit. When you're fit, you can do things other people cannot do, and this gives you a sense of power.

You can walk up a flight of stairs and not be winded. You can walk up these stairs faster than a colleague at work. When you arrive at the top feeling fine and hardly breathing, while your colleague follows a moment later, winded and gasping for breath, you've made a personal statement of sorts.

Power is one reason why men spend so much time hefting weights in the gym and women attend aerobics classes. Being fit improves your perception of yourself. It also shapes how other people look at you and how they think of you. Together these translate into an increase in power.

Is there something wrong with this? Not at all. Power itself is a neutral value (although, as has been noted, it does tend to corrupt over time). You can be a person of great power and use it to destructive ends. Or you can use power in the service of others. It depends on what you make of it.

One thing is certain: this feeling of power, this renewed sense of health and strength and possibility, is one of the joys of running. Never deny it or hide from it. Enjoy it.

Resolved: I relish this growing sense of personal power that comes with being fit.

September 15

"Good and beautiful things may easily be spoiled by suggestions of rights and duties."

—A. C. Benson, writer

There are so many "musts" and "shoulds" in life that it can make a person crazy. You must go to work. You should get there on time. You must turn in that report by the deadline. You should come back from lunch by 1:30, and so on.

Try not to let must and should spoil your running. You don't have to run today. There are no musts or shoulds attached to it. It's not mandatory. There are no laws obligating you to run. You can always run tomorrow when you feel more up to it.

Running gives you a sense of freedom. When you fill it up with musts and shoulds, you can dilute or even destroy that sense of freedom. It becomes less of a pleasure and more of a duty or habit.

Of course, you may feel like running today. It's not a must-do in your mind; it's a want-to-do. Still, you may be running along and think, "I don't feel so hot today. I think I'll cut it short," only to be seized by a second thought: "But if I turn around now, I won't be doing my normal distance. I should run more."

Run more if you feel like it. But let *that* be the governing principle, not a sense of should or must. A sense of duty can be a wonderful thing, but it need not overpower the pleasurable aspects of running.

Resolved: If I want to run today, I run. If I don't, I don't. But I keep "must" and "should" out of it.

September 16

"In my business hours I avoid fatigue. I do this by not doing too much work—the only trustworthy recipe."

—E. V. Knox, writer

You've worked hard today. It's time to do the old "push away": push yourself away from that desk, turn out the lights, lock the door on your way out, and do what you love to do.

It's practically dark outside. But there's still time. Maybe you're the type who carries running togs in the car. Toss them on in a hurry, and aerate the heart and lungs for a while. Sure, there's work left to do. There's always work to do. But it will be sitting right where you left it come tomorrow.

Surveys show that Americans are working harder and longer than ever, and you can personally vouch for it. You get up early and go home late. The company gets more than its money's worth; that's for sure.

If you have kids, you know your work isn't over when you get home. It doesn't stop until they go to bed. By then it's nine or ten o'clock at night, and you're almost too tired to appreciate the little bit of downtime you've been allowed.

If you're lucky, you'll log seven or eight hours of continuous snooze time before the alarm rings and you have to get up and pay those dues all over again. It's like what Merle Haggard says: you work to make a living, but the living never entirely gets made.

You work hard, damn hard. You deserve to do something for yourself at the end of the day. Time to quit, and go for a run.

Resolved: I always make time for myself—running time—at the end of a long day.

September 17

You may run in an ugly neighborhood with ugly streets and buildings. In which case it makes sense to rush through without taking note of the surroundings. But if you run in a pretty place with flowers and trees and birds, what's the hurry? Why the rush?

If you give yourself to running, running will give back. It's the same with nature. Open yourself up to the green world around you, and you will receive plenty in return—an abundance, in fact.

People who are bored with running put blinders on themselves. They focus only on the mechanics of the act—their footfall, the distance they have to go, their time, whatever. If they took off the blinders, their boredom would vanish in a snap.

The trees are full of birds: did you notice? And they're making all kinds of noise. You can't call it singing exactly, but it is musical. Be quiet, and listen. There's a vibrant, living, thriving world outside of yourself and your concerns. You'll be amazed by what you can see and hear, once you open your eyes and ears.

Shhhh. Take a moment of quiet to drink it all in. Before you run, or after, or even during. Even if you have been running in the same place for years, you will discover things you never imagined. And come to know it as if for the first time.

Resolved: When I run, I give myself a moment of quiet to appreciate my surroundings.

September 18

"Seeing is believing, but feeling is God's own truth."

—Irish proverb

If you're like most runners, you probably have a pretty good idea of how much you run each day. You may even have an *exact* idea, having measured it precisely at some point.

It's comforting to know how much you run. There's a feeling of accomplishment in being able to say you ran 2.5 miles, or 4.3 miles, or whatever it happens to be.

Today is going to be a little different. Today you're going to run until you feel like stopping. (Then again, you may resent being told what to do. Fair enough. Run your usual route as always. Just file these thoughts away for later use.)

Instead of your normal pattern of running a preestablished distance regardless of how you feel, you're going to run, in essence, as far as you feel. If you feel like running less than normal, you're going to do that. But you may also feel like running farther than you usually do. If so, run farther.

And if you don't feel like running at all, well, you're going to skip it today. And not feel guilty about it either. Running less than normal (if you do) may inspire you to run more the next time you go out. Running farther than normal may surprise you and show you that you're stronger than you think. The idea is, listen to your feelings (and your body speaking through those feelings). Feelings have a truth of their own. Let them tell you how far to run today.

Resolved: I run until I feel like stopping.

September 19

"Runners need to take responsibility for the health of their muscles, not just how fast they go. Recovery has to be an integral part of training."

—Linda Jaros, massage therapist (whose clients include many runners)

A lot of this comes down to a matter of respect. Respecting your body, respecting yourself.

If you abuse your body, you are abusing yourself. You can abuse your body through running. Every runner knows that.

Your body has been with you from the very beginning, ever since you were a little tadpole in your mama's womb. The formation of self has coincided with the formation of your body. One could not have occurred without the other. As adults, we tend to emphasize our intellectual and emotional selves to the neglect of our physical side. We see the latter as inferior to the other two. This is a foolish and ultimately false view. It's all of a piece—intellect, emotion, body. All are connected; all work together. If one breaks down, the other parts are affected.

A one-time sportscaster turned news anchor, Jan Hutchins, had a favorite expression: "The body is the temple of the soul." He used it to sign off his sportscasts, to encourage people to take care of their bodies, until viewers objected to it for both religious and nonreligious reasons. Appropriate or not for the evening news, Hutchins had a point: can you respect what's inside the vessel (soul, intelligence, emotion) if you do not respect the vessel itself? Food for thought on today's run.

Resolved: I respect my body; I respect myself.

September 20

"I have realized that the past and the future are real illusions, that they exist only in the present, which is what there is and all that there is."

—Alan Watts, philosopher

In running a marathon, the goal is not to run 26 miles, 385 yards. The goal is simply to run one step at a time.

If you contemplate a marathon in its entirety, it is a mammoth undertaking. Think of it as one step at a time, and it becomes a much easier one. How many individual steps in a marathon? Thousands upon thousands, to be sure. But you'll become lost and discouraged if you focus on the totality. Think only about making one step and following it with another step and another.

No, check that: you don't even have to do that. Forget the second and third and fourth and fifth steps and all the steps that follow; they are only abstractions. The only step that matters is this one, the one you are making now.

Is there such a thing as the future? Only as an abstraction, for when you reach the future, it's no longer the future; it's the present. It's the same in running. The second and third and fourth steps—the steps that come later—are only abstractions. When you reach those steps, they transform into the step you are taking at that moment.

There's no need to look ahead in running. Take it one step at a time.

Resolved: I run one step at a time.

September 21

It's fun to travel. It's fun to go to Tokyo or London or Honolulu to run marathons. A race being held in a faraway locale can serve as a great motivator. Buy your discount airline tickets early, and go for it.

But you don't have to go anywhere to run if you don't want to. Everything you need is right here at home.

The adventure of running is in your body and mind. If you're looking for adventure in faraway places, you're looking in the wrong spot.

Herman Melville said that the greatest adventure of all was the adventure of a person's spirit, the soul's journey. In running terms, this may be expressed as the journey of the soles.

This is such a liberating idea when you grasp it fully. Everything you're looking for from running, everything you want to achieve, is available now. You don't have to send away for it or fly on a jet six hours to find it. It's here, in the adventure of your own body and mind.

Not only do you not need to go anywhere, but you don't need anyone else either. Although it's nice to run with people and get their support, it's not necessary in order for you to achieve what you want. You can do it all on your own.

Resolved: I understand that the greatest adventure in running is an adventure of both the body and spirit.

September 22

"The individual is what he is and has the significance that he has not so much in virtue of his individuality, but rather as a member of a great human community, which directs his material and spiritual existence from the cradle to the grave."

—Albert Einstein

Running is such a solitary activity at times. Especially when you're struggling, it seems as if you're a stranger in a strange land. No one to help you, no one to offer support or encouragement, no one to extend a friendly hand.

But, in fact, there exists a vast community of runners out there, people who understand what you're going through and who can provide support and assistance.

But how do you find it? Well, there are a number of ways. You can hook up with friends who are runners. You can join a running club or enter races. You can go where runners go, such as coffee shops or pancake houses where they meet after Sunday-morning runs. Running-shoe stores, which often function as unofficial headquarters in local running communities, are one more way to connect with runners.

In the days of yore, running *was* solitary. Runners were as rare as exotic birds—and like exotic birds, almost always seen alone. People who ran were branded as eccentrics or worse and widely mocked by the sentient world.

Those days, thankfully, are long gone. If you're struggling, if you feel alone, if you have questions, if you need support, or heck, if you just want to make friends and have a good time—a diverse community of runners is out there. All you have to do is tap into it.

Resolved: If I start feeling cut off as a runner, I tap into my local running community.

September 23

"Then summer fades and passes. We will smell smoke then, and feel an unsuspected sharpness, a thrill of nervous, swift elation, a sense of sadness and departure."

—Thomas Wolfe

Runners spend lots of time outdoors, so they know better than most meteorologists what's up with the weather. They know that the seasons never begin and end when the calendar says they do. Some years it seems as if spring takes place on a single day (blink, and you miss it), while the summers go on and on and on and on. (Winters can feel like that, too.)

Fall is a wonderful time for runners because the weather gets cooler. The enervating heat of summer has gratefully passed, and yet the sharp coldness of winter with its harsh extremes has not yet set in. It's a pleasant balance.

When it's been hot for a while, and the weather breaks and it's suddenly cool, it's like a gift. Maybe it happens overnight. You fall asleep with a couple of blankets on the bed, but in the middle of the night you get cold and snuggle in closer to your lover. Then you wake up, and it's gray and overcast outside, and you feel like singing.

Isn't that one of the most delightfully perverse characteristics of runners? While much of the rest of the world gets gloomy when the sun goes away, runners become as giddy as children on Christmas morning. As the season of the cool begins, enjoy.

Resolved: I relish the coolness of fall and go for a run.

September 24

"Duty does not have to be dull. Love can make it beautiful and fill it with life."

—Thomas Merton, writer

You're down and feeling awful. You've got the Monday-morning blues (even if it's not Monday). You don't feel like getting out of bed, much less going for a run.

Let your routine save you. Your routine, which includes running, is constant. Fall back on it, and let it carry you when your inspiration flags.

The conventional view of routine is that it is deadening. People don't know why they do what they do; they just do it. They have no energy or interest in it. All that impels them forward is their deadly dull, life-sapping, blood-draining routine.

Routine *can* have this effect, but not always. Sometimes it can get you out of bed when you don't feel like it. Sometimes it can make you put on your shoes and run anyway. After all, it's part of your routine.

And you know what happens? You're glad you did. You're glad you got out of bed; you're glad you ran. Though you were listless and slow in the beginning, you gradually got into it. In fact you ended up having a pretty decent workout, far better than you anticipated.

Make running part of your routine. When the inspiration lags, fall back on that routine.

Resolved: I let my routine work for me and run even when I'm not feeling supermotivated.

September 25

"Do it the right way, which is the long way. You can't cram for a marathon, because the final exam for a marathon will never allow you to be successful if you take shortcuts."

—Bill Wenmark, running coach

There are no shortcuts in running, no skipping steps. You must pay your dues. It's very fair in this regard.

You put in the time (and miles), and you will reap the rewards according to your ability and desire. There are no poseurs in running, at least not in the front ranks. The poseurs—the people who have not put in the time, who are seeking to skip steps—are always exposed come race day, wilting as surely as a tulip under the hot sun.

Runners are not elitists in general. They welcome all manner of persons to their sport. But they are elitist in this respect: they see only one way to run, and that is the long way.

The long way means putting in the time. It means spending an inordinate amount of your waking hours alone or with other similarly afflicted souls, pounding the pavement. It means coping with a variety of aches and pains and small physical indignities to achieve a greater sense of health and well-being.

There is only one way to happiness in running, and that is the long way. There are no shortcuts. Take the long way to happiness in running, and you'll be sure to find it.

Resolved: I run the right way, which is the long way.

September 26

"At the end of my daily jaunt I was totally exhausted. Then, gradually, a strange thing happened. I began to realize that it was taking me less and less energy to run a mile. I was beginning to get in shape."

—David Burhans Jr., runner

If you run regularly, strange things will happen to you, too. You will be able to run a mile without feeling winded. You will, in fact, feel better at the end of the mile than you did at the start. Your stamina will grow over time. You will be able to run two or three or four miles without stopping. You truly will consider it a strange phenomenon, worthy of Ripley's. Even as you run more and more, it requires less and less energy from you. Amazing.

But here's the kicker: in order to achieve these gains from running, you must keep it in the schedule.

You're a busy person who leads a busy life. Busy in the morning, busy in the afternoon, you barely have time for lunch. Work makes impossible demands on you. After work, family makes still more demands on you.

Simplifying your schedule is an excellent idea. But not at the expense of running. Whereas work drains you of energy, running restores it. Whereas work steals your time, running seems to create it. When you run, you work more efficiently, which in turn gives you more time for doing things.

Only by running will you get into shape. Only by running will you become a stronger, faster runner. But you must keep it in the schedule.

Resolved: I always make time for running, however crazy my schedule gets.

September 27

"People should be encouraged to prepare properly. We need to teach them to put less emphasis on trying to perform well, and more on having fun, and staying within their range."

—Dr. John Bagshaw, advising runners prior to a race

It's easy to tell runners to put less emphasis on performing well "and more on having fun." But the advice really goes against human nature. Most people want to perform well *and* have fun. For them, performing well is having fun. How can you have fun and not perform well? Why can't you have both?

Here's a thought on how to have both: stay in your range. If you stay in your range as a runner, you are going to perform well—or, more precisely, as well as you can. You probably won't win the race. You may not even finish in the top 2,000. But if you performed as well as you possibly could—if you did your best—what complaint can you have?

Furthermore, you didn't go out too fast and falter at the end. Nor did you hold back for most of the race, saving up for a big finishing kick. You ran your pace, all the way through, and even held a conversation with the runner alongside you while you were at it. You finished with such a good feeling that next time, you think you might be able to push your limits a little further and expand your range.

You can perform well and have fun. Stay in your range as a runner, and you will.

Resolved: I stay in my range when I run.

September 28

"In a marathon I never let myself think, I've got 26 miles ahead of me. You have to think of your race as it is then and there. At the same time you keep in mind the prospects for the future."

—Bill Rodgers, marathoner

One foot in front of the other, and you're there.

New York.

Boston.

Honolulu.

The Empire State Building (bottom to top, every step).

Falmouth.

Peachtree.

Tokyo.

Bay to Breakers.

The bottom of Mojave, the top of Whitney.

Los Angeles.

Chicago.

Fifty miles.

Seventy-five miles.

One-hundred-mile Ride and Tie.

One foot in front of the other, and you're there. The future is now.

Resolved: One foot in front of the other.

September 29

"Nothing helps me sort out problems better than lacing up my shoes and taking a turn around the park."

—Judith Kaye, runner

There is no problem so difficult that a run around the park won't cure.

Why are you sitting there, looking so troubled? Quit worrying. The answer is waiting for you at the park. Lace up your shoes, and go find it.

You've wracked your brain enough. You've got to look someplace else. That someplace is the park. All those people running around the park just like you? They're looking for answers, too. It's like a giant Easter egg hunt for runners, only the answers aren't hidden. They're in the open, available to all.

Ever see *It's a Mad, Mad, Mad, Mad World*? It's a classic, starring Jonathan Winters, Sid Caesar, and a bunch of other great old-time comedians—definitely a rental. Anyway, they're all on this crazed hunt for stolen loot, which is buried in a park under "the sign of the W."

Not to give the movie away, but suffice it to say that they all look straight at the W and can't figure it out. The answer to the riddle is staring them in the face, yet they almost miss it. It's the same for you. The answer is waiting for you at the park. Running will lift the veil from your eyes and help you see it.

Resolved: I take a turn around the park and sort out my problems.

September 30

"He has to try running fast and slow, learn from his mistakes, and then figure out his own magic formula."

—Roger Bannister, legendary miler,
on how runners succeed

Try running fast. Try running slow. Try running fast *and* slow.

Gradually build your distances. Run a little bit, then a little bit more. Progress from there until you find what's comfortable for you. When you find it, stick with it for a while.

Vary your workouts from time to time. Run intervals on a track. Run long, slow distances at a conversational pace. Get off the pavement. Run cross-country on dirt trails thick with pine and oak.

Run once a week. Then run twice a week if it feels right. Run even more if you're up to it. Keep tabs on your body. How is it doing?

Learn from your mistakes. Learn from your successes. Always, keep learning. You'll work it out. Over time you will find what works for you—your "magic" formula, if you will—though there will definitely be times when it doesn't seem like magic at all, just a lot of hard work.

Today, go out and run. Do the work. Who knows? Maybe there will be some magic in it.

Resolved: As I run, I continue to look for the right running formula for me, magic or not.

October 1

"The right word spoken at the right time sometimes achieves miracles."

—Anonymous

It's the first of the month. *First* begins with *f*—the same as in *forward*. Move forward on the first. Now, there's a theme for the day!

Sometimes that's all you need to get going—a little word-key, or mantra, that you say to yourself; it possesses such force of energy that it pushes you out of your chair, makes you pull the running shoes out of the closet, and stirs you into action.

No one else hears it or knows it. You say it softly to yourself, yet it is powerful enough to drive you out into the street and set your legs a-churning. Sometimes the word-key is even useful while you're running. As you begin to tire, you recite it to yourself and find new spring in your legs.

Move forward on the first. If it works, use it. If not, use something else. The important thing is not the mantra but the action it engenders.

Perhaps you think it's silly. It's cheerleading, you say. Who needs it?

Perhaps not you. What do you use, then? There has to be something—some mental process that knocks over the internal trip wire that launches you onto the roads. Maybe it's the idea of health, or energy, or power. Whatever it is, whatever gets you going, grab onto it and use it.

Today's the first. When you run, you move forward. What better word-key than to combine the two?

Resolved: I move forward on the first!

October 2

Bill Cosby tells a story about his son, who was having trouble with his homework. He'd start on it but soon grow bored with it and put it down. After a while he'd come back to it again. But boredom would descend, and his interest would waiver anew. Finally his dad offered some advice:

"A jet plane burns its greatest energy taking off, but once it reaches its cruising altitude, it burns less fuel," Cosby said. "If you're constantly taking off and landing, you're going to burn more fuel as opposed to taking off and staying up there and maintaining that altitude."

This is wonderful advice for students as well as runners, dieters, writers, building contractors, and anyone else working on a project that requires big chunks of time. Constantly starting and stopping only wastes precious energy and resources.

People tend to jump into a new project with lots of enthusiasm and energy. But when it doesn't admit to an easy, quick solution, they grow disenchanted with it.

See your big job as a series of small jobs. That will help boil it down to a manageable size. Then get started on it. Once you start, find a rhythm and pace that's comfortable for you—in Cosby's terms, your "cruising altitude." Once you do that, you will have more energy and be less prone to wasteful stops and starts.

Resolved: I avoid the tendency to start and stop and settle into a good cruising altitude when I run.

October 3

Jeff Galloway, the runner and writer, offers a nice suggestion to normally solitary runners: go on a group run at least once a week.

Group running offers lots of advantages: For one, you're not alone. There's safety in a pack. You can go almost anywhere, at any time. Another advantage is that you have lots of potential conversation partners. When you get bored talking to one, you can move on to someone else. One never lacks for conversational diversity in a group run.

Group running can be as competitive or as noncompetitive as you like. A few of the members can push the pace if they feel so inspired. If you're not one of them, you can hang back with the easy gliders. The entire lot of you can meet up again later in the run or at Sam's Place, where you're having brunch afterward.

When you're lacking motivation, as Galloway suggests, the group energy will pull you along. Almost certainly someone in the group will have a good joke or story that will brighten the morning.

Group running requires more planning than going solo. But it offers its own distinctive pleasures. Nowadays there's a big herd of runners in almost every community across the land. Go run with the herd, and reap the rewards.

Resolved: I call up some friends and do a little group running for a change.

October 4

"If individuals can get into the habit of starting workouts at a certain time every day, they will accept them as part of the regular daily schedule. Exercise will become habitual and the day won't seem complete without it."

—Barry Franklin, exercise physiologist

Check out your schedule for today. How does it look? Pretty bad, huh? No time to run? Oh well, what about tomorrow?

What's that, you're afraid to look? Go ahead; it's all right. You never know: you could get lucky. Yikes, it's even worse tomorrow?

You say you've got some time a week from Thursday, in the late afternoon? Well, that's a hopeful sign. Put it down. Once it's on the schedule, it's inviolate. No one can move you off it. Cast in concrete, you bet. Uh-oh, is that the phone? Better get it. Sure, I'll wait.

So, who was on the line? A client? What's up? What? What do you mean you can't run next Thursday? Are you sure that's the only time he could get together? Oh man, when are you ever going to run?

OK, I know. It happens. But have you ever thought of dropping something out of the schedule to make a little room for running? That maybe everything isn't so important after all, and that maybe you could uncomplicate your schedule—and life?

All right, all right. Don't get excited. It was just a thought. What about the third Wednesday of next month, around midnight? What, you're busy? OK then, how 'bout . . .

Resolved: I think about dropping something from my schedule to make time for running.

October 5

"Running is a kind of play. When you are moving well, you feel like a spectator enjoying this movement of your own. If there is a great crowd with you, you are moved."

—Joshua Kimeto, runner

Want to be moved? First pick up a running magazine and flip to the calendar section. You'll find dozens and dozens of races that a person could enter in any one month.

For those who want to go the distance, there is the New Hampshire Marathon in Bristol, among several marathons set for this month. The Pumpkin 5-Mile in Doylestown, Pennsylvania, is one of many pumpkin-themed races. Additionally there are races with a fall or harvest theme: Fall Classic 5K, Harvest Run 5-Mile, Apple Harvest 5-Mile, Fall Foliage 5K, and Harvard Pilgrim 5K.

For runners who like to dress up, Halloween races—Trick or Trot 5K, Monster Dash 5K, Halloween Hustle 10K, Beaches Halloween 5K—are always a possibility. Runners with a less frivolous bent might want to enter a race with a good cause, such as Run for the Children 10K, Rebuild the Family 5K, Iowa City Hospice Races, and Run Against Cancer 5K.

If you're a fan of reggae music, there's the Reggae Run 5K in Cincinnati, and many races in a natural or outdoorsy setting: the Humboldt Redwoods Marathon, Run with Nature 10K, and Signal Mountain 6.8 Mile.

It's fun flipping through a calendar and looking at all these races. Even imagining yourself jumping onto a plane and showing up at, say, the Cuyamaca Ride & Tie or the Autumn Woods 10K. So, what's stopping you?

Resolved: I flip through the pages of a running calendar and pick out a race I'd like to run over the fall or winter.

October 6

It's amazing how many runners enter races without knowing
a thing about the event itself. A friend calls up out of the blue
and says, "Hey, I'm running in the Pumpkin Patch 10K on Saturday. Wanna come? It'll be a kick." The runner on the other
end of the line thinks about it for a moment before replying,
"All right. What the heck. Sounds like fun."

Her enthusiasm is to be commended. With energy and
enthusiasm, a person can do almost anything. But a little
knowledge isn't a bad thing, either.

What's the course like? Are there any hills? How many
runners will there be? How many aid stations? How far is 10
kilometers anyway? It doesn't hurt to collect a little data about
an event before you enter it. This will help you answer an
even more fundamental question: Am I ready for this?

Longtime runners, not just novices, would do well to heed
this advice. Every race is different, as Bill Rodgers and others
have noted. The more you know, the better off you are. Good
runners are always learning. They often drive a course prior
to running it, so they're familiar with the twists and turns.

Keep that enthusiasm alive. It's a good thing. Couple it with
a little knowledge, and you'll be unbeatable.

Resolved: If there's time, I do some homework about the
course and the event before I run it.

October 7

"Brains are the only things worth having in this world, no matter whether one is a crow or a man."

—The Scarecrow, from *The Wizard of Oz* by L. Frank Baum

The Scarecrow, as is well known, had no brains, so he didn't have enough sense to avoid the holes on the Yellow Brick Road. When he walked, he always tripped and fell in the holes.

But since he was a scarecrow, after all—made not of flesh and bones but of straw—falling never hurt him. He'd get right up and not think twice about it. Wouldn't it be nice if runners were made of straw—no more bruised chins and scraped knees!

Then again, if having straw insides means giving up your brains, maybe that's not such a good idea. Brains are good things. Even a simple scarecrow can see that. What's more, brains are an unsurpassed motivational tool. (A great aphrodisiac, too.) When you're feeling low, they will get you up again. When you're in trouble, they will get you out of trouble. When you're losing, they will help you find a way to win. When you're stumbling in darkness, they will lead you to the light.

It's said that people use only a tiny percentage of their potential brainpower. Exploit your brains to the utmost, and you can go anywhere you want (to Kansas and beyond), although you still may encounter a few potholes along the way.

Resolved: I use my brains to find ways to motivate myself and stay fit.

October 8

Running is about friendships. Call up a friend, and go for a run together.

Running is about people. Call up a bunch of friends, and go for a group run.

Running is about nature. Get off the pavement, and run on a woodsy parkland trail.

Running is about sweat. After you work up a good one, take a long, exquisitely hot shower.

Running is about pleasure. Treat yourself to a tasty fruit shake after you run.

Running is about health. Run comfortably, without strain, and exercise the heart and lungs.

Running is about clearing your head. When you change into your running togs at the end of a long day, change your state of mind, too.

Running is about getting away from everything. Lay down your burdens and duties, at least for a while, and do something for yourself.

Running is about having fun, just as you did when you were a kid. Running around like crazy, feeling free.

Running is about lots of things besides how fast you run. Today leave your watch at home and get reacquainted with those other things.

Resolved: I leave my watch at home today when I run.

October 9

*"Athletics, because it enables one to move to a better state of
being, can be viewed as a branch of medicine, but one which
fortunately finds room for spontaneity, ingenuity, and judgment."*
—Paul Weiss, philosopher

You must show discipline in running—that's one of the hardest things about it. You must run regularly to receive the full benefits of it. But if you run every day (or close to it), you can't go all out. Your body won't take it. You must show restraint—not run too fast or too hard. Otherwise you'll risk injury.

There is that side of running—the one that requires discipline, will, self-restraint, constancy. But if you emphasize that side too much, you will kill your desire to run.

You've got to be willing to let go, too. Take all the "musts" and "shoulds" out of it. Running can't always be associated in your mind with obligation, duty, self-denial. It must feed your soul as well as your body. There has to be fun and pleasure in it. When you run, there has to be an element of play to it.

Fact is, you need both elements—play and work—to survive and thrive as a runner. In a word: balance.

Strike a balance when you run between freedom and control. What'd you do yesterday—work hard? Well, then, play a little today. Have you been goofing around the last few days? Well, maybe you need to do a little grinding today. Use your judgment, and always seek a balance.

Resolved: I strike a balance in my running between freedom and control.

October 10

"Training is my creativity. I wouldn't want a coach even if I could have one. The fun is in trying to figure things out for myself."
—Edward Epstein, runner

If your toilet backs up, you will probably need a plumber. If your car breaks down on the highway, you may need to call a tow truck. If you want to build an addition to your house, it's advisable to talk to a general contractor. (More than one, in fact.)

There are many events in life that require outside assistance. But running is not necessarily one of them. You can find the right answer on your own. You really can.

Listen to your friends. Listen to a coach (if you have one). Read the magazines and books. Watch other runners, and talk to them. Do all these things, and then unleash your natural creativity as a runner. Only this will bring lasting success.

What creativity, you ask? It's there. It may be buried or need a good feather dusting due to lack of use. But it's there. If you've got a goal, you have what it takes to reach it. Call it natural creativity, call it resourcefulness, call it whatever you want. But you've got it.

You may not be an expert runner. But you are an expert on one topic: you. Go back to that seemingly intractable problem. The solution is there. Unleash your natural creativity on it, and you will find it.

Resolved: I unleash my natural creativity on my running and find my way out of any situation.

October 11

Consider the passion of one Luis Jorge Obando Ramirez of Colombia. He once ran 5,000 miles up through South and Central America to appear at the New York Marathon.

Beginning in June in his hometown of Bogotá, Ramirez left with $800 in his backpack and a ton of desire. He needed every ounce of it—and more. In Costa Rica, insects attacked him. Rain in Central America came down so hard at times that he could not see between the drops.

When he reached Mexico, authorities gave him a 30-day visa, forcing him to turn in 75-mile days to make it across the border before his time expired. He passed into Laredo and on to Houston, where an aching calf sat him down for four days in September.

In the United States Ramirez often ran all day and spent his nights in the jail of the town where he stayed. Without money, that was the only place that would put him up for the night. He wore out five pairs of running shoes on his five-month-long run. "Many times I wondered if I'd make it," confessed Ramirez. But he did. And after all that, he completed the marathon in 3 hours, 15 minutes, and 53 seconds. Then he flew home and slept for a very long time.

Next time you get tired, next time you feel like quitting, remember Luis Ramirez—and keep on trucking.

Resolved: I keep running; I keep plugging away.

October 12

*"Perhaps the most valuable result of all education is the ability
to make yourself do the thing you have to do when it ought to
be done whether you like it or not."*

—Thomas Huxley, biologist

It's not unpatriotic to admit that there may be a thing or two
about running that you don't like. It doesn't matter how many
times you do it, you still don't care for it. And yet, you know
that this thing is good for you or needs to be done.

So, do it. Quit squawking, quit procrastinating, quit paint-
ing your toenails, quit finding other things to do that help
you forget this one objectionable thing. Go out and get it done.
The quickest way to get rid of a thing you don't like, but know
you have to do, is to do it. There's no other answer. You can't
wish or hope it away. It's there, in all its ugly eminence, like
the proverbial 800-pound gorilla in the living room.

Maybe you hate running in races, even though you realize
the competition is good for you. Maybe you hate running on
a track, even though you can see the results when you do.
Maybe you simply hate getting up in the morning to run.

Don't go crazy about this. Don't do hateful things to spite
yourself. If you really have deep-seated dislikes about a certain
thing in running (or about running in general), maybe you
ought to take up another hobby, like model boat building or
embroidery. But if it's a manageable thing—a simple thing you
dislike from time to time but know you need to do—here's
how to make your life instantly easier: do it. Then forget
about it.

Resolved: I do the thing I know I need to do in running, even
though I may not like it. Then I leave it alone.

October 13

"Nature takes care of us. Time heals most of the damage done in the marathon."

—Dr. David Costil, who has studied the impact of running on the body

Runners compete against time in a race, but after the race is over, time becomes their ally.

Time allows you to heal. You have spent two or three hours or more breaking down your body. Time gives you the opportunity to build your body up again.

To be a runner, you must know how to wait, for after a race, waiting is a necessity. You must wait before entering another race. Your body demands it.

Sometimes this is a struggle. You love to run, you love the charge you get out of it, and you want to get back into it as quickly as you can. Proceed with caution. Running is a matter of learning about your body, and one aspect of that is knowing how long your body needs to rest between exertions.

Is it possible to rest too long? One supposes, but most runners make the opposite mistake of coming back too fast. One of the most difficult times for a runner is the period after an injury in which he or she has recovered enough to feel like running again. If you come back too fast, you can aggravate the injury and delay your recovery.

Take today off. Take tomorrow off. Let time work its magic for you.

Resolved: I give it a rest today.

October 14

"I cried twice out there. It was beautiful. The people all along the way, standing there, cheering, yelling to you. I couldn't help myself. I cried twice."

—Walt Ganty, running at Boston

Runners often have emotional reactions when they participate in a race. Spectators, too. They break down at the finish, just completely exhausted and happy, and tears spring forth as if from an underground spring.

It's a tremendous release (and relief). People are often understandably and justifiably overwhelmed by what they've accomplished. They've worked so hard, for so long, to achieve this goal—and now they've done it. They can finally let go.

Sometimes the tears aren't directly related to running, but rather to an unresolved issue in the person's life. Perhaps a runner is in mourning over the loss of a loved one. She expends so much energy in the race, her barriers come down. This allows her to release her emotions and possibly even to let the healing begin.

There are lots of ways in which people find emotional release in their lives. Through church, through therapy. Others find the release they so need by a simple, solitary run through the woods at dawn.

Whatever it is you're hanging on to, whatever weighs you down emotionally, whatever touches your heart with sadness, running can help you with it. Run, and let it go.

Resolved: I run and let it go. I just let it go.

October 15

"In running, you're successful just by doing it. You learn how far you can take yourself and how to compete within yourself. When you do that, you start feeling good about yourself."
—Sue Stricklin, runner

Want to feel good about yourself? Want to feel better than you do now? Well, then, put down this book and go for a run.

All the talk about the benefits of running boils down to one essential thought: it makes you feel better. Who can say, really, whether running prolongs a person's life? But it certainly does improve the quality. If you feel lousy, it will make you feel good. If you feel good, it will make you feel great. Don't you want to feel good, or even great, today? Go out and run, and you've got a shot at it.

In what other areas of life can you make such a claim? Eat a bowl of ice cream, and you will feel great while you're in the middle of it, but after a while those chocolate scoops will begin to sit like rocks in your stomach. If you have a glass of Bordeaux, it will taste lovely and give you a little buzz—before the inevitable letdown, that is. There's even a letdown after great sex.

But what's the downside to running? If you were told that you could do something that would instantly make you feel better than you do now, wouldn't you at least consider it? Well, consider this: a nice gentle run around the park will do exactly that. Absolutely guaranteed.

Resolved: I go for a run—and feel great.

October 16

"I don't think they give any awards for workouts. To the best of my knowledge, there are no gold medals for 'Most Mileage.'"
—Craig Virgin, three-time Olympian

When you run, you need to keep time in perspective. If your only focus is going faster—getting a better time—you're going to miss much of the pleasure that derives from running.

It's the same with distance. It's natural to keep tabs on how much you run, but never let that take precedence over how you feel. As Virgin says, they don't give medals for mileage.

Some runners affix mystical qualities to certain distances—say, 100 miles a week. But Virgin never thought there was anything special in that number. If he ran 98 miles in a week and felt satisfied, he stopped right there. He didn't run 100 miles just for the sake of doing it.

Other runners not in Virgin's class fall into a similar trap. For example, if they've run 18 miles in a week, they'll make the extra effort to reach 20. Or if they've run 27 miles, they'll make the push to reach an even 30. It puts them in a different category, they think; it raises them to a more exalted level.

Stick to how you feel. Stay in tune with that. If you feel satisfied with yourself, the numbers will take care of themselves.

Resolved: I run to feel satisfied and let my mileage take care of itself.

October 17

"In all experience there is the consciousness of something which lies deeper than experience."

—John Lancaster Spalding, writer

Experience is the best teacher. The longer you do a thing, the more you know. And the more you know, the better off you are.

That's what the experts say, and there is a ring of truth to it. Someone who has been running for five years knows more about himself and his capabilities than someone who just started.

Still, it is possible to know a thing so well that you don't know it at all. You've been doing it so long that you've become tired and cynical. You know all the angles—or think you do—and you've stopped growing.

It's always good to retain a little naïveté about running. When you're a little innocent, you still have that childlike enthusiasm and energy. It still seems fresh. You don't know it all, nor do you pretend to. You're still learning. In fact, you're jazzed about how much there is to learn, even though you've been running for years and years.

Experience is a great teacher. But innocence teaches, too. When you're new to a thing, you are drawn to the feeling it excites in you. Experience gives knowledge, which tends to create distance from that feeling. Never become so knowledgeable in running that you outgrow its joys, its pleasures, its innocent dreams.

Resolved: I never outgrow the innocent pleasures of a run through the park.

October 18

"There is nothing so easy to learn as experience and nothing so hard to apply."

—Josh Bilings, writer

Wouldn't you agree that it's almost always harder to do something the first time? Whether it's running a marathon, writing a novel, performing a play, building a house, or anything else you can name, the first time you do it is usually the hardest.

You're working out the kinks, feeling your way as you go forward. There is inevitably wasted motion, wasted effort. You're learning, and that always involves bobbles and stumbles. The second time around, it's usually much easier. You put that knowledge you gained to use. You're more efficient and more relaxed. You've done it before, so you know what to expect. You can handle surprises in stride.

Why, then, would you stop running marathons (or 5Ks or 10Ks or Ride and Ties) after just one? You can benefit from the lessons you learned that first time only if you do it a second time.

Never be a one-time-only runner. Even before you run a marathon, allow for the possibility that you might do it again. Doing it a second time helps you consolidate your gains and improve, transforming what was a difficult thing into a more manageable one. (Running a marathon is never "easy.") And telling yourself before the race that this is not the only time you're going to do it, that you're coming back again, will ease the pressure on you.

Resolved: I never settle for once in running. I always do it twice.

October 19

"Life is a desperate struggle to succeed in being in fact that which we are in design."

—José Ortega y Gasset, philosopher

There's more stress on you than ever before. You're being challenged in ways you've never been—in virtually all areas of your life.

Know that you can respond to the challenge.

You've never been busier at work. You know that it represents an incredible opportunity, but there are lots of stresses that come with it.

Know that you can respond to the challenge.

Your home life is in an uproar, as usual. Everyone is healthy (thank God), but there are plenty of other "issues" to deal with. Because these issues involve other people and their perceptions, it's pretty sticky stuff.

Know that you can respond to the challenge.

Perhaps because it's your way of coping with these stresses, you're running more than you ever have before. Really pounding out the miles. Running is the one area of your life in which there are clear-cut victories and losses, tangible benefits, and undiluted pleasures. You run, it makes you feel good, and so you run some more.

Know that you can respond to every challenge. The stresses in your life aren't going away; in fact, they'll probably only get worse. But you *can* handle them. Keep after it. You can become the person you want to be.

Resolved: I keep after it, knowing that I can respond to all the challenges in my life: at work, at home, and in running.

October 20

"Enjoy it, because you never know when it's all going to be taken away."

—Michael Jordan

Do you enjoy running? No? Well, then, why the heck are you doing it?

Stop right this minute. Throw those running shoes into the trash. Burn your shorts and socks and overpriced jogging suit. Cancel your subscription to *Runner's World.* There's no point to any of it.

So what if you just won a trophy in the Poughkeepsie 10K. Nice going, but awards mean little if they are not accompanied by joy.

Enjoy, enjoy, enjoy. Each moment, to the fullest. That's the best running motto. Why, what's a better one? Punish yourself, risk injury, collect plaques?

You know that feeling you get when you run? Pursue it. Go where that feeling takes you. Within that feeling lies your potential as a runner.

And when you have that feeling—that "runner's high," as it's called—appreciate it, cherish it, worship it. Even though it passes quickly—sometimes in the blink of an eye—its impact ultimately lasts far longer than any of the trophies or ribbons or awards you will ever collect.

Resolved: Today, when I run, I enjoy each moment. To the fullest.

October 21

"The best athletes display a gift for control. Their success depends upon bending—but not breaking—the body to their will."

—Kenny Moore, marathoner and writer

Some years ago, when Tom Landry was coaching the Dallas Cowboys, he referred to the Cleveland Browns as a "rubber band" defense. "They bend, but they don't break," said the gruff Texan.

Landry meant it as a compliment, but Browns fans were outraged. They saw it as an attack on their team's—this is football, remember—power and toughness.

Most runners would agree with Landry, however, for "bending, not breaking" is what they aspire to do. In fact, having a mental image of a rubber band is not a bad one for runners.

"Bending" might be defined as going as far as you can go without going over your limits. When you go over your limits, you know it right away because injury is often the result. Injury stops you, which is something you don't want to have happen. You want to keep going, keep improving, keep learning. Only by running do you continue to progress. But the progress must be gradual and incremental, and that's where the ability to stay in control comes into play. Discipline is crucial.

In simple terms, it's a push-pull kind of thing. Learn the limits of how far you can push your body before you need to pull back, always staying within yourself.

Resolved: Like the Cleveland Browns of old, I bend but never break as a runner.

October 22

"Thirty miles a week automatically gets me into inner harmony."
—George Sheehan, philosopher-runner

We all lead busy lives full of distractions. It's hard to concentrate on any one thing for long. As soon we focus on one thing, something else grabs our attention.

To a certain extent, this is understandable. No one is fully in charge of his or her life. Interruptions are inevitable whether you're at work or at home with family.

Running is almost unique in that it provides solitary, uninterrupted time. When you go for a run, there is an unbroken span of time in which you can think, sort out the problems of the day, and steady yourself. When you return to the world of everyday concerns, you feel stronger and calmer.

What's also great is that you can begin a run wrestling with a problem in your mind, and, by the end, find a solution for it or at least feel better about your ability to manage it. You return with a feeling that, whatever happens to you or your family, you can cope with it. Your problems don't seem quite so overwhelming. Running gives you a better perspective in looking at your life and puts it more in balance somehow.

Chances are you will not be retiring to a Buddhist monastery anytime soon. But a run today will enable you to make a kind of peace with yourself and your world, if only for a while.

Resolved: I seek some inner harmony this afternoon. I go for a run.

October 23

"Only two rules really count: never miss an opportunity to relieve yourself; and never miss a chance to rest your feet."

—Duke of Windsor

The aristocratic Duke was talking about how to survive the English social whirl, not succeed at running, but his advice applies all the same. There are only two important rules of road racing, and he hit on both of them: never pass up an opportunity to relieve yourself, and always rest when you get a chance.

First things first. No one ever feels like running if other things are weighing on his or her mind—or bladder, as the case may be. In this regard men have a distinct advantage over women runners, for they can drop trou far more easily.

You see this in evidence prior to a running race. There are long lines of anxious women waiting for the next portable toilet to open up. While men also use these facilities, they have other options—namely, the trees and bushes. Go into the bushes near the start of any road race, and you will find men (and an occasional desperate woman) obtaining comfort at last.

Before a race, runners are generally too nervous to sit down; but by the end (and sometimes during) they relax enough to heed the Duke's second rule: find a place to rest. Some runners have no choice; they simply must lie or sit down afterward.

Remember the Duke's immortal advice: relieve yourself when the opportunity presents itself, and sit down frequently. These are the keys to a happy and well-balanced running life.

Resolved: I never miss an opportunity to relieve myself before I run and to sit down afterward.

October 24

"Real freedom begins deep down in the consciousness of the individual. It is the stuff of variation and growth, the fuel of life."

—Holbrook Jackson, philosopher

It's time; that's all. It's just time.

Time to get away from the phone. It's been ringing off the hook, driving you nuts.

Time to push away from the desk. You sit there so much that you can almost feel body parts spreading.

Time to shut down the PC. They say it's a labor-saving device, but you always seem to have too much to do.

Time to bid a temporary adieu to your coworkers. They're a great group, all right, but you see them more than you see your own family, and that's enough.

Time to escape from the office. It's stuffy and claustrophobic and dominates your life as it is.

Time to let go of demands and responsibilities, if only for a while. Don't worry: they'll be waiting for you when you return.

Most important perhaps, time to get away from the feeling that time is always sitting on you like a big weight, pressing you down.

Time to be free. Time to get away and run.

Resolved: You're right. It's time. I'm going for a run.

October 25

"Now is the time of illuminated woods. Every leaf glows like a tiny lamp; one walks through their lighted halls with a curious enjoyment."

—John Burroughs, writer

Do they call it "fall" because that's when the leaves fall from the trees? Ah, just a thought. Anyhow, it's happening again—this annual vibrant shedding of foliage—and how wonderful it is.

The leaves have turned and are turning, and now they're scattered across the trail like torn pieces of gray and black and orange and red paper. Some are pressed into the soil, already returning to their native earth. As you run, you see the leaves actually dropping from the trees. The wind comes up, and a dozen flutter to the ground.

City runners, not just trail runners, experience these sights, too. They watch as the leaves of their favorite trees turn orange and red and drop to the ground, scattering across the sidewalks and streets before brooms and sweepers whisk them away.

In the fall the trees lose the leaves they formed in spring. In spring they return. Because you run, you feel a part of this natural cycle of things. You feel a certain humility, and awe, when you witness it. It's like when you were a kid walking home from school. You'd find a leaf on the sidewalk and take it home to press it between the pages of a book. It was magical, as if you'd somehow captured a ray of light.

Resolved: When I run, I feel the satisfying crunch of leaves underfoot.

October 26

"Running should be viewed as a wonder drug. It has profound potential in preventing disease and in rehabilitation after various illnesses. However, just like other wonder drugs, it has the potential for abuse."

—William P. Morgan, Ed.D.

You have easy days and hard days when you run. But unfortunately, there's a tendency among some runners to see only the hard days as beneficial to them.

When they've worked hard, when they've really logged some serious miles—that's when they feel good about themselves. This in part leads them to abuse their bodies. If they'd take it easy for a day or two and lighten up on the self-recriminations, they'd be a lot better off.

In a way, this view is almost puritanical: only through hard work do we obtain virtue. But in running and athletics, that's simply not true. Your easy days are often just as productive as your hard ones.

When you have an easy day, take advantage of it. Enjoy it. See it as a mental and physical break—one that's probably long overdue. Use it as a way to lift your spirits and get out of your usual rut. Maybe you run five miles normally. Well, today run two instead. It's not sloughing off; you're giving your physical *and* mental muscles a rest, and that's important.

Cotton Mather has been dead for hundreds of years. Do yourself a favor, and lighten up. You'll be amazed how good it will feel.

Resolved: I take it nice and easy today and enjoy the break.

October 27

Endings mean a lot. If you finish a run strong, you may feel good about what you did even though the time isn't the best.

A good ending can salvage an otherwise mediocre performance. You may not have it the first 10 or so miles of a half-marathon. Then something kicks into gear the last mile or two, and what was previously a strain now becomes pure, effortless joy.

A good ending provides hope. It makes you think you can do better, much better. Look how strong you were at the end! It gives you the feeling that there's more there, that you haven't exhausted your potential, and that you can run faster or longer or both.

It doesn't make sense to save up your energy for a boffo ending. To put together a complete race, you need a solid start and middle, too. That's the best running strategy. But it can't hurt—and it may do some good—to give a little extra at the end.

There's a natural tendency to do that anyway, whether you're in a race or on a Sunday-afternoon run. Sensing the end, you pick up the pace a little. We all love to finish with a flourish.

Take that natural tendency and seize upon it: be a strong finisher. Even if you've given everything over the entire course, give a little bit more. It's there. Reach for it. It's amazing what we discover when we press ourselves.

Resolved: I give a little extra at the end and finish with a flourish.

October 28

"Breathing is like ethereal drinking. It is a luxury simply to exist."

—Henry Ward Beecher, writer

Breath is life. Life is breath.

If you have any doubts about the truth of those two sentences, stop breathing for a moment. Life ends when breath ceases.

Books, philosophies, branches of religion have centered on the miracle of breath. It's everything. All of a person's life is contained in a single breath. Breath is the key to physical vitality and a gateway to the spirit.

When a baby is born, what characterizes him or her as living, as having entered the world, is breath. If the child is breathing, the child has entered. The newborn is alive.

A baby boy breathes his first; an old man breathes his last. Every person on Earth is sustained by the air we breathe. It is one of the things that unites us all. It's said that few people really exercise their lungs when they breathe. They breathe shallowly as a rule, never exercising their full capacities. They take the gift of breath for granted.

Not runners. They know its sacred importance. Every time they run, they experience the value of deep, truly cleansing breaths that fully engage the lungs and heart. It is one of the joys of the sport.

Live life, breathe deep, and run.

Resolved: I go for a run today and take some deep, truly cleansing breaths of air.

October 29

"Nobody running at full speed has either a head or a heart."
—W. B. Yeats

You're a buzz saw of activity. You've got more balls in the air than a Cirque du Soleil juggler. No one can keep up with you. You can barely keep up with yourself.

Slow down, and run.

Moving faster than the speed of light is sometimes necessary in this hyperdrive, warp-speed world of ours. But it's madness to fly at those speeds all the time. Eventually the heat-reflecting shields of your personal spaceship will crack under the pressure, catch fire, and blow up, hurtling you into the void.

OK, so I got carried away. But you get the idea: you've got to get some sanity, some perspective, in your life. Running will help you do it.

Running helps you reset your internal clock. It slows your bodily mechanisms down even as it supplies them with more energy. Maybe you're wired from coffee and a lack of sleep and thoughts of all the things you've got to do today. Running restores your body—and mind—to a semblance of balance or at least sets the process in motion.

Just the fact that you are taking an hour out of your schedule to run—this alone—teaches an instructive lesson to your mind and body. Sometimes speed equates with efficiency. But sometimes not. When you jump back into the swift-running current of your schedule after taking time for a run, you will work more efficiently and possibly enjoy it more.

Resolved: I slow down today and run.

October 30

"In the deep of the night, lying on my back, I ask myself what life is and I see that I do not know; but I also see that it is a royal thing to be alive."

—C. F. Ramuz, philosopher

It is indeed a royal thing to be alive—and to be a runner at that. When you're a long-distance runner, the whole world opens up to you. You can:

Run for a bus as it's pulling away from the stop and reach it in time to get on.

Run after your lover after saying something that you regret and apologize before he or she gets away.

Run to a gas station if your car runs out of gas. (Thanks to Bill Rodgers for that one.)

Run and beat someone to a cab after you both hailed it at the same time.

Run from an angry rottweiler.

Run outside and jump into the getaway car after robbing a bank. (This is not recommended for all.)

Run into the backyard and over the fence when a creditor appears at your front door.

Run up the steps when the elevator at the mall breaks down.

Run down the corridor when the passenger-conveyor system at the airport malfunctions.

Run to the front door to receive your million-dollar winner's check from Publishers Clearing House.

Resolved: I always run after my lover to apologize if I've said something hurtful.

October 31

"Running is not a religion. It is, however, a way of becoming an adult."

—George Sheehan, philosopher-runner

Yes, but not today. Today's Halloween. Tomorrow you can return to being a sober-minded adult.

The origins of All Hallows' Eve date back to medieval times, to a Celtic rite associated with the beginning of winter. In certain parts of the British Isles, people lit bonfires in the countryside and told stories about witches, goblins, and ghosts. Nowadays, of course, runners have jumped into the rite with both feet.

Lots of clubs organize Halloween runs. Throw on a costume, and go for it. It's a kick. Or call a bunch of friends, and dress up on your own. Scare the neighbor kids as you jog by.

Some runners are more social and don't like always doing it alone. Well, here's your chance to mix with other people who, like you, may take a more relaxed approach to the sport. (Although certainly lots of red-hot runners like to dress up on Halloween, too.)

Running is not finding a cure for cancer, after all. There's no reason to take it so seriously. Anyway, how can you not crack a smile when Herman Munster is running next to you?

The appeal of Halloween is much the same as that for Mardi Gras: it's a chance for people to take on identities other than their own. For runners, it's a chance to have a little crazy fun. What's the harm in that?

Resolved: I have a little crazy fun. I put on a costume and go for a Halloween run.

November 1

"There is something healthy and invigorating about direct action."

—Henry Miller, writer

It's November 1, the first day of the penultimate month of the year. Time is running out. Winter is on its way. Get off your duff, and get going.

What, you wanted subtlety? Subtlety, schmutlety. Sometimes what a person needs is a good, stiff kick in the rear, and this is it. Ouch!

Don't stew, don't fret, don't pine, don't try to work it into your schedule. Just get out of bed, and get going. Or if you're at work, unstick yourself from that chair, pull yourself away from that game of computer chess you're playing, and go.

You may be thinking, "This is boot camp stuff. I'm not being subtly guided toward my divine inner light. I'm not learning about the yin and yang of running here. This is like when my high-school coaches used to get in my face, yelling at me to dress for P.E."

Yeah. You got a problem with that?

Enough subtlety. Enough gentle coaxing. Enough yin and yang. There comes a time, and you've reached it. Get off yer butt, and get going.

Resolved: Ok already. But do you have to be so . . . abrupt? I get off my duff and run.

November 2

"Who promised love should be happiness? Nature may have some other end."

—Mark Rutherford, poet

You can't keep it inside you; you have to let it go. If you keep it inside, it will tear you up.

Sometimes it seems as if loss defines life. Certainly it's part of it, but it's not all of it. Joy is a part of it, too, a big part.

Though it may not seem like that right now. You're upset, angry, shocked. Those are all understandable emotions. You have a right to feel the way you do. What happened is unfair; it's not right.

But he's not coming back. No matter what you do, he's gone for good.

Go for a run. That will help a little bit, though of course it won't change the situation. But while you're running, you'll be able to think. Or maybe you won't think about it at all, which might be the best thing that could happen to you right now.

You'll always miss him. That will never change. But you will get better, and life will go on. Loss is part of life, to be sure. But joy is part of it, too. And running will help you find it again.

Resolved: I go for a run and don't think about him for a while.

November 3

"The richness and rightness of our spiritual vision depends largely upon the keenness and careful use of our eyes."
—Charles-Damian Boulogne, philosopher

Ever watch a cat at rest? He's a picture of relaxation, all stretchy and sleepy on his blanket on the couch. He can barely open his eyes, as if his eyelids have weights on them. If there's a slight disturbance in the room, he might open his eyes halfway to see what it is, before letting them wearily fall shut again.

Let a child's pet rat come into the room, however, and watch this same cat respond. His eyes get big as saucers. The rat is prey, and its presence touches something deep inside the cat, something primal and instinctive. The languor vanishes; he's all eyes, and they're fixed on one object only. He sees nothing but the rat; he can think of nothing else. His senses have been vitalized.

The same thing happens to people when they run. Before a run, you feel like that sleeping cat. You can barely keep your eyes open; they're tired and droopy. Then the rat enters the room—that is, you run—and your senses are vitalized.

Your dopiness and fatigue are blown away in an instant. That's why some people don't like to run in the evening; it wakes them up so much that they can't sleep. You're suddenly awake and buzzing, and your eyes are no longer weary. They're sharp and as wide open as the cat's. You feel vital and full of energy, as if something deep within you—something primal and ancestral—has been stirred to life.

Resolved: I run today and feel as clear-eyed as a cat eyeing its prey.

November 4

"Genius is just another way of looking at things."

—William James, philosopher

Fascinating stories are told about Morihei Ueshiba, the founder of the martial art of aikido.

It was said that the diminutive Ueshiba could disarm any attacker, put 10 opponents on their backs simultaneously, and pin them without ever laying a finger on them. This isn't comic-book stuff; these things all supposedly happened, according to aikido followers.

Ueshiba did not overpower his opponents physically; he converted and deflected their hostile energy, using it against themselves. He did not butt heads with his opponents; that would have brought him down to their level and methods and thus would have defeated him. He developed techniques to mentally sidestep his opponents and wrap them in their own energy, as if tying them up with an invisible rope.

Today, use a little of Ueshiba's methods to give you the space to run.

Make time work for you, not against you. See your obligations not as interfering with your running but as motivations for it. Simplify every complication; sidestep every potential conflict. Disarm opponents without butting heads; turn their energy against themselves and free yourself, thus giving yourself plenty of time to run.

Resolved: I convert any negative energy today and allow myself plenty of time to run.

November 5

"The moment we pass out of our habits, we lose all sense of permanency and routine."

—George Moore, philosopher

Running is daily; it's ongoing. It's a habit that provides a sense of permanency to our lives. That's one of its chief appeals.

Have you ever had anyone (a nonrunner, naturally) express disbelief at what you do? "Geez," he will say, "I don't see how you do it. Every day, you run. That's amazing."

Amazing? Runners would use a variety of words to describe what they do, but that is probably not one of them. What they do is, well, *what they do*. There's no mystique to it. There's nothing superhuman about it. It's what runners do; that's all. It's like what astronaut Jim Lovell said after the United States landed a man on the Moon: "It wasn't a miracle. We just did it."

Same with you and all those miles you've logged over the years. It wasn't a miracle; you just did it. And you're still doing it. You lace up the shoes—those beautiful, beat-up shoes—you throw on a pair of shorts or sweats, you open the front door, and off you go.

Other people may see that as amazing. But you're not one of them. In fact, that may be why those other people don't run and you do. They see it as some strange and exotic activity that requires amazing powers. But it's just running; that's all.

Today, do what you do. And let other people react in wonder.

Resolved: I keep doing it; I keep ticking off the miles.

November 6

"An old lady said to me the other day that she had set too much value all her life on positive obligation. I am going to begin to practice a little negative obligation, and boldly say there are things I can't do."

—A. C. Benson, writer

Truly, what was ever accomplished in a meeting? It's a negative obligation if there ever was one. People talk and talk some more. When they're done talking, and sometimes even when they're not, everyone leaves, and the meeting is over.

Skip the meeting, and run. Meetings come and go. They're held every day of the year, in every office and workplace around the globe. If meetings are so important, why are they so routine? Almost every meeting is skippable.

Once a year, if you're lucky, you'll sit in a meeting in which something actually gets accomplished. Mostly everyone agrees to come back and discuss things later, postponing any decisions until the next meeting, when they are sure to avoid making any decisions again.

Some meetings start in daylight and end in darkness. Missing some all-day bore-a-thon with the boss is hardly the equivalent of turning down a ticket to see Ralph Fiennes play Hamlet. If you miss a meeting, you can always find out what went on from someone who was there. And there is sure to be another.

Meetings are seldom productive. Running, however, is always productive. Isn't it a law of business that nonproductive activities should give way to productive ones?

Anyhow, blow off the meeting today, and run.

Resolved: I skip the meeting and run.

November 7

"I changed my belief from an external focus—beating others—to an internal focus. My self-worth was based on doing my best. I would compete only with myself."

—Henry Marsh, steeplechaser

Henry Marsh is one of the world's greatest steeplechasers, but he was hardly great in his first years at BYU. He was pudgy and out of shape and bored with competing.

When he realized that running wasn't fun anymore, he quit. That lasted about two weeks. When he came back after this short hiatus, he decided to change his training habits, becoming, as he says, "something of a maverick."

He set his own workout schedules, he lost weight, he tried new things. He became a toe runner instead of a heel runner as he had always been. By trial and error he figured out what worked best for him, and he rapidly improved, nearly winning the NCAA steeplechase title and qualifying for the first of four U.S. Olympic teams.

The most important ingredient in his success was a change in attitude. "When I changed my belief, I changed my behavior," he says. His self-worth was no longer based on winning, but on doing his best. "I redefined my definition of winning—from beating others to getting the best out of myself."

Everyone can take a cue from Marsh. Define success based on what others are doing, and it will always be elusive to obtain. Define success based on your own goals and aspirations, and you may yet find it.

Resolved: I define success in running based on what I do, not on what others are doing.

November 8

It's over and done. There's nothing more you can do, except try to figure out the whys and wherefores. You did your best. You gave it everything you had. No one will ever accuse you of a lack of effort. Still, you came up short. Life is like that sometimes.

You've replayed it in your mind a hundred times. You've wondered to yourself, "What if I had done something different? Would that have produced a different result?" You'll never know. What happened happened. No one will ever be able to change it, certainly not you.

Maybe you were up for a new job. It came down to two candidates—you and someone else. Then you got the news: they picked the other person. What can you do? Well, one thing you can do is go out and run and put a little distance between you and the event. As you're running, you may realize that any company that misses the chance to hire you doesn't know what it's doing, and therefore you're better off without the job. It's a thought, anyhow.

Running won't change what happened. Nothing will. But after you run and put the event behind you, you will feel a little bit better, and that will help.

Resolved: I put it behind me, and I run.

November 9

"One of the most important factors is the ability to direct one's whole energies towards the fulfillment of a particular task."

—Field Marshal Erwin Rommel

You've set your mind on a particular task. It's important that you finish it. Keep your focus, and you will.

Imagine yourself at the end of the task. See the finish line in your mind's eye. You're almost there. Let nothing distract or impede you.

You're tired. You're ready to quit. You were ready to quit miles ago. In the beginning of the race you needed to keep your focus. It's even more true now that you're tired and approaching the end.

Do you realize how hard it is to concentrate on a single thing these days? And yet you've concentrated on this one thing for days, months, years. Here, today, is the culmination. You deserve so much credit. What you're doing is not easy to do.

And yet, it's not over. You must keep going, stay fixed on your goal. You must have the vision of an archer, narrowing her eyes as she draws back her bowstring. There can be nothing in her sights except that target.

Be like that archer. Even at this late date, there are distractions, things that can knock you off course. Ignore them. Stay true to yourself and your goal. That picture in your mind of you crossing the finish line? Keep your focus, and it will become a reality.

Resolved: Focus, focus, focus. I keep my focus and complete my goal.

November 10

"You can succeed by finishing last."

—Joe Henderson, runner and writer

You can learn a lot from a first-place finisher at a road race. But you can learn a lot from the last-place finisher, too.

The last-place finisher occasionally wins a ribbon or a prize. But that's not his primary motivation. For him, running is personal. Winners always get strokes for their accomplishments. The last-place finisher must find his satisfaction from within. Look at the extraordinary patience and endurance he shows. He's out on the course for hours . . . and hours . . . and hours. The race is usually packed up and put to bed long before he finishes, and yet finish he does.

Spectators applaud and cheer him—the ones who stick around, that is. But his tiny steps also cause some to jeer and laugh. He turns a deaf ear and keeps on running.

Younger, swifter runners fly by him. Cars honk at him to get out of the way. He suffers indignities that front-of-the-pack runners never experience. On he runs, undaunted. The last-place finisher is often elderly, a person who's been running a long, long time. Running makes him feel good, and he's going to keep doing it as long as he's healthy.

Anyone can finish first. Go to the head of the pack at a race and you will see all sorts of contenders (and pretenders). But it's a rare breed who can finish last with dignity. Note his facial expression when he finally crosses the line: you will see a picture of contentment to which every runner may aspire.

Resolved: I run with the indomitable patience of a last-place finisher.

November 11

"In our ever-more mechanized society, marathoners want to assert their independence and affirm their individuality. Call it humanism, call it health, call it folly. Whatever it is, our ailing world could use a lot more of it."

—Erich Segal, marathoner and novelist

It's Veterans Day, and today is a perfect day for a run, whether you're a veteran or not. Any day is a perfect day for a run, actually, but today especially. Today is set aside as a national holiday to honor the men and women who have fought and died for this country in our nation's wars.

Life, liberty, and the pursuit of happiness. It's still all about that. And if you're one of those benighted souls whose definition of happiness includes running, what better day to pursue it?

Running is an expression of freedom, an assertion of independence and individuality. For a very long time, long-distance runners were branded as crazy eccentrics. Only in the past two decades have the sport and its participants moved into the social mainstream. But running's essential nature remains unchanged. When you run, you separate yourself from the masses: you step away. This is an American quality.

People who run are often also passionate about self-improvement—another uniquely American characteristic.

It's a serious day, a day to take pause, but these are way too somber thoughts for a simple run. Go out today, and think a few thoughts of your own.

Resolved: In honor of Veterans Day, I run.

November 12

*"We nurse a fiction that people love to cover up their feelings,
but I have learned that if the feeling is real and deep they love
far better to find a way to uncover it."*

—David Grayson, writer

Let running take you somewhere today, whether it be to a
physical place, a state of mind, or an emotion. Let running
lead you there today, and follow it.

Follow it if it wants to take you to the top of that fire trail
you've passed so many times on your usual route. You've
always wondered where that trail goes. Well, today is the day
to find out.

Maybe there's a grand vista at the top of the trail or a lovely
grove of oak and pine. Maybe a red-shouldered hawk makes
its nest in the trees there. Maybe you'll surprise a doe and her
fawns feeding there. Or maybe there'll be nothing except a
bunch of tall grass and weeds and the trail winding off into
the distance. But that's something, isn't it? For a runner, a
long and winding road is an invitation.

More important even than knowing what's at the end of the
trail is the feeling that you're being responsive to whim. You're
indulging in the spirit of adventure, and that's fun in itself. In
what other areas of your life can you let that spirit guide you?

Resolved: Today I let running lead me wherever it wants
to go.

November 13

*"All day my mind has reached out and out. There are certain
days when one seems to have the strength of some gigantic
prehistoric monster. It has been so with me today."*

—Sherwood Anderson

Today: think Godzilla. There are some days when you're meek
as a church mouse. Today is not one of them. Look out, Fay
Wray. King Kong is coming to town.

You know the *T. rex* in *Jurassic Park*? You could send it
back to prehistoric times all by yourself. You feel so good, you
could give a whupping to Apollo Creed today.

If you were an ancient Greek warrior, you'd be Achilles.
Only without the wimpy heel. Achilles with good feet, that's
who you are today.

You're the king of the jungle, a lion with nerve. If you were
an eagle, you'd be bald. If you lived in the sea, you'd be a
sperm whale. If you were a snake, you'd be a cobra. If you
were a spider, you'd be a tarantula.

Nobody messes with you. You know that scene in *Taxi Dri-
ver* when Robert De Niro as Travis T. Bickle is talking to himself in front of the mirror? "You talkin' to me?" he says. "You
talkin' to me?" Nobody's talking to you today, not if they
know what's good for them.

If you were the leader of a Mongol horde, you'd be Genghis
Khan. If you were an Egyptian queen, you'd be Cleopatra. If
you were a writer, you'd be Milton. If you were a rapper, you'd
be Tupac. If you were a runner—wait a second: you *are* a runner. Well, then, just be yourself. But have a good time with it.
And be kind.

Resolved: Today when I run I think: Godzilla.

November 14

"I look at running as a good mental break. After a hard day at work, a good run always makes me feel much more centered and relaxed."

—Greg Barton, Olympic-gold-medal kayaker

Want to know how to end a hard day? Aw, you already know. You go for a run. Well, then, what's stopping you?

You know how it goes. You have a miserable day at work. You move from job to job, meeting to meeting, phone call to phone call, without ever pausing to breathe. In the five minutes you allow yourself for lunch, you gobble a banana and yogurt at your desk before you're besieged by yet another person making more demands on your time.

At the end of a day like that, there is a way to get straight. There is a way to clear your head. There is a way to quiet all the noise, at least for an evening, and obtain some rest and peace. It's a sweet irony: the body heals the mind. By moving your body, working up a sweat, and getting the heart and lungs expanding and contracting and expanding, you can achieve actual serenity, actual peace of mind.

But take it easy on yourself. You've killed yourself all day at work; now be nice to yourself for a change. Take a nice, easy run followed by a warm bath. Do that, and the next morning you may even have the energy to get up and fight the wars all over again.

Resolved: I take an easy run after a hard day at work.

November 15

"The great winds howl and swoop across the land: they make a distant roaring in great trees. All through the night there is the clean, the bitter rain of acorns, and the chestnut burrs are plopping to the ground."

—Thomas Wolfe

The bad weather is starting. Who knows, maybe it's already started in your part of the country.

The rain.

The cold.

The sleet.

The wind.

Heck, even the acorns and plopping chestnut burrs.

Not a pleasant prospect, is it? Winter is on its way. Whatever your feelings about this, however, it is likely that the weather hardly notices or cares. The weather will do what the weather will do, and there's very little that anyone can do about it.

Except, perhaps, maintain a good attitude. An attitude that whatever the weather is like this winter, you're going to keep running. That doesn't mean you run when it's 40 degrees below and storming. It just means that you make every effort to run, whenever you can.

Let the weather do what it will this winter. You keep running.

Resolved: Bad weather or no, I keep running in the coming months.

November 16

"A good rest is half the work."

—Yugoslav proverb

You've been banging and banging your head against that wall, and the wall never budges. And what do you have to show for it? A headache, that's all. Give it a rest, and run.

You're tired. You can hardly think. You've put in a hard day's (week's) work, way more than your share. Tomorrow you'll be back at it. Of course you will. You always are. But now it's time to give it a rest, and run.

Your eyes are bleary. Your head hurts. Your back is aching. Your hands are throbbing. Your body is telling you loud and clear: time for a break. Listen to your body. It's like your mother: it always knows.

If you can't give it a rest when it's time to give it a rest, when will you? It's time now. When you come back to it in an hour (or a day or a week or whenever), you'll be fresh and able to see it with clear eyes.

Even work you love, when you let it drag on too long, drains the blood out of you. Running puts it back in. It gives you energy. You need a rest from your work, and running will help you get it.

Now put it down. Whatever it is you're doing, whatever is bugging you and causing your head to pound, give it a rest. And run.

Resolved: OK, OK. I give it a rest and run.

November 17

"If a thing is worth doing, it is worth doing badly."

—G. K. Chesterton, writer

You can have a terrible day of running and still get a big boost from it. It's like what fishermen always say: their worst day of fishing is always better than any other day because at least they're doing what they love.

If you're running today, how bad can it be? Beats work, doesn't it? And if things are bad, they'll be a little bit better after you run. Or at least they'll *seem* better, which often equates to the same thing.

How can it be bad for you to do something you love, something that feels so good? Well, sure, if you take it to extremes. But every day of running is a good day on some level. You may have other things happen during the day that aren't so terrific. But the running part of it—that's a plus, which then casts the rest of your day in a new and better light.

Everyone who runs knows how difficult it is. But that can be a good thing, too. If you walk away from a run without learning something, you're not paying attention.

Badness is relative. You don't have to be a world-class runner to receive world-class benefits. You can finish last in a race and be thrilled. And you can finish first and be disappointed by your time. Good, bad, bad, good—the important thing is to run. Do it badly, do it well, just do it.

Resolved: Every day of running is a good day on some level. I always keep that in mind, even on the bad days.

November 18

"Our society puts us into boxes, and we do the same to ourselves. We tell ourselves, 'I'm a business person, so I'll leave art to the artists.' But it doesn't have to be this way."

—Shaun McNiff, therapist

Boxes, boxes, boxes. We live in little pink boxes, we work in tall skyscraper boxes, and we stuff our potential as human beings into invisible boxes.

You may think to yourself, "I'm not an athlete. I've never been terribly athletic. So, I'll never become a very good runner." That's a box.

Or you may think to yourself, "I'm OK about running the shorter distances. But a marathon? I don't think so. That's too hard." That's another box.

Sometimes boxes are imposed on us from without. You get stuck in a certain thing, say building widgets, and once that happens, you have to fight like hell the rest of your life to convince people that you can do something else.

"Wait," you tell them. "I can do other things. I can *design* widgets, too."

Boxes are also imposed from within—that is, by ourselves. Sometimes this occurs because of what society tells us, and we internalize this message. But let's be honest: sometimes we climb into boxes and pull the cover tight because it's safer in there. It's cozy and warm inside the box, and that's where we want to stay.

Are you in a running box? If so, isn't it about time you busted out of it?

Resolved: I do some soul-searching to see if I'm in a box in running.

November 19

Your life is like an overflowing drawer. "Clutter" does not begin to describe it. But you've finally cleared a little space to fit in a run.

Enjoy the run, and enjoy the clarity.

Scientific research has affirmed how beneficial running is to the heart and lungs and other bodily systems. But there's more to it than that, far more. One of its benefits is the clarity it brings. Our lives are so busy and full these days. There's always something to do, some new demand being made upon us. Running brings all of that into sharp focus.

You will be faced with tough decisions in life. All you can ask for, all you can hope for, is clarity. If you can see the situation clearly, you have a better shot at making the right choice. Running can supply some of that badly needed clarity. If you were an artist, it would be like giving yourself the chance to paint or sculpt. You've cleared away the distractions, the noise and clutter, and you've at last gotten down to what matters, what counts.

Running provides many benefits in addition to the physical. Clarity is one of them.

Resolved: I enjoy the run, and I enjoy the clarity it gives me.

November 20

"How singular is this thing called pleasure, and how curiously related to pain, which might be thought to be the opposite of it. Yet he who pursues either is generally compelled to take the other."

—Socrates

Feel the pleasure of running. Feel the pain. Both are essential to the experience.

You can't run without experiencing pain at some point (many points?) along the way. You're a fool if you expect only pleasure, and yet, some people apparently do.

They expect to run without blisters, sprains, achy muscles, soreness? What are they thinking? Longtime runners generally accept pain as part of the bargain. It's almost religious in nature. They know they've got to suffer a little in order to reach running salvation.

The key, clearly, is to maximize the pleasures and minimize the pain. Too much pain is a definite no-no, because it forces you to stop running. But it's not entirely negative—depending, of course, on how you respond to it. The pain you're feeling in your shin may be sending you an important message. Seek to understand the message, and heed it. Ignoring it will only cause greater problems.

Nothing good in life comes without struggle. Pain is a symbol of that struggle. But it's not the enemy. Don't fear it. Like pleasure, it's a natural part of running, and it can teach you great lessons.

Resolved: I do not fear pain. I respect it for what it can teach me.

November 21

"The man is blessed who every day is permitted to behold
anything so pure and serene as the western sky at sunset,
while revolutions vex the world."

—Henry David Thoreau

A runner who spends a lot of time ogling the sky isn't going to get very far. Runners must pay attention to what's in front of them, not above them.

But before or after a run—or even during, if it presents itself to you—remember to check out the sky every now and then. It puts on a pretty good show much of the time.

Runners are, by their nature, of a philosophical bent. Perhaps this is because they spend so much time under an open sky. The sky puts things in perspective. Your toil and troubles, however significant they may seem, always look slightly different when cast against the overwhelming vastness of the sky.

The sky unites every runner and every person. Runners in Atlanta and Oxford and Hong Kong and Sydney and Rio and Nairobi all run under the same sky.

An indoor person may view the sky as dull and uniform. Runners know different. They may encounter a series of atmospheric changes—cloudy and gray, to dark thunderclouds, to bright sunshine—in the course of a single run. Runners are forever scanning the heavens. They take a look out the window, see what's going on, and decide to go for it. What's it look like out your window?

Resolved: I remember to check out the sky when I run.

November 22

"Contentment comes as the infallible result of great acceptances, great humilities—of letting life flow through us."

—David Grayson, philosopher

Some days you're going to feel like pushing it at the end. Turning on the afterburners and driving hard to the finish and certain glory.

Not today, though. Put it in cruise control, and ride it all the way to the end.

Let life flow gently through you today. There's no need for a big push, anyway. If you put in your hard work in the middle, you won't need to make up for it at the end. Save the show-stopping finales for Broadway.

Coasting in to the finish leaves you with the feeling that you've got something left in the tank. That's a good feeling, and a good note upon which to conclude: you've got more, but you're not desperate to show it. You'll be back tomorrow.

Anyone can end with a mad dash, because afterward you're going to stop and rest. Pick up the pace in the middle, and keep it going for a while—that's the real way to build endurance.

It's a state-of-mind thing, too. You can be contented with how far you've come, even as you know you've still got more work to do. You're doing what you need to do. You have nothing to prove to anyone, least of all yourself. End on an easy, contented note today. You deserve it.

Resolved: I coast in for an easy landing today.

November 23

"All good organization tends to simplicity."

—Sir Arthur Helps, philosopher

You woke this morning with a plan of how your day would go, and that plan included running. But everything that has happened since has conspired to knock you out of your plan and stop you from running.

Stick to the plan, and run.

True, it may be a fight. True, you will have to hustle. But it's what you want, right? Well, then. Stick to what you want, and find a way to do it.

Some days will flow smoothly, and running will fit neatly into them: no fuss, no bother. But you have to expect that every day won't be like that. There will be days when running is the proverbial square peg in the round hole, impossible to fit.

If that's often the case, your schedule may be too crowded. Think about how you can organize your life to allow more time for yourself and more time for running.

Now, some days, it's true, there's just no time. It's too much trouble; there's just too much going on. But make no mistake: today is *not* one of those days. You're making a stand; you're fighting like hell. Your schedule has thrown down the gauntlet, and you've picked it up. You're not giving in; you're not caving. The plan includes running, and you're sticking with it.

Once you adopt this attitude, you will probably find a way to run.

Resolved: I stick to my original plan today and run.

November 24

"Work is a dull thing. The only agreeable existence is one of idleness."

—Rose Macaulay, writer

You've heard of don't-bother-me Fridays. Well, today is a don't-bother-me day.

You know how it goes. A don't-bother-me day is the day before a holiday or three-day weekend. You don't want people calling you, you don't want work dumped on you, you don't really want to do anything at all.

All you want is to be out of there. But you can't just cut out; you've got to stick around and at least appear to be working. Then at the earliest opportunity, you grab your hat and coat and scram.

Running is a kind of don't-bother-me experience. All you want to do when you run is get away from things, at least for a while. Get away from phones and faxes, worries and responsibilities. Go outside, be among the trees and birds, and clear your head. When you come back to the world, you feel a lot better about everything.

A run is a perfect way to end a don't-bother-me day. Maybe you're not in such a good mood after work. So, you take a run (as some people take a drink), and you feel transformed. You're in a holiday frame of mind as you greet your family with open arms.

The perfect solution for a don't-bother-me day? Take a don't-bother-me run.

Resolved: I end a don't-bother-me day with a run and feel much better for it.

November 25

"Who does not thank for little will not thank for much."

—Estonian proverb

When you look around, you've got a lot to be thankful for, don't you? Here are just a few of the things:

Your new running shoes. So clean and cool, they make you feel like Michael Johnson.

Your previous pair of running shoes. They did their time, and they did it well. They were good soldiers.

All those pairs of beat-up, old running shoes piled in the closet. They're like old friends, and it's hard to part with any of them.

Your shoelaces. Admittedly a little thing, easily ignored, but how could you run without shoelaces? So, thanks to them, too.

Podiatrists. What would we do without them? Make a note to take yours to lunch.

Tom, your running partner. What a great guy. You run together every morning, and if there's time, the two of you have breakfast after. Come to think of it, though, when was the last time he paid? Better ask him about it.

Your family. They never complain when you're gone for hours at a time pounding the pavement. Well, not too much, anyhow.

Weekends. God bless weekends, the best time for running.

And oh yes, much thanks for your health and your life. Where would you be without those?

Resolved: I give thanks for all the blessings in my life, and I run.

November 26

"Hell is full of the talented but Heaven of the energetic."
—Saint Jane Francis de Chantal

Perhaps you feel sluggish and uninspired today. Run, and you will feel better instantly.

That's the way it is with this amazing activity. Whatever your mood, running will put you in a better one. It creates energy.

If you're tired, it will give you pep. If you've got plenty of pep already, it will give you an extra dose.

If you're feeling down, it will lift your spirits. It's the greatest antidepressant of all. And if you're already feeling good, you'll feel so good after you run that you won't be able to stand yourself.

If you're pressed for that most precious commodity, time, running will create some for you. You work more efficiently when you run, and by working more efficiently you will carve out more time for the things you do.

Running can even make money for you. You think better and more creatively when you run, right? On your next run, think of some creative money-making opportunities. Who knows: maybe you'll invent the next Power Bar.

Let running create energy for you. And let that energy carry you to great places in your life.

Resolved: If I'm feeling sluggish or uninspired, I run and give myself a shot of energy.

November 27

"Clouds today—great archangel wings across the sky."
—Anne Morrow Lindbergh

The sky is dark and ominous. Thunder clouds range to the north and west. It's not raining yet, but rain seems to be an inevitability.

You have your doubts, but you decide to run anyway. You hope you can get it in before the skies open up.

You drive to your usual spot and start up the trail. The light is soft. It's cool, and there's moisture in the air. You feel almost as if you're racing an unseen enemy, but you keep your pace steady and even.

The clouds are moving implacably in your direction. In fact, you can see across the straits to the north: sheets of rain already falling. But it's kind of fun, being chased by rain. It gives you a little charge, and you pick up your pace. You wonder if you're going to make it back to your car before you get dumped on.

As you turn down the trail back along the creek to the end of your run, you feel a drop of rain. Then another. And another. It's starting to happen. You pull your car door shut behind you just as the skies part and the downpour begins.

You've made it. You've run under darkening skies, and it's a great feeling. It's almost as if you got away with something. You flip on the windshield wipers as you drive off, glad that you did not hesitate for long and that you were willing to give it a go.

Resolved: I never delay for long. When the skies start to darken, I get my run in.

"My rule is if you let things go to the final sprint, it's the worst guy who ends up winning. Waiting and kicking may work in the 1,500, where the whole field can stay close, but not the distances."

—John Chaplin, running coach

Runners who wait and kick are a common sight at marathons or half-marathons. They are often middle- or back-of-the-pack stragglers who put on a final finishing kick to beat another runner to the line.

They are applauded mightily for their effort, as well they should be, although their strategy may be questionable. When you leave things to the very end in the distances, you can never be sure what will happen.

The other problem with waiting and kicking is that you run the risk of holding something back when you race. And if you have something left at the end, you may not be running as hard as you can during the race.

Now, you may want to hold something back to make sure you last the entire distance. You don't want to give your all for 10 miles and then be forced to drop out at mile 15 because you have nothing left. Or you may see the race as an extended training run.

Still, you never want to run a race in earnest and think afterward, "What if I had run harder?" It's an empty feeling to cross the finish line with something left in your tank and yet be disappointed in your performance. Give everything you have, leave it all on the course, and you'll never have reason to be disappointed.

Resolved: When I race seriously, I leave it all on the course.

November 29

"Madness need not be all breakdown. It may also be breakthrough. It is potentially liberation and renewal."

—R. D. Laing, psychiatrist

There is a long-distance runner from Indonesia named Ruwiyati—one name only—who has an interesting motivational technique. She sucks the blood of her running coach. "As soon as I reach the finish line, I suck my coach's blood from his finger," she says. "I feel refreshed." Her understanding coach's name is Alwi Mugiyanto, who once let his star pupil suck some blood from his neck before the Indonesian national games.

As strange as this practice may be—except, of course, in Transylvania, where it's a well-established custom for members of Team Dracula—it's hard to argue with results. Ruwiyati won the Southeast Asian Games Marathon in 2 hours, 46 minutes, and 20 seconds and has won other races in the region.

So, what can the rest of us learn from Ruwiyati? Well, if you don't have a coach with a willing carotid artery, you're going to have to find other motivational techniques. We've talked about this before, but it's worth repeating. Doesn't matter how crazy. Doesn't matter how the rest of the civilized world views it. If you find something that works for you, use it.

Maybe doing cartwheels gets you in a running mood. Maybe you like to sing an aria from *Carmen*. Maybe you like to flap your wings like a chicken. Maybe you like to hear from your mother in Dayton who wishes you good luck. Maybe you like to carry a lucky penny. Whatever it is, if it works for you, use it.

Resolved: As crazy as it may seem to others, if I find a motivational or training technique that works for me, I use it.

"I like to think of thoughts as living blossoms borne by the human tree."

—James Douglas, philosopher

You suddenly have a nifty thought about your running. You think, "I'm going to fly to Tokyo and run the marathon." But, for whatever reason—lack of time or money or follow-through—it doesn't happen. The thought remains just that: a thought.

That happens to everybody. We all have grand schemes and plans that never blossom.

Still, if an idea keeps popping into your head, you may want to listen to it. If you missed the Tokyo Marathon one year, but the prospect of running in it still appeals to you the next year, and the year after that, there is clearly something about the idea that resonates with you. Ideas that last are generally good ideas, worthy of follow-up. What does it say about you if you keep turning your back on ideas that appeal to you?

Here's an idea: always follow the fresh thought. Thoughts are like bread: at some point they grow stale. Treat your thoughts like fresh bread from the oven. Let it sit for a moment, then dig in.

What's your latest thought about running? Buy new shoes? Find a new place to run? Enter the 10K on Saturday? Call up a friend to go running together? Fly to Tokyo for the marathon? Whatever your latest thought about running, follow it, and see where it takes you.

Resolved: I follow my latest running thought to see where it takes me.

December 1

"To make life living, we must descend to a more profound and primitive level. The good of seeing and smelling and tasting and daring and doing with one's body grows and grows."

—William James, philosopher

It's the first day of the last month of the year. What better way to usher it in than with a run?

Last month dragged a little. Perhaps because the weather got colder, and you got tired. But that was last month, and it's over now. This is a new month. Bring fresh energy to it.

Generally runners don't tend to draw distinctions between days, or even months. They're going to run today, and if they don't make it today, they'll run tomorrow—and what's the difference, anyhow? Every day is good for running.

They're right, of course. Every day is good for running. But not every day is the same, nor every month. We tend to lump the days together because of the dreary familiarity of work. But each day offers the chance for a fresh beginning, a new chance to smell and taste and dare and do with one's body.

If you view this calendar year in terms of a race, you're on the final stretch drive. Bring new energy to it, and finish with a bang.

Resolved: It's the first day of December, and I'm going for a run.

December 2

"For we have in the dream forsaken our allegiance to the organizing and controlling forces of the world. We have sworn fealty to the wild, incalculable, creative forces, the Imagination of the Universe."

—Isak Dinesen, writer

You'll get no peace from yourself until you do it, so you might as well do it. You've been on your back long enough, and you're getting heavy, too heavy to carry anymore. It's time to take a load off yourself.

Sometimes your boss rides you. Sometimes it's your spouse or your kids. Lots of times it's your mother. But they're not involved this time. This time, it's just you.

You've bugged yourself long enough. You've let it gnaw at you long enough. You've wanted to do this thing—this crazy, mixed-up, impossible-to-explain, possibly insane thing—for so long that you can't remember how it got started, or when. The idea seems as old as you.

You've tried to get rid of it, but you can't. It's lodged into your head, and nothing you do ever seems to shake it loose or out. It's like the Terminator: nothing can kill it. It's become a permanent part of your anatomy, like your eyes or ears.

The solution? Quit trying to get rid of it. Rather, get rid of it by plunging deeply into it. That's the only way you'll ever be free of the idea: by giving yourself up to it.

Resolved: You know this crazy, hare-brained idea I keep thinking about in running? I'm doing it.

December 3

"Freud was 36 before he began to do the work that made him famous."

—Lionel Trilling, literary critic and writer

One of the biggest misconceptions about youth is that it is a bold and adventurous time. In fact, as others have pointed out, young people can be extremely conservative in their habits, beliefs, and goals.

Some runners think to themselves, "If I'd only started earlier, think how good I'd be now." But this isn't necessarily true. For one, if they'd started earlier, they might have burned out on the sport or gotten hurt. And their inexperience and youth might have held them back if they'd gotten serious at that time.

Often people do not begin to take risks—that is, do the things they really want to do and damn the consequences—until their 30s and 40s. They've lived a little by then, and they're more willing to take chances. They're less worried about screwing up and looking bad. They're less concerned about what others think and more interested in what *they* think.

Here's today's thought: you're right on time. For whatever reason, running wasn't right for you in the past. But it's right now. And you *can* do it, even if you're in your 30s or 40s or 50s or 60s or 70s or 80s. You think you're old? You're not old; you're just getting started.

Resolved: I'm not old; I'm just getting started.

December 4

"If you tell yourself that your goal race is going to hurt and that it won't be any fun, your expectations will probably come true. Instead tell yourself that there will be challenges, counterbalanced by feelings of joy and satisfaction."

—Jeff Galloway, runner and writer

Some runners think of road races as deadly serious affairs that allow no room for play. Jeff Galloway, an accomplished road racer and author, is not one of them. He thinks that races can be just as enjoyable as your everyday workouts. He suggests a couple of "mind games" that runners can play to keep things light and enjoyable:

- Have fun on a hill, especially after you've reached the top. As Galloway says, "See how far you can glide onto the flats using the momentum of the previous hill." Instead of viewing a hill as an insurmountable obstacle, use it as a slingshot that propels you forward.
- In the second half of a race, pick out a runner who's slightly ahead of you. Put her in your sights, and slowly, over the course of the race, reel her in. Then, if there's time, pick out another person and pass him. This will spur you on, even if you're in the rear of the pack.

Even in a race, says Galloway, "the possibilities for play are endless." Not only will the miles go by more quickly, but you may even run faster. You tend to think less about yourself and your narrow concerns. It is not all hard work and grim determination; there is joy and fun in it, too.

Resolved: I use the momentum of a hill to slingshot me forward in a race.

December 5

"Be yourself. You are the things you grew up with, the things your parents taught you. For years I tried to figure out who I was, where I came from. Now I just feel it's important to be Dan O'Brien."

—Dan O'Brien, Olympic decathlete

Use what you have. Use everything you have, and that includes your past and who you are as a person.

You may not be an athlete. Running may be the first sport you've ever done seriously. Even so, there are things in your past that can be helpful to you now. Think about what those things could be. Find them, and put them to use in your running.

You may have been a great athlete when you were younger, only your sports were baseball and basketball, not running. Nevertheless, there are things in your past that can be applied to running.

Your mom or dad may have taught you something as a kid. Something may have happened to you 20 years ago that still speaks to you today. If so, put it to use. All your past plays a part in forming who you are. Some past events are negative. Becoming aware of yourself also means becoming aware of the negative patterns that have shaped your life and how you can change them.

You are who you are. And who you are is unique. No one else has your individual experiences, past, knowledge. You're a resource even larger than the Internet, and you're all there, available for the taking. Tap into those internal resources, and make yourself the runner you want to be.

Resolved: I use everything I have to make myself the runner I want to be.

December 6

How often in life do you score a big victory? Win the lottery? Sign a seven-figure contract? Claim the title, and walk off with the girl (or guy)?

If you're lucky, it happens every once in a blue moon. In the meantime, we must learn to be content with small victories.

You're not always going to run a personal best. But running your fourth-fastest time ever is nothing to sneeze at, either.

Ok, so you didn't walk away the winner. But you finished in the top 50, and that's pretty darned good.

It's disappointing, to be sure, not to run your fastest time every time you run a marathon. But this last marathon marked your sixth lifetime marathon, and how many people can claim that? And you ran it under 2 hours, 50 minutes. That's fantastic. Think about where you started as a runner and how far you've come.

Special occasions are how you define them, for every achievement in running is potentially a bird on the wing. It can be a special occasion just to run, and complete, a race. You don't have to win or finish high. It's like owning an expensive set of Tiffany silver. If you bring it out only for wedding showers and anniversaries, it will remain mostly in the closet. There are small victories worth recognizing, too. Be sure to celebrate them as well.

Resolved: I celebrate both my big and small victories in running.

December 7

"People say, I believe, that in anger a person says things that are a caricature of the truth, but in that caricature you can find truth about yourself that you could never find any other way."

—Katharine Butler Hathaway, writer

You've no doubt heard the phrase "Don't get mad—get even." Well, sometimes just getting mad—really ticked off—about some aspect of your running can be highly motivational.

You get mad at your inability to run a marathon under three hours.

You get mad because someone you don't like beat you in a race.

You get mad because some other runners, who started about the same time as you and who are less athletic, are progressing faster than you.

You get mad because you're stuck on a plateau and can't seem to get off.

Now, obviously you will need more than just anger in the long run. Sometimes a person gets mad and decides that a change is in order. But after the initial anger subsides, interest and enthusiasm fade with it.

If you've reached a point in running where you're getting mad at yourself or a situation, that's a signal that change is in order. Don't hide from it; recognize it, and seek the sources of it. The anger you feel can be a catalyst for long-term positive changes.

Resolved: When I get angry about something in running, I look to the causes of that anger and seek a remedy.

December 8

"The first fall of snow is not only an event but it is a magical event. If this is not enchantment, then where is it to be found?"
— J. B. Priestley, writer

When the first fall of snow comes this winter, why not celebrate by going for a run?

Let everyone else bundle up indoors. You go for a run and turn up the heat on your internal thermostat.

Is anything in nature more beautiful than a first snow? There's magic to it, an enchanted quality. When you go to bed, as Priestley has noted, the world looks one way. When you wake up the next morning after a fresh snow, the world has slipped on a new coat of white and been miraculously transformed.

Since it's still early and you're not yet in the throes of winter, perhaps it's warm outside and the snow isn't sticking. It lands lightly on the pavement, melting on contact. Flakes fall against your face, and you stick your tongue out to taste them. You grin and laugh with the sheer joy of it.

It reminds you of when you were a kid and built a snowman with the other neighbor kids on your front lawn. You feel a surge of freedom. Some people passing look cold and uncomfortable, hustling to get indoors. You feel almost a little pity for them. Do they know what they're missing? You run and run and run, hoping the experience never ends.

Resolved: At the first snowfall of the year, I go for a run.

December 9

One of the great things about running is that it can make you warm while everyone else is cold. It can be a chilly day in December. You're dressed in layers to fight off the chill. You go out and run, and suddenly you become a lot warmer.

You start out in your cold-weather gear. But as you run, you shed your parka. It's as if you've turned on the pilot light for your body, and you're starting to generate your own heat. By the time you're done with your run, you're sweaty and hot.

You especially notice the change after you're back in your civilian clothes. It suddenly doesn't feel quite so cold outside. Then you return home (or go back to work). The room immediately feels hot and stuffy when you walk in. Before your workout you kept turning the temperature up; now you turn it down or shut it off.

Everyone else is wearing clothes on top of clothes, and they still can't get warm. Now you're walking around in a T-shirt or shirtsleeves and saying what a beautiful day it is outside. It's a great feeling. You clearly see and feel how running gets the blood pumping and how good that is for your body.

If it's cold outside, don't stay indoors and hug the fire. Go outside for a run, and turn on your body's pilot light.

Resolved: On a cold day, I warm myself up with a run.

December 10

"Start slowly, and taper off fast."

—Popular slogan of Dolphin Running Club
of San Francisco

There was the Ali shuffle, and the shuffle off to Buffalo. But runners know a different kind of shuffle: the marathon shuffle.

The marathon shuffle is a kind of long, slow distance-running "technique," although that may be too highfalutin a term for it. You see it done all the time by marathon runners, especially ones in the middle or back of the pack.

The marathon shuffle is slow dancing for runners. People who do the shuffle are most likely going to dance their way to the end of the marathon, albeit at their own unhurried pace. They may not get there fast, but they get there.

Older runners do the marathon shuffle, but younger runners like it, too. If you're not sure whether or not you can finish the entire 26-mile distance, find someone who's doing the shuffle. He or she will guide you the rest of the way. And if you can't immediately see anyone doing it, slow down. A shuffler will be coming along eventually. Shufflers are indomitable as fate.

It may not be fancy, but it gets results. If you want to be sure to finish what you start, do the marathon shuffle. The results will be positively inspiring.

Resolved: I do the marathon shuffle, starting slowly and tapering off fast.

December 11

One time Paula Newby-Fraser, the greatest female triathlete of all time, was locked in a tight race in the Hawaii Ironman with a close rival. The swimming and bicycling were over, and they were running the last leg of the event, the marathon.

The race was very close. Her rival made her move with about 13 miles to go. She surged forward and steadily pulled away, almost daring Newby-Fraser to go with her.

Newby-Fraser, however, did not take the bait. The native South African has studied Buddhism and incorporates some of its tenets into her life and athletics. "Now is all there is," she chanted to herself, "now is all there is," staying on her pace and refusing to follow her rival even though she had lost eye contact with her.

Her patience and discipline paid off. She kept chanting this mantra to herself—"Now is all there is, now is all there is"—and with three miles to go, she passed her rival and won the Ironman easily.

Next time someone passes you, know that you don't have to go with him. Do as Newby-Fraser did, and tell yourself: "Now is all there is, now is all there is." Know that, *understand* that, and you will be fine in every race of your life.

Resolved: Now is all there is; now is all there is.

December 12

"We all die. Not living is the failure."

—Sidney J. Winawer, M.D.

You feel it every time you run, and that is ultimately why you run.

You don't feel it when you wake up in the morning, groggy and tired.

You don't feel it reading the paper or listening to the traffic report on the radio.

You don't feel it as you cinch up your tie or put on another boring business suit.

You don't feel it on the drive to work, playing bumper cars with the other commuters on the freeway.

You don't feel it on the subway or bus, jostling with the other passengers for a seat and trying to avoid their eyes.

You don't feel it sitting in front of a computer or talking on the phone or reading a report or attending a meeting.

You don't feel it when you come home at the end of another day that was strikingly similar to yesterday and a probable foreshadowing of tomorrow.

You don't feel it when you fall asleep in front of Letterman, channel changer slipping from your hand as you nod off.

You don't feel it any of those times, but you do feel it when you run. Every runner does. Now's the time. Go out and feel the feeling.

Resolved: I run and feel life surging inside me.

December 13

"If I were to wish for anything, I should not wish for wealth and power, but for the passionate sense of the potential, for the eye which, ever young and ardent, sees the possible. Pleasure disappoints, possibility never."

—Søren Kierkegaard

It's gray outside, a melancholy, overcast day. You set out on your usual run, expecting to be covered by a blanket of gray all day long. You start at the bottom of the draw near where you park the car. There's a creek that runs through there, and sometimes in the summer cattle laze around in the shade under the oak trees.

You run along the fire trail, flanked by the creek on one side and brown rolling hills on the other, gradually making your way up the draw. There's a short, steep section at the end that makes you work, and you feel good when you reach the top. You're not paying attention to what the sky is doing; you're just running and concentrating on that. But when you stop to catch your breath at the top of the draw, you notice it.

It's suddenly blue above you. The sky has changed colors. The seemingly omnipresent grayness has melted away, as if someone poured hot water on it. There are still mopey gray clouds around the edges, but in the center of the sky it's blue, an impossibly rich and vivid blue.

How nice, you think; what a nice surprise. The change in the sky's mood seems to lift yours, and after you've rested, you push off again down the trail, running now under a sparkling patch of blue.

Resolved: I believe, always, in the possibility of a break—of blue skies, for example, suddenly appearing on an overcast day.

December 14

"Where the unaided intellect fails, the body now reveals. As I run up that hill, I am a pupil, an observer. My body is my tutor."

—George Sheehan, philosopher-runner

You know more at the top of every hill you run than you did at the bottom.

You know more at the end of every run than at the start.

You know more at the end of every marathon you finish than at the beginning. You know more at mile 5 than at mile 1 and more at mile 20 than at mile 15.

Running teaches you something every time you run. When you return to the house after a run, you know more about yourself than when you left. You're a different person in some way. You've changed.

These changes may not be dramatic or even noticeable by you, but they're there. That you're not immediately aware of them doesn't mean they don't exist.

The benefits of running are not merely cumulative. The fact that you are not the same runner you were five years ago or even five months ago is not the result of years of running; it is the result of a series of *days*. The changes that have occurred, and are occurring, occur in small but meaningful ways each time you run. You do not have to wait years and months for these changes; they can take place in the time it takes to go from the bottom of a hill to the top.

Resolved: I recognize that I am changing each time I run.

December 15

"You gotta hang in there. You don't know what's ahead. You don't realize the potential you have. You keep asking yourself, 'Is it really worth it?' But you gotta hang in there."

—Brenda Morehead, sprinter

Kevin Kline tells a wonderful story about how he came to play *Hamlet* on Broadway.

When he was a struggling actor in New York, he met Donald Madden, who had played the Danish prince in the longest-running production of the play in Broadway history. At the time, Madden was starring in *Richard III* in Central Park, a performance in which young Kline's duties consisted of carrying a spear and little more.

Kline asked him how he had prepared for the role of Hamlet, and Madden said, "If you want to play Hamlet, start now. Get a pocket-size edition of the play. Carry it with you everywhere." And that's basically what Kline did. He read and studied the play for 15 years until, finally, he performed it to rave reviews on Broadway.

If you have a dream in running, start now. It may take just as long to accomplish. Cut out a picture of the Boston skyline, and stick it in your purse or pocket. (Or New York or Sydney or wherever.) Whenever you feel the dream fading, pull that picture out, unfold it, and study it.

No one knows what lies ahead for you. Nor do you really know how much potential you have. But you're not going to find out the answers if you don't hang in there. Keep the dream present in your life, and never give up on it.

Resolved: I hang in there. I don't know what lies ahead, but I'm hanging in there.

December 16

You're pooped, you're beat, you're whipped, you're fried. The tank is empty. You're running on fumes.

Run a little bit more.

You're tired, you're sore, you're achy. Your feet and shins and back are screaming in agony. You don't want to die, but you feel as if you might.

Run a little bit more.

Your head—ah, your head. You'd rather not think about it because it hurts to think. It's pounding, pulsing, throbbing, booming, blasting. It feels as if a brass band (complete with clashing cymbals) is playing inside your skull.

Run a little bit more.

Runners are passing you. Senior citizens in walkers are passing you. It's as if everyone is in fast motion and you're standing still. Race officials have disqualified you for going too slowly.

Run a little bit more.

You feel terrible, miserable, horrible. You've never felt this bad in your entire life. Still, you know that you will feel even worse if you quit. You can't even stomach the thought. That's the lowest of the low, the worst idea of all. Run a little bit more.

Resolved: I don't kill myself, but I keep going. I run a little bit more.

December 17

"Learn to listen to your body. It will tell you when you've done enough work."

—Gayle Barron, marathoner

Running can almost be seen as a contest between the body and the clock. Those who pay too close attention to the clock sometimes ignore the commands of the body, train too hard, and suffer because of it. On the other hand, a runner who simply runs and runs, without any regard for his or her time, has a tough time going any faster. He or she doesn't improve or takes much longer to do so.

Great runners, of course, listen to their bodies yet also pay attention to the clock. One spurs the other to greater and greater heights.

What they have is what all runners aspire to: a balance. Everybody wants to turn in a good time. But to do so while tearing down your body is foolhardy.

Similarly, when you're in a race, you must stay focused on the moment while simultaneously looking ahead to the finish. You don't want to push too hard, but you must stretch your limits a little to improve. And successfully stretching your limits involves an awareness of time. It's not really a contest after all. When everything is clicking for you as a runner, body, mind, and clock are working together as if on the same team.

Resolved: I seek a balance between the dictates of my body and the dictates of the clock.

December 18

"There is no way to explain the feeling properly. It's one of those rare feelings that cannot be told to anyone who hasn't been there. It's simply the best feeling I've ever experienced."

—Mark Osmun,
after finishing his first marathon

Read a book about running (including Osmun's fine book on the Honolulu Marathon), and you'll get a certain feeling from it. That's true if you watch a movie or TV show, too. Even better is to go out and watch a road race. That's a pretty special experience as well. It's inspiring to see other people achieve their dreams.

But nothing replaces direct experience. Not reading about it, not watching a movie, not seeing it in person. You have to be there. You have to do it. You have to experience it for yourself.

How else do you know the taste of water unless you drink it? How else do you know what it feels like to run a marathon unless you do it? Finishing a marathon may be the most dramatic experience a runner will ever have. Nothing is quite like it.

But you can also get the feeling in a shorter race. It just depends on how much you put into it, for feeling usually corresponds to effort. The greater the effort, the more intense the feeling. And, at the end, despite possible doubts along the way, the feeling almost always justifies the effort.

Ah, but these are mere scratchings on paper. You want to feel the feeling? Go for a run. All else is a paltry substitute.

Resolved: I accept no substitutes. I seek always direct experience in running.

December 19

"You want to know how to make God laugh? Tell Him your plans."

—Anonymous

Every runner has dreams. But sometimes those hopes and dreams don't come true, despite your every effort.

You can visualize positive outcomes. You can do everything humanly possible to achieve them. But the outcomes won't always be positive in running or in life, no matter what you do.

You can plan to run New York. You can train for it and work hard. Everything can be right and ready to go. Then the night before your flight, you can throw your back out.

Those things happen. Sometimes even worse things happen, things you never would have imagined could happen to you or your loved ones. Maybe if you're lucky, you'll be able to look back on those things and say that you learned from them, that it was right the way things happened, and that if they hadn't happened the way they did, some other good things that happened after that would never have occurred.

Then again, bad things do happen. They're bad when they happen, and they stay bad even when you look back at them from the safety of years. There's nothing you can do about these things except, perhaps, look inside yourself and know that when they do occur, you will get through them. You will get through them, and you will be a stronger person because of them.

Resolved: Whatever happens to me, even if it's something really bad, I know I can get through it.

December 20

It's a big decision. There's a lot at stake. You're not sure what to do. Your very future is up for grabs. Not only that, but also lots of other people's lives will be affected by what you do.

Before you commit, take a run.

You've never been in a situation like this before. You almost wish it had never come up. No, that's not true. It's a wonderful predicament to be in. Sort of. At least that's what you think most of the time. Because your mood, of course, changes from moment to moment.

Before you commit, take a run.

You look at some couples and think, "That's not so bad. I could do that." Then you look at other completely miserable couples, and you think, "Absolutely not. Tar and feather me and ride me out of town on a rail, but don't make me do that."

You've grown a lot as a person, and sometimes you think you could handle it. Then there are those times when you feel as if you're 12 years old again, and you know there's no way.

But you've got to make up your mind at some point. That much is clear. Push has finally come to shove. You can't let this situation drag on and on and on. You've simply got to decide— one way or the other. Should I ask her to marry me, or not?

Resolved: Before I do anything drastic, I take a run.

December 21

"The ability to be aware of one's body has a great importance all through life. It is a curious fact that most adults have so lost physical awareness that they are unable to tell how their leg feels, or their ankle, or any other part of the body."

—Rollo May, therapist

Are you tensing or "holding" a part of your body when you run? Lots of runners do, though they may not be aware of it.

We all react to stress. Some people clench their jaws. Others clench their hands or tense their backs. What occurs, in general, is a tightening of the body, a kind of clamping down. The body is being put under stress, and it naturally responds by tensing and holding the muscles in place.

First comes awareness. Do you clench your jaw when you get mad at your kids? Does your back stiffen up when a new assignment gets dumped on you at work? You have to become aware of how you respond to pressure before you can change your response.

This has obvious applications to running. Do you unconsciously tense up when you run? Does your body feel under stress, and does that make you stiffen up somewhere? Observe yourself when you run. See if you can turn what has been an unconscious act into a conscious one. See how you're holding your body.

You might be carrying tension over into your running, and as a result you may be working harder than you need to. By your recognizing this tension and then changing your response to it, your running will become easier and more relaxed.

Resolved: I watch for signs of tension in the way I hold my body when I run.

December 22

Small smooth movements. That's today's mantra: small and smooth.

People think in terms of fast or slow when they run. Instead: think small and smooth.

You may be running 15 miles today. But the way you're covering that big distance is by small, smooth steps. Look at all the top road racers. It's how they run. They don't take giant strides. Their strides are compact and regular as the action of a metronome. They gobble up the pavement and move at impossibly fast speeds through small, smooth movements.

How do you win a marathon? How do you attain a high and mighty aspiration? Lots and lots and lots of small, smooth movements. You don't have to be a big person; you don't need a long stride. Make small, smooth movements, turn them over rapidly, and you will be challenging the leaders at the front of the pack, if that's your dream.

Make every stride as smooth as possible. If that's hard to do, you may be going too fast. Slow down a little—always a good idea in running—and think small and smooth. That will get you there faster in the long run.

Resolved: Small, smooth movements. Always, small, smooth movements.

December 23

It's been said before, but it's worth saying again: in running, less is more. Today, when you run, do less. Tomorrow, do less. Always, do less.

The way to accomplish more in running is by doing less. It's a contradiction with the power of truth.

The more you strain, the slower you will go. And the more you will expose yourself to possible injury. Work within your limits; don't fight against them. See your limits as warning signs at the edge of a dangerous cliff. If you ignore the signs and get too close to the edge, the dirt may crumble under your feet, and you may fall off. Play it safe. Stay away from the edge of the abyss, and remain on solid ground.

If another runner ever tells you, "No pain, no gain," know that that person is a fool and probably will be on the sidelines before long with an injured calf or shinsplints. Fact is, you can't learn when your body is in pain. All that pain teaches is pain. Your body cannot heal itself until the pain goes away.

Do less, and learn. Do less, and stay away from the pain. Do less, and keep running.

Resolved: I stay within my limits and do less.

December 24

One day you go out and surprise yourself at how fast you run and how good you feel. The next day you go out, and you just don't have it. Your legs feel like lead, your intervals are terrible, and you can't understand why.

There is still so much to learn.

You go with a friend to a new place where you've never run before. It's beautiful. For a while you drop your obsession about times and performance, and you just enjoy the heck out of the day.

There is still so much to learn.

You watch the top runners at a road race, the ones competing for the prize money. They don't look as if they're having any fun at all. While the older runners, the ones in the back of the pack, seem to be having the time of their lives.

There is still so much to learn.

You enter a race and encounter a friend you haven't seen in a while. He's running really fast. You talk to him about his training techniques, and he gives you a couple of good tips you'd like to try.

There is still so much to learn.

You're feeling isolated as a runner. Finally you overcome your inhibitions and join a club. You meet lots of great people. You realize that running is not such a lonely pastime after all, and you wonder why you didn't do it before. Apparently there is still much more for you to learn.

Resolved: I keep my mind open, and I keep learning.

December 25

This is a big day, for fairly well-known reasons, and no doubt
you have lots of things going on. Church possibly, opening
presents, spending time with family, having a big meal, celebrating with friends and neighbors and extended family.

These are all important things, worthy things, things you
must do and probably love to do. But at some point today, after
your family obligations are over—or if there's a break in the
festivities—you may want to practice the fine art of slipping
away for a run.

This is a good survival skill for the holidays in general or
for any stressful time. In the last month, to be sure, you've had
commitments piled upon commitments. Parties to go to, shopping to do, events to attend. It's been crazy.

Slipping away for a run is a sure cure for the holiday madness (and the holiday blues). You slip out the door, and no one
notices you're gone until you're down the block and in fine,
full stride. By then, it's too late.

Today, slip away for a run. And while you're out there,
think of all the blessings in your life. That will surely fill your
heart with gratitude and joy.

Resolved: I slip away for a run and think of the many blessings in my life.

December 26

"Great things are not done by impulse, but by a series of small things brought together. And great things are not something accidental, but must certainly be willed."

—Vincent van Gogh

You stuck to your guns, and you did it. And it wasn't easy to do. Is there a more satisfying feeling in all of life?

You did all the small things, which added up to a great big thing. There were times when you felt like quitting, and yet you didn't. There were times when hope seemed lost, and yet you stayed with it.

You had this idea of doing something heretofore unimaginable for you: running a 10K/marathon/hundred-mile ultra (choose one). People thought you were crazy. Even you thought it was a little crazy. You certainly had no idea how it would all turn out when you started.

But it was something you wanted to do, deep inside you. No, it was more than that: you *had* to do it. To turn your back on it would be to ignore the deepest parts of your being. This wasn't about people. This was about you. This was about dreams and desire and what was true and right. And you did it. When the going got tough, you got going. You hung in there; you did not bail. You fought the good fight, and you won.

So, give yourself credit. Take a moment. There won't be many times in life when you can claim this, so enjoy this one while you can. You stuck to your guns, and you did it.

Resolved: Hurrah for me. I stuck to my guns, and I did a great thing.

December 27

"Goals must continually be refined. Runners need to know the big picture, rather than just haphazardly go from race to race."

—Doug Renner

As this year draws to a close, it's natural to think about what lies ahead for the next year. Renner, who's a running coach, wants runners to do even more than that. He wants you to look not just at next year, but to the year after it, too. In fact, he recommends a two- to four-year plan to improve your running.

Now, that may seem like an awfully long time, and it is. Sometimes it's hard to know what you're doing tomorrow, let alone two or three or four years down the road.

Still, a small shift in thinking may be beneficial. Instead of focusing on a race or a run as an end in itself, think of it as a building block in a longer process. For example, if you enter a 10K next week, enter it not so much with the idea of winning it or achieving a personal best, although those would be nice. Rather, see it as part of your long-term training for a marathon that will occur 36 months from now.

In a sense, this replicates the vision you must have as a runner. In a race you must concentrate on what you're doing now—this step—while thinking ahead to make sure you have enough left to finish.

Appreciate today, in the context of building for tomorrow. That's the message, in a nutshell.

Resolved: When I run, I appreciate today while building for tomorrow.

December 28

"Work hard. Be dedicated. That's all."

—Charles Foster, track hurdler, on the secret of success

You want inspiration? Do the work. You'll find plenty of inspiration then.

There are no shortcuts to success in running. You must do the work, put in the time. There is no other way. Inspiration equals perspiration. If you do not perspire, you will not be inspired. It's the people on the sidelines who always seem to lack inspiration. The runners in the race, the ones who are sweating and laboring, draw their motivation from what they are doing, the simple fact of it.

There is not an exact corollary between the miles a person runs and the success he or she has, but it's close enough. The more you work, the better the results. The better the results, the more inspired you will be. Keep working, and you will get results.

Will you always get the results you're seeking? Always win the race, always run a personal best? Of course not. That happens only in the movies. But if you do the work, if you put in the time, you will generally get the results you deserve.

Running is a "no B.S." sport, as one runner has noted. You earn the success you achieve. There's no way to fake it. You've been doing the work. Now keep doing it.

Resolved: I work hard. I stay dedicated. Always.

December 29

"Once he started running, he never stopped."

—Quote about Steve Prefontaine,
from the movie *Prefontaine*

You may not have much in common with distance legend Steve Prefontaine, but let there be this: once you start running, never stop.

Keep after it. Keep going. If the enthusiasm drains out of you and you grow road-weary, go back to what attracted you to running in the first place. Rekindle that feeling, and your spirit will be restored.

Running is about being fit and keeping your heart pumping and staying healthy. But it's also about feeling that feeling, that anything-is-possible feeling of youth and adventure and challenge. People who run do it because they love it. They're running for that feeling as much as for the physical benefits. Having the feeling helps them receive the physical benefits, which in turn makes the feeling even more pronounced. It's a lovely cycle to be caught up in.

You can stop for a while. You don't have to run and run and run and run and do nothing else. It doesn't have to be an obsession. In fact it's better if it isn't. Running is not a form of slavery. You choose to run. The fact that you choose to run increases the pleasure and the benefits derived from it.

Think not about tomorrow or next month or next year. Just think about having a good run and a good time today. Do that, and you will never stop running.

Resolved: Once I start running, I never stop.

December 30

"Each race is a new challenge. They're all different."

—Bill Rodgers, marathoner

Here's a racing challenge for you: How about a midnight run tomorrow to ring in the new year?

All races are different, and a midnight run is more different from most. First of all, it's at night. It's pitch black outside and possibly very cold. Not only that, but also it's at a time of day—er, night—when you're normally sacked out in bed logging zzzz's.

One compensation is that there will be other like-minded souls out there with you, also missing their beauty sleep for a chance to usher in the new year in crazy style.

Would you rather run or watch the ball drop in Times Square the way you usually do? Would you rather celebrate in a unique way or gaze dumbly at Dick Clark? Would you rather meet new people or watch them blow up another building in Vegas? These are not even close calls.

While the rest of the so-called civilized world is overeating and overdrinking in an annual ritual of forced frivolity, you will be running. Who will have the better time? Again, not even close.

Check out your local racing calendar. Lots of running clubs around the country sponsor midnight runs on New Year's Eve. It's a great way to start the new year right.

Resolved: I go for it. Tomorrow I ring in the new year with a midnight run.

December 31

*"If you are doing something you would do for nothing, then you
are on your way to salvation."*

—George Sheehan, philosopher-runner

This is it, the last day of the year, the grand finale (though, of
course, the journey of running never ends). When you look
back at this year, how'd you do, running-wise?

Did you run a marathon or achieve a personal best? How's
your health? Do you feel fitter than you did last January? And
what about your state of mind? Do you feel good about yourself and what you've done?

Here's the main question, in my mind: Are you enjoying
yourself? If you are—if the act of running fills you with joy,
from the top of your head to the bottom of your feet—you've
got the thing wired. Records and times are mere marginalia;
the reason you run, what motivates you, is: you love it.

When you run for nothing, as Sheehan says, you're on the
road to salvation. He continues, "And if you could drop it in
a minute and forget the outcome, you are even further along.
And if while you are doing it, you are transformed into
another existence, there is no need for you to worry about the
future."

There *is* no need to worry about the future. You've got it all,
right now, in the sheer enjoyment you feel in moving your
body, in running. Follow that joy, and you will never go
wrong.

Resolved: I make next year the greatest year of my running
life.

About the Author

Kevin Nelson is the author of 13 books, including *The Angler's Book of Daily Inspiration* and *The Golfer's Book of Daily Inspiration*. He lives with his wife and children in the San Francisco Bay area.

Index

372